THE EMERGENCE OF KURDISH NATIONALISM AND THE SHEIKH SAID REBELLION, 1880–1925

THE EMERGENCE OF KURDISH NATIONALISM AND THE SHEIKH SAID REBELLION, 1880–1925

By
Robert Olson

Introduction by William F. Tucker

UNIVERSITY OF TEXAS PRESS, AUSTIN

First Edition, 1989

Requests for permission to reproduce material from this work should
be sent to Permissions, University of Texas Press, Box 7819, Austin,
Texas 78713-7819.

The paper used in this publication meets the minimum requirements
of American National Standard for Information Sciences—Permanence
of Paper for Printed Library Materials, ANSI Z39.48-1984. ⊛

Library of Congress Cataloging-in-Publication Data

Olson, Robert W.
    The emergence of Kurdish nationalism and the Sheikh Said
Rebellion, 1880–1925 / by Robert Olson : introduction by William F.
Tucker. — 1st ed.
        p.   cm.
    Bibliography: p.
    Includes index.
    ISBN 978-0-292-72085-5
    1. Kurds—Turkey.   2. Turkey—Ethnic relations.   3. Kurdistan—
Politics and government.   4. Great Britain—Foreign relations—
Middle East.   5. Middle East—Foreign relations—Great Britain.
1. Title.
DR435.K87044   1989
956.1'0049159—dc19   88-38738
                                                           CIP

*For Wadie, who introduced me to
the studies of Middle Eastern peoples:
to his teaching, scholarship, friendship,
encouragement, and conversation.*

*To Bill for his understanding, support, care,
and common concerns.*

*And to Judith, Becca, and Manda:
three beautiful women whom I cherish and
who are amazingly tolerant and understanding
of me and the Middle East.*

Contents

Preface

I FIRST became aware of the Sheikh Said rebellion when I was studying Middle Eastern and Islamic history at Indiana University from 1965 to 1973 with Wadie Jwaideh. Professor Jwaideh was the first historian to write a comprehensive history of the Kurdish nationalist movement and his students were the first beneficiaries of his research. My fellow student and friend Bill Tucker first wrote a graduate paper on the rebellion. Because I knew Turkish and Bill did not, he asked me to collaborate with him; we co-authored an article that was subsequently published in *Die Welt des Islams*. This article appeared before Martin van Bruinessen published his *Agha, Shaikh and State*.

While I was on sabbatical in Great Britain in 1979–1980, I decided to see if there were any documents concerning the Sheikh Said rebellion as well as British policy toward the Kurds during the years 1921 to 1925. To my amazement, I found literally thousands of documents, especially in the Air Ministry files. The Air Ministry files concerning the rebellion have never been used before. Air Ministry files 23/236, 237, 238, and 239 were, in fact, ensconced in four manila files entitled "Shaikh Said Rebellion." These four folders alone included some 304 enclosures covering the period 26 February 1926 to January 1927. As the notes indicate, these documents were only the core of a substantial amount of documents and materials concerned with the rebellion in the Air Ministry files.

The Colonial Office records were also very rich. It should be pointed out that the Colonial Office records and documents concerned directly with the rebellion, in most instances, originated within the Air Ministry. Air intelligence in Iraq was the main source of information on the Kurds, Iraq, and eastern Turkey from 1922 until the rebellion in 1925. In turn, many Foreign Office records dealing with the rebellion were based on reports to the Colonial Office, which had received them from the Air Ministry.

These records provide the basis for the publication of this book, which is the first account of the rebellion based on contemporary sources. The Air Ministry records are enriched further by the fact that British intelligence in Iraq and French intelligence in Syria and Lebanon exchanged information regularly with regard to the rebellion. There are numerous French intelligence reports incorporated into the Air Ministry records. This compensates partially for my inability, because of lack of funds and teaching duties, to investigate the French archives, which are undoubtedly rich in data concerning the rebellion other than those provided to the British. There is also, I am sure, much information concerning the rebellion in German and Soviet archives. I hope that my book will encourage other scholars to investigate these records. The archives of Turkey, when they are opened to scholars, will also provide rich information. In the meantime, I hope this book will contribute to our knowledge of the Sheikh Said rebellion and to the historiography of the post–World War I Middle East.

Robert Olson
Lexington, Kentucky

Acknowledgments

EVEN THE dedication of this book cannot indicate my debt to Wadie Jwaideh not only for his teaching, friendship, and encouragement, but also for his "The Kurdish Nationalist Movement: Its Origins and Development." After nearly thirty years, it still remains unsurpassed in its treatment of the early stages of the development of Kurdish nationalism. This book also would not have been possible without the work of Martin van Bruinessen, as the notes make clear. I am also grateful to Dr. van Bruinessen for giving me permission to adapt a version of the map on p. 157 of his "Vom Osmanismus zum Separatimus: Religiöse und ethnische Hintergründe der Rebellion des Scheich Said," in *Jahrbuch zur Geschichte und Gesellschaft des Vorderen und Mittleren Orients 1984*, ed. Martin van Bruinessen and Jochen Blaschke (Berlin: Express Edition, 1985). It has been a deep and profound pleasure for me to know and work with Wadie Jwaideh and Martin van Bruinessen, two of the foremost scholars of Kurdish history and society of the nineteenth and twentieth centuries. From them I have learned that great scholarship produces generous people.

I wish to thank the Public Record Office, Kew Gardens, Great Britain, for allowing me to quote from documents in its archives and for providing a comfortable place to do research during my stay in 1979–1980. Professors Stefan Wild and Werner Ende, editors of *Die Welt des Islams*, kindly granted permission to use portions of my "The Second Time Around: British Policy towards the Kurds (1921–1922)" (27 [1987]). Kemal Karpat, editor of the *International Journal of Turkish Studies*, graciously permitted me to use material from "The Churchill-Cox Correspondence Regarding the Creation of the State of Iraq: Consequences for British Policy toward the Nationalist Turkish Government from 1921–23," which will appear in volume 5, number 1, of that journal. I also wish to thank Paul Dumont, editor of *Turcica*, for permitting me to use material from "The Sheikh

Said Rebellion in Turkey in 1925: Estimates of Troops Employed,"
which will appear in a forthcoming issue in 1989.

A book such as this that is dependent on foreign-language materials can only be done at a university such as the University of Kentucky that has no Middle Eastern language holdings with the stellar
performance of the Interlibrary Loan staff. Roxanne Jones, head of
Interlibrary Loan Services, and her staff were helpful beyond the call
of duty although sometimes amused by my requests for publications
in such "weird" languages. But they always managed to procure the
requested books. Jennifer Marie Geran was especially adept, per-
sistent, and expeditious in obtaining the books that I needed. I also
wish to express my appreciation to the Interlibrary Loan Services at
the University of California, Los Angeles, which managed to fulfill
all of the requests that I made.

Pat Howard performed the laborious task of putting the manuscript on a word processor in her usual extremely capable and effi-
cient manner. Despite her hectic schedule, she managed to ferret
out spelling, grammatical, and other needed changes along the way.
She also did all of the work necessary for printing the manuscript on
a laser printer.

Gyula Pauer, director of Cartography Laboratory at the University
of Kentucky, somehow found time in his busy schedule to make the
maps personally. He was insistent that the book have at least "two
good maps."

Professor William F. Tucker, gentleman and scholar that he is, did
not waive his right to anonymity as one of the readers of the manuscript and as a result I prevailed upon him to write the introduction. He agreed to do so by abandoning his own research for several
weeks, not to mention shortening his summer vacation. One of the
pleasures of being a Middle East historian is to be the constant re-
cipient of the generosity of one's colleagues. I am grateful to Professor Tucker.

Frankie Westbrook, humanities editor of the University of Texas
Press, was most gracious in extending advice to an excited author
and in expediting the production of the book. I am most grateful to
Kathy Lewis, my copy editor. She found errors that I am convinced
no one else could have. The helpfulness of the entire University of
Texas Press staff made it a real pleasure to have a book published
in Austin.

Note on Spelling and Names

I HAVE generally followed modern Turkish orthography in the spelling of names and places because Sheikh Said's rebellion took place in Turkey and most secondary sources concerned with the rebellion are in Turkish. In modern Turkish the letters ö and ü are similar to the German letters. The letter *i* is pronounced like "sit" in English. There is also an undotted *ı* in Turkish, which sounds like the *u* in "stadium." The letters ç and ş are similar to the *ch* in "church" and the *sh* in "should." The *c* is pronounced like the *j* in "John." In modern Turkish, the Ottoman, Arabic, and Farsi letters *d* and *b* are rendered as *t* and *p* at the end of words (thus, *Mehmed, Ahmed,* and *Receb* in Ottoman Turkish become *Mehmet, Ahmet,* and *Recep* in modern Turkish). Turkish also has a letter ğ, which has the effect of lengthening the preceding vowel and sometimes obviates the need to pronounce the following consonants, as in *ağa* (large landowner). In Ottoman and Arabic, the word is generally spelled *agha* with the sound of the letter *ghain* in Arabic.

I have taken some liberties with the transliteration when certain names or places would be more familiar in a slightly different rendering. For example, I spell "sheikh" as I do rather than use the Turkish *şeyh* or the Arabic *shaykh* because it is closer to the English "sheik." I also spell Sheikh Said's name with a *d* rather than a *t*, because that is the way he spelled it. His rebellion occurred before the Turkish language law of 1928, which mandated Latin characters for the Turkish alphabet.

In other instances, I do not adhere to modern Turkish orthography if the meaning of a word, place, or name would be better understood or more in uniformity with the Arabic, Farsi, Kurdish, or Ottoman if rendered differently or, as in the appendixes, given as written in the documents. I have sometimes omitted the umlaut over certain letters in order to make the words easily comprehensible to readers and speakers of Arabic, Farsi, Kurdish, Turkish, and Ottoman (e.g., *Abdulhamid, Huseyin*). I also generally use the appellation "beg" for Kurds and "bey" for Turks to aid the reader in distinguishing between the two, when it is possible to do so.

For the transliteration of Arabic, I have used the Library of Congress system.

Introduction

IN HIS masterful study of relations between Europeans and non-European peoples (*Europe and the People without History*), Eric Wolf refers to Western concepts of so-called primitive peoples as "without history," that is, populations supposedly isolated from the external world and from one another (a fallacious view as he goes on to show). One might also speak of peoples with "denied history." The application of such a phrase and idea to the peoples of western Asia in fact makes a great deal of sense when one thinks of the Palestinian Arabs, Armenians, and especially the Kurdish people in the last hundred years. The modern history and political struggles of this last group form the subject of this book.

As Middle East specialists are well aware, the Kurds are a separate and distinctive nationality living, except for exiles, in an area often referred to as Kurdistan, in which they make up the majority of the population—a region comprised of eastern Anatolia, extreme northeastern Syria, northern Iraq, northwestern Iran, and parts of southern and southeastern Soviet Armenia. In addition to having occupied this area for centuries, the Kurds also share a common language, which, although related to modern Persian, is a separate Indo-European tongue; the majority of its speakers speak three dialects: one variously known as Kurmanci or Kirmanci, another as Sorani, and the third as Kurdi. A minority of Kurds speak another dialect most often called Zaza. Whatever the dialect, the Kurdish language is distinct with respect to its grammar, syntax, and vocabulary. In addition, the Kurds possess a folklore and literature of long standing, including chronicles, poems, and, since the late nineteenth century, journalism.

Although it is impossible in a brief examination of this sort to devote a great deal of attention to the early history of the Kurds, which is in any case complex and even controversial, it should be emphasized that they have resided in a fairly compact and homogeneous fashion in Kurdistan since ancient times, at least since the time of the Medes. Living in the mountainous areas of the Taurus and the Zagros and adjacent valleys, the Kurds were exposed, like other peoples, to various waves of invaders and to different governments, but they managed to enjoy periods of relative autonomy or quasi-independence, thanks to topography and the declining fortunes of one or another ruling dynasty. After the Islamic conquests of the Middle East, the Kurds came under the authority of the various Islamic dynasties; but by the tenth century, as elsewhere in the eastern Islamic world, the Kurds had begun to experience much greater freedom from the writ of caliphal governments, and Kurdish chieftains and leaders had become active in the establishment of small, virtually independent dynastic principalities. The Mongol, Safavid, and Ottoman invasions wrought much devastation and dislocation among the Kurdish population, but Kurdish notables and local rulers were able to utilize Perso-Turkish disputes in their own interests for at least a part of the time between 1514 and the late seventeenth century.

By the early eighteenth century, the Ottoman Empire was experiencing such difficulties at the level of central government that local Kurdish princes were able gradually to assert themselves and to enjoy virtual autonomy. It was only with the reform and centralization efforts of Sultan Mahmud II (1808–1839) that the Kurdish emirs (e.g., Muhammad Paşa of Rawanduz and Bedir Khan Beg of Bohtan) were brought to heel. After the suppression of the princelings, effective power and leadership in the Kurdish community passed into the hands of a new kind of political leader—the sheikh.

Through piety, charisma, matrimonial alliances, and wealth, sheikhs associated generally with the Nakşbandi or Qadiri Sufi orders came to enjoy much power and prestige by the 1870s. After the Ottoman defeat of the princes, disorder and lawlessness prevailed in Kurdistan and the sheikhs were the only moral force capable of restoring any sort of peace and order. As a result, one sees the rise of the sheikhs of Şemdinan, Barzanca, and Barzan by the 1850s. As Professor Wadie Jwaideh has shown, the rise to prominence and power of the sheikhs demonstrated the desire of the Kurdish people to fill the power gap caused by the fall of the princes. The rise of Sheikh Ubaydallah in the late 1870s is illustrative of the great role the sheikhs had come to play in Kurdistan. Ubaydallah's revolt, however, was also significant for another reason—it marked the emergence of a political force directed toward unification of the Kurds and their rising (unsuccessful, it must be noted); the sheikhs played a role of considerable magnitude in Kurdish nationalism and Kurdish autonomist political and military movements. One must not belabor the obvious, but it must be appreciated that for the Kurds nationalism and religion became intertwined, in effect, from the beginning. One must understand the role of the sheikhs and of this mixture of nationalism and Islam in order to appreciate this book and, for that matter, the modern history of the Kurdish people.

After the Young Turk revolution of 1908, Kurdish political clubs and societies were established in a number of cities within the Ottoman Empire, including Istanbul, Mosul, Diyarbakır, and Baghdad. In addition, young Kurds, especially members of prominent families such as the Bedir Khan and Baban, began to travel outside the Middle East (e.g., to France and Switzerland) for their educations. Inevitably, members of this emerging intelligentsia became acquainted with Western-style nationalism and other political concepts, leading to a heightened awareness of their own national traditions and values. Some have argued that these intellectuals and their ideas were generally viewed with suspicion and distaste by traditional political and religious leaders in Kurdistan. In fact, the research of Jwaideh and Olson shows that nationalist ideas were not rejected out of hand by leaders in Kurdistan. In fact, nationalist concepts came to be accepted and propagated by the religious brotherhoods and the sheikhs of Kurdistan.

This last development was of paramount importance for the evolution of the Kurdish national consciousness and movement. Since the sheikhs were so closely identified with the Kurdish masses, their espousal of nationalist ideas was a major avenue for the spread of a Kurdish national identity and programs among the masses. The diffusion of such ideas was facilitated by the fact that they came from traditional Islamic leaders who stood in opposition to the secularism clearly identified with Turkish leadership and government circles after 1908. In fact, as Olson demonstrates, the secularism associated with the Young Turks and then with the Kemalist reforms was a primary factor in the ideology of Sheikh Said's revolt.

In the aftermath of World War I when the Ottoman Empire had disappeared and the situation in the Near East was fluid and uncertain, to say the least, it seemed that the Kurds and other nationalities might benefit greatly from the new order that the victorious Allies seemed ready to impose upon the Middle East. In fact, a spokesman chosen by Kurdish nationalist organizations attended the Paris peace conference, and it looked as though the Kurds were going to realize their fondest dream—a national state. The Treaty of Sèvres, signed in August 1920, dealt with Kurdish affairs in articles

62–64. Article 64 in effect gave the Kurds the opportunity to form an independent state in Kurdistan, at least in those parts formerly belonging to the Ottoman *vilayet* of Mosul. Unfortunately for the Kurds, the treaty was rendered inoperative by the actions of Mustafa Kemal and his forces. The Kurds had come up against two of the brutal facts faced by so many nationalist movements before and since—competing nationalisms mean trouble for smaller or less powerful groups and offer keen instruments for diplomats and politicians of the great powers.

As Olson shows, the Kurdish nationalist cause provided a tool for at least potential manipulation and *Realpolitik* on the part of strong states within and outside of the Middle East. One of the major themes of the book, in fact, is the way in which the Kurds were used as pawns in the policy struggles between Britain and Kemalist Turkey. One sees not only the Turkish fear of British designs on the Middle East but also the nature of the struggle that threatened to break out over Turkish-Iraqi borders. Interestingly enough, however, this book shows quite clearly that the rebellion of Sheikh Said was a Kurdish matter, not a British put-up job to use against the Turks in the interests of an Iraqi Mosul. In addition, Olson provides extremely important information about the role the Kurds played in British imperial policy, divergencies and disputes among makers of that policy, and the nature of the techniques employed to sustain that policy, such as the use of air power. Sheikh Said and the Kurds were of far greater interest to the British than they probably ever realized.

In the final analysis, however, this book is a story of the relationship between Turks and nationally conscious Kurds since World War I. It is very important to understand how the rebellion affected the future of the Kurds in Turkey and, for that matter, other potential opponents of Kemalism within the Turkish state. The nature and number of Turkish army campaigns in Kurdish areas should be particularly noted; more Turkish military actions have been carried out in Kurdistan than in any other area of Turkish concern, foreign or domestic. Obviously, the Sheikh Said rebellion left a legacy of bitterness, mistrust, and suspicion that has subsisted for decades. Those observers familiar with Turkish military actions in eastern Anatolia within the past few years will undoubtedly find much of interest in the present volume. The hostility and suspicion of the Turkish government toward dissenting or opposition groups also becomes much more significant in light of the information provided here. The Said rebellion made possible and even seemed to justify draconian measures against opposition groups, whose ideologies were seen as constituting a major challenge or threat to Kemalism.

Sheikh Said and other leaders were executed, the rising was put down forcefully, but the problem did not simply vanish. Other Kurdish rebellions occurred in the late 1920s and early 1930s, and Kurdish desires for independence or autonomy have not disappeared. The issue of conflicting nationalisms has not gone away: in all likelihood, it will not do so. Furthermore, the Sheikh Said rebellion showed many years ago something that some observers have associated only with Iran in recent times—the possibility of a symbiotic relationship between nationalism and religion. In fact, long before Ayatollah Khomeini began his crusade in 1963, it had been quite effectively shown that nationalism in its seemingly modern Western sense (shared language, cultural forms, history, contiguous territory, etc.) and religion, in this case Sunni Islam, were by no means incompatible, at least at the level of political policy and struggle.

William F. Tucker

THE EMERGENCE OF KURDISH NATIONALISM
AND THE SHEIKH SAID REBELLION, 1880–1925

1. The Emergence of Kurdish Nationalism: Sheikh Ubaydallah and the Kurdish League

THE SHEIKH Said rebellion that occurred in the spring of 1925 in eastern Turkey was the culmination of four distinct stages of Kurdish nationalism. Each of the stages had its own developments, but some patterns persisted throughout—for example, the dominance of the nationalist movement by sheikhs or religious figures rather than nonreligious personages such as emirs or tribal chiefs who had ruled the Kurds prior to the rise of Sheikh Ubaydallah. The four major stages of Kurdish nationalism can be delineated as follows: (1) the movement led by Sheikh Ubaydallah of Nehri and his Kurdish League, which marked the emergence of the sheikhs as the most important leaders among the Kurds, ending with his death in 1883; (2) the role of the Hamidiye Light Cavalry from its creation in 1891 until the outbreak of World War I; (3) the events of World War I to the Treaty of Sèvres (10 August 1920); and (4) the aftermath of World War I and postwar developments through the rebellion of Sheikh Said.

Sheikh Ubaydallah's rise to prominence marks the first stage of a greater consciousness of Kurdish nationalism. A sense of community had previously existed among the Kurds, but the sheikh's open declaration that he wanted to create an independent Kurdistan distinguished his rule from that of his predecessors such as Emir Bedir Khan Beg of Bohtan, who had ruled over much of the same area in southeastern Turkey and northeastern Iraq from the 1820s to the 1840s that later came under Sheikh Ubaydallah's jurisdiction.

Since Ubaydallah's rule was characterized by nationalist goals and that of Bedir Khan Beg was not, it is important to note some of the differences between their reigns.[1] The most notable is their titles. Ubaydallah was a sheikh, a title designating his religious functions as head of the Nakşbandi order (tarikat).[2] As sheikh, Ubaydallah exercised influence even in areas under the rule of other chieftains. Ubaydallah's position as a powerful sheikh allowed him to infuse religious phraseology full of millenarian and messianic symbols into his nationalist objectives in a way that Bedir Khan Beg as a non-religious leader was unable to do in spite of the fact that he was a *mir* (prince) or paramount chieftain of a confederation of tribes. Some Kurdish nationalists are of the opinion that after the defeat of the Ottomans in 1839 by Ibrahim Paşa, son of Muhammad Ali of Egypt, Bedir Khan "started planning the establishment of an independent Kurdistan," but "there is nothing in the historical record which indicates this."[3] It seems what Bedir Khan Beg desired was greater autonomy under Ottoman administration.

It is possible that Bedir Khan Beg's consolidation of power and his wars against the Nestorian Christians in 1843 and 1846, which allowed the Ottomans to interfere in Kurdish affairs more than they had been able to do previously, also encouraged the Kurds to try to prevent such interference and manipulation in the future.[4] The most important difference between Sheikh Ubaydallah's nationalist aims and the traditional, autonomy-minded Bedir Khan Beg was his publicly stated goal of establishing an independent Kurdistan. In July 1880, Ubaydallah wrote the following letter to British Vice-Consul Clayton in Başkale:

> The Kurdish nation is a people apart. Their religion is different (to that of others), and their laws and customs are distinct. They are known among all nations as mischievous and corrupt. . . . The chiefs and rulers of Kurdistan, whether Turkish or Persian subjects, and the inhabitants of Kurdistan (the Christians) one and all are united and agreed that matters cannot be carried on this way with the two governments, and necessarily something must be done so that the European governments having understood the matter shall enquire into our state. . . . We want our affairs to be in our hands. . . . Otherwise the whole of Kurdistan will take the matter into their own hands, as they are unable to put up with these continued evil deeds, and the oppression which they suffer at the hands of the two governments of impure intentions.[5]

Other than Sheikh Ubaydallah's self-proclaimed desire for independence, British consuls in the area thought he had "a comprehensive plan for uniting all the Kurds in an independent state under himself. . . ." Wadie Jwaideh considers the rise of Sheikh Ubaydallah "as the emergence of a new type of leadership among the Kurds. He was the first and probably the greatest of the religious-secular leaders of Kurdistan."[6] Ubaydallah's position as sheikh granted him the prestige held historically by sheikhs in Muslim society. A sheikh, simply by attaining the position, set himself apart as a leader of men as well as a servant of God. Besides piety, august morality, and an often charismatic personality, a sheikh also needed all the abilities of a modern politician. He had to be able to effect compromises, settle disputes, and provide succor in such a way that none of the aggrieved felt shortchanged. Such acts of arbitration and conciliation were often best achieved by men of nonlocal origin, who had not participated in local feuds that would have been thought to have tainted their judgment. The sheikh's reputation was based on his family's saintly genealogy, sagacity, charisma, and nonlocal blood lines. Sheikh Ubaydallah himself could claim descent from Sheikh Abdul Qadir al-Gaylan, the famous thirteenth-century saint from Baghdad.

In Kurdistan, in particular, it was the role of the sheikh as a holy man that allowed him to become so powerful. Many of his illiterate and fanatically religious followers (*murids*) could readily see their sheikh as a *mahdi* (messiah), a savior come to bring justice and a better life. Such devotion and demands increased in times of social and political malaise and famine and economic hardship. Sheikh Ubaydallah's rise to power in the late 1870s and earlier 1880s and that of Sheikh Said in the 1920s occurred in such circumstances. The sheikh was thought able to perform miracles through his special grace (*keramet*), which could persist after his death. This belief contributed greatly to the importance of worship at the tombs of dead sheikhs. The sheikhs also performed medicinal as well as psychic functions. In short, the sheikhs fulfilled the roles of doctor, lawyer, priest, and psychiatrist. While a sheikh or sheikhly family could rise to prominence by defending an exploited class or group such as the peasantry, this was only one way. Sheikh Ubaydallah gained great power because many tribal chiefs owed him allegiance through marriage, as followers (*murids*), or for services rendered. Some of the greatest tribal chieftains of the time addressed Sheikh Ubaydallah as "Your Highness."[7] A sheikh also consolidated his power through marriage to daughters of village authorities. By the time a sheikh and his progeny were able to contract daughters of tribal chieftains in marriage, he probably had achieved some wealth. This was necessary because a sheikh was expected to be generous and hospitable, depended upon for survival in times of need. He required money to attract and hold his followers. There was a direct relationship and reciprocity between the number of a sheikh's followers and the food, livestock, money, and land he received from them.

In addition to this wealth acquired through gifts of all kinds and through marriage, sheikhs also had control over *vaqf*s or pious foundations established to provide revenues for the upkeep of mosques, wells, and *medrese*s (religious schools). Many of the sheikhs treated the *vaqf* lands as their own properties. The Ottoman Land Code of 1858 also contributed to their wealth by increasing the amount of land they owned as individuals.[8] Along with *ağa*s (large landowners), tribal chiefs and leaders, government officials, and rich merchants, sheikhs were the chief beneficiaries of this land code by virtue of their increasingly dominant position in Kurdish society after the crushing of the emirates in the 1830s and 1840s. Granting land to sheikhs and tribal leaders after 1858 also served the political function of achieving the centralization of power that the Ottoman government desired in the latter half of the nineteenth century in eastern Anatolia and in Iraq.

The suppression of the semi-independent Kurdish principalities by the Ottoman government, especially during the reign of Mahmud II (1808–1839), paved the way for the emergence of Sheikh Ubaydallah as a national leader. The disappearance of the emirs resulted in increased lawlessness and banditry that sometimes verged on anarchy. Released from the strictures placed upon them by the emirs, local petty chiefs pursued their own vendettas and feuds. In spite of its intentions, the Ottoman government was unable to centralize control. Encumbered by massive problems in western Anatolia as well as in its European and Arab provinces and by increasing challenges and demands from European countries, the Ottomans simply could not fill the vacuum left by the disappearance of the emirs. Thus, the political as well as the religious situation was ripe for a shift of power to the sheikhs. Wadie Jwaideh has observed that "the rise of the shaykhs to a position of national leadership among the Kurds does not merely indicate the great reverence in which the shaykhs were held on account of their religious character, it also indicates that, after the overthrow of the great princes, there was no secular person capable of commanding sufficient prestige among the people. The readiness with which the Kurds accepted the shaykhs as leaders shows the extent to which the Kurdish people felt the need for filling the power vacuum left by the disappearance of the emirs."[9] The absence of some paramount figure undoubtedly seemed incongruous to the Kurds.

A sociological view supports the conclusion that the reduction of the Kurdish emirates to smaller tribal units paved the way for sheikhly rule. For a period of thirty years or so after the destruction of the emirates (1847–1880), the Kurds, as van Bruinessen suggests, were less integrated into a state, whether Kurdish or Ottoman, and less able to move toward a state structure of their own. Van Bruinessen believes the abolition of the emirates did not mean greater direct (by which he seems to mean participatory) rule and hence was a step backward in social evolution, away from the creation of a potential state. The proclivities toward tribal rule were still too strong to allow such a development. But it was, it seems to me, the very lack of "direct rule" by the Kurdish emirs in the wake of the demise of the emirates that allowed Sheikh Ubaydallah's independence movement based on the popular appeal of the religious brotherhoods (*tarikats*) to be realized.[10] The Ottoman government— which had pursued an increasingly secular orientation throughout the nineteenth century that its successor, the republic of Turkey, continued to pursue throughout the twentieth century, with the exception of the two-decade rule of Abdulhamid II (1876–1909)—fostered the type of nationalism led by religious leaders, which held sway from Sheikh Ubaydallah to Sheikh Said. While it was the suppression of the emirates and its consequences that provided the context for the emergence of sheikhs as political leaders, it was the aftermath of the Russo-Turkish war of 1877–1888 that encouraged Ubaydallah to declare his nationalist program. The war had brought devastation, famine, and general hardship accompanied by disease, banditry, and violence. The peoples of the eastern provinces of the empire were in desperate straits.

The precipitant cause of Ubaydallah's publicly declared independent Kurdish state was the Treaty of Berlin signed on 13 July 1878 as a conclusion to the Russo-Turkish war. Article 61 stated that the Sublime Porte would undertake "improvements and reforms demanded by local requirements in the provinces and inhabited by the Armenians, and to guarantee their security against the Circassians and Kurds."[11] The European powers were to oversee the implementation of the reforms. Jwaideh states that "fear of the Armenian ascendancy in Kurdistan appears to have been one of the most powerful reasons behind the shaykhs' attempt to unite the Kurds."[12] Rumors were rife in eastern Anatolia that if an Armenian state were to be established it would be in the same area or overlap the area where a Kurdish state would be established. Upon hearing of article 61, Sheikh Ubaydallah is reported to have said, "What is this I hear; that the Armenians are going to have an independent state in Van, and the Nestorians are going to hoist the British flag and declare themselves British subjects. I will never permit it, even if I have to arm the women."[13] From this point onward, Sheikh Ubaydallah seemed more than ever determined to resist reforms that would lead to the establishment of an Armenian state and preempt a Kurdish state. His statement that he would arm the women, which he apparently made in earnest, is indicative that he was indeed a new kind of Kurdish leader. The arrival of British consuls in Kurdistan as stipulated by the Convention of Defensive Alliance of 4 June 1878 to oversee the reforms exacerbated already-intense Kurdish fears. These fears were not misplaced—contemporaries, indeed, the consuls themselves, thought this would inaugurate the "Protectorate of Asia Minor." The consuls were "a beacon of hope to the oppressed and repressed Christians of Eastern Turkey, encouraging them to crave for justice. . . ."[14]

In order to prevent the reforms that would allow more power and possibly independence for the Armenians and Nestorians, Sheikh Ubaydallah launched a sophisticated diplomatic strategy that included the creation of the Kurdish League—the first Kurdish alliance of its kind. Jwaideh argues that one of the main reasons for the success of the short-lived Kurdish League was that it was supported by the Ottoman government because of its resistance to reforms that would lead to loss of more Ottoman territory. Previous reforms throughout the nineteenth century had led to a steady erosion of Ottoman authority in its Balkan possessions and, as the Treaty of Berlin and the Cyprus Convention make clear, in Egypt. The Armenians were positive that the objective of the Kurdish League was "to stifle the Armenian question by raising a new one, that of the Kurds."[15] Even a rebellion against the government in 1879 did not deter Ottoman support for Ubaydallah and the Kurdish League's activities. After all, Sheikh Ubaydallah and his forces had been a significant aid to the Ottomans in their recently fought war (*jihad*) against the Russians. The sheikh's forces still possessed the weapons, including Martini rifles, provided by the Ottomans for that endeavor. The Ottomans thought that the Kurds could be used to good advantage once again.

In 1880, Ubaydallah invaded Iran to increase the territory under his authority. His Kurdish brethren lay just across the border. Iran was weak and the Iranians were Shi'is. Although the Ottomans supported the Kurdish League, it is possible that once Ubaydallah had consolidated his power in Iran he planned to use his newly found power against the Ottoman government to facilitate the establishment of an independent Kurdistan. Ubaydallah's plans and dreams came to naught in Iran. His army was defeated soundly by the Iranians. Even the Ottomans took action against him upon his return, probably for two reasons: they were forced to do so by European public opinion and they realized that support of Kurdish nationalism could easily get beyond their control. Ubaydallah was captured by

Ottoman forces and taken to Istanbul in July 1881. After several months there, he escaped and made his way back to his home town of Nehri. But the European powers, still outraged by Ubaydallah's actions against the Christian Nestorians, prevailed upon the Porte to send a force against the sheikh. Ubaydallah was captured and exiled to the Hijaz. He died in Mecca in 1883.[16]

Ubaydallah's invasion of Iran also made the Kurdish movement for independence an international issue, viewed unfavorably by the powers of the time and indicative of such future efforts. Russia did not want to be robbed of the territories, some of which were largely Kurdish, in eastern Turkey that it had obtained by the Treaty of Berlin. Neither did it want a Kurdish state on its Caucasian borders, especially one animated by the religious fervor of the Nakşbandi order. Russia had its fill of such movements with Shah Şamil in the 1840s, whose movement had been suppressed with great difficulty. Great Britain was opposed to Ubaydallah's movement because it did not want a situation that would draw Iran closer to Russia. Such a development would complicate its imperial policies in central and southwest Asia. The only large power in support of Ubaydallah was the Ottoman Empire, which wanted to use Ubaydallah's Kurdish League against the reforms, and hence the European powers, especially Great Britain and Russia. It also wanted to use the Kurds to stifle the Armenian independence movement. It is possible that the Ottoman government wanted to compensate for losses sustained in Europe by reconquering the Kurdish, Sunni regions of Iran and the Turkish-speaking, although Shi'i, regions of Azerbayjan.[17] At the end of this first stage of Kurdish nationalism, all of the European powers, as emphasized in the Treaty of Berlin, were opposed to Kurdish independence movements. In addition, as indicated, Great Britain and Russia had their own reasons for opposing such movements. Only the Ottoman Empire had good reasons for supporting Kurdish independence movements, but not, of course, an independent Kurdish state.

The Hamidiye

The creation of the Hamidiye Light Cavalry Regiments (Hamidiye Hafif Süvari Alayları) delineates the second stage of Kurdish nationalism. Bayram Kodaman suggests that Abdulhamid II's creation of the Hamidiye reflected the four major objectives of his regime: centralization, Islamic unity, the politics of balance, and the politics of reform. Stephen Duguid sees the post-1878 period as representing "a fundamental shift in the Ottoman self-view."[18] Abdulhamid's creation of the Kurdish Light Cavalry was an effort to help realize his four major political objectives. It would tie the empire more firmly to its Muslim roots and provide a defense against Russia and the Armenians, both increasingly aggressive after 1878, and the Kurds could be used as a balance against the urban notables and the provincial governments. The successful implementation of these policies would allow the government further to centralize its authority.

The creation of the Hamidiye was also a result of the relations between Abdulhamid II and the tribes of eastern Anatolia. After the failure of Ubaydallah's movement, Abdulhamid attempted to draw the Kurdish tribes closer and to organize them against the Armenians and their backers, the British. The Russians became amenable to this policy after 1883; they were also opposed to the creation of an independent Armenia. By 1884, *valis* (governors of provinces) personally appointed by Abdulhamid and responsible to him were soliciting the support of the tribal leaders and supplying them with arms. Kodaman argues that during the period 1885–1890 the Porte was able to get some control over the tribes through this solicitous policy and that the Ottomans also took pains to pay attention to the demands of the Armenians. Most historians of this period see little Ottoman concern with the demands and concerns of the Armenians.[19] Whatever the intentions of the Ottoman government toward the Armenians from 1885 to 1890, increased Armenian independence activities after 1890 threatened, in the view of Abdulhamid, not only the state, but also his tribal policy and hence all of his desired reforms.

The creation of the Hamidiye was not solely for the purposes of using the Kurdish cavalry against the Armenians. Kodaman and Duguid suggest that creation of the Hamidiye has to be placed in the context of the larger objectives of Abdulhamid's policies: to establish central authority; to create a new social-political balance to make the government more effective in eastern Anatolia; to take advantage of tribal forces for military purposes; to use the cavalry against the Armenians and to equalize the balance of power, at least military power; to protect against Russian invasion and impede or stop Great Britain's policies of penetration in eastern Anatolia; and to implement the policy of Pan-Islam.[20] All of these objectives were compatible with the fundamental shift in Ottoman politics to try to establish greater Muslim unity: the Hamidiye and the Kurds were to be part of this policy. In spite of the several objectives that the Ottomans hoped to achieve by the establishment of the Hamidiye, it was established in direct response to increased Armenian activities in 1891. Also, Abdulhamid had been in power for thirteen years by

1891: if the Hamidiye was such an important catalyst to his reform, why had it not been implemented before?

The regiments were to be under the command of Müşir Zeki Paşa, who was married to a sister of Abdulhamid, and were to consist of not less than four companies and not more than six. Each regiment was to have at least 512 men and not more than 1,152. Large tribes were able to commit enough men to make an entire regiment; smaller tribes were given the right to commit enough men for one company. The regiments were forbidden to unify except in times of war and only at the order of the commanding general. The tribes were to submit population figures to the Interior Ministry on all men between the ages of seventeen and forty. The officers of the regiments were sent to a special school (Hamidiye Süvari Mektebi) in Istanbul. While a Kurd could rise to the rank of colonel, his assistant had to be a regular (Ottoman) soldier.

The tribes that were granted the right to create a regiment or a company of men gained many advantages. In the competition the larger tribes, especially those that had some record of loyalty to the state, were favored by the Porte. The tribes had to be Sunni to fit into Abdulhamid's Pan-Islamic policy. Once a tribe reached Hamidiye status and received weapons, in addition to increased prestige, its ability to dominate and at times to intimidate and terrorize smaller tribes increased markedly. Also, a large and strong tribe out of favor with the government could be brought to heel by being excluded from participating in the Hamidiye. Alternatively, a Hamidiye tribe could be sent against a recalcitrant tribe. To be excluded from the Hamidiye meant those tribes were available for conscription into the regular army. This is the first time that Kurdish tribesmen were required to serve in Ottoman forces, not necessarily in Kurdistan. This conscription, which paralleled the creation of the Hamidiye, spurred interest and a desire to serve in the Hamidiye.

After the creation of the Hamidiye, it was deployed on two fronts. The first was between Erzurum and Van and the second in the Mardin-Urfa region: one against the Russians and the other against the British. Both regiments were attached to the Fourth Army under the command of Müşir Zeki Paşa, who "acted as 'protector' of the Kurds against their main enemies, the local governments."[21] Zeki Paşa's protection of the Kurds against the *valis*, themselves appointed by Abdulhamid, indicates how frustrating and difficult it must have been for the *valis* to implement reforms in eastern Anatolia. The sultan's close ties with Zeki Paşa also suggest that his main goal may have been to use the Kurds against the Armenians. The employment of the Hamidiye in the Erzurum-Van and Mardin-Urfa regions would have enabled it not only to be used against Russia, with whom relations were not threatening at the time, or Great Britain, but also to be employed both north and south of the Armenians. For example, in spite of Hamidiye atrocities against the Armenians in Sasun on 22 September 1893, recruitment continued unabated. By 1895, the Hamidiye consisted of 57 regiments.[22] If we calculate 512 as the least number of men in a regiment and 1,152 as the most, that would mean that between 29,184 to 65,664 Kurds were serving in the Hamidiye. At an average of 832 men in each regiment, the total figure would be some 47,000 men—all well armed. In 1896, in the wake of increased Armenian revolutionary activity, the Hamidiye was sent against the Armenians, which resulted in much bloodshed for both parties. Some Armenians were massacred.[23] These events in many ways marked the culmination of the tension and suspicions between Armenians and Kurds since 1878. Their struggle had assumed the characteristics of a civil war, with the Ottomans supporting the Kurds and the Russians and the British the Armenians. More bloodshed was to follow.

The Hamidiye continued after the deposition of its founder and benefactor, Abdulhamid II. Between 1908 and 1910, the regiments were reorganized and the name was changed to Tribal Regiments by Mahmud Şevket Paşa, the commander of the Third Army, who had led the attack against the counterrevolution of 13 April 1909. For a while, it was contemplated to change the name of the regiments to Oğuz Alayları, but Mahmud Şevket Paşa was of the opinion that *oğuz* would be construed as *uyuz* (mangy or weak)—a play on words the detractors of the regiments would obviously relish.[24] The word *oğuz* referred to an early Turkic tribal confederation and conveyed a sense of strength. The fact that the early Oğuz confederation contained no Kurds did not seem to bother Mahmud Şevket Paşa. It is interesting that the word *oğuz* was considered. It had much more of a nationalist (Turkish) than tribal meaning. It does indicate, however, that the Young Turks were to follow essentially the politics of Abdulhamid II in terms of harnessing the Kurdish tribal regiments to the cause of the Young Turks and increasingly to Turkish nationalism. Perhaps assigning the name of the earliest Turkish tribal confederation to Kurdish tribal regiments could also have been more than the budding Turkish nationalists thought desirable.

The Young Turks also considered using the Kurdish cavalry regiments in guerrilla warfare. The regiments continued to grow under the Young Turks, expanding to 64 in August 1910. Calculating each regiment at 832 men, this would mean that over 53,000 men were enlisted. Three tribal regiments from the Urfa and Viranşehir regions alone were sent to fight in the Balkan wars. With the outbreak of World War I, the regiments were sufficiently armed and organized to play a major role, especially on the eastern front, where they were attached to the Third Army and fought loyally in the Ottoman forces. The creation of the Hamidiye had both negative and positive consequences for the evolution of Kurdish nationalism. Among the most negative consequences were the intertribal Sunni-Shiʿi rivalries that were created. The regiments were enrolled from only Sunni tribes in accordance with Abdulhamid's Pan-Islamic policy. This greatly weakened the position of the Shiʿis and/or Alevi tribes and increased the hostility between the Sunnis and Shiʿis generally. Şerif Firat, who chronicled some of these conflicts, indicates how this situation led to unremitting hostility between his own Alevi tribe, the Hormek, and the Sunni Cibran tribe, which formed four Hamidiye Regiments. This hostility continued until the Sheikh Said rebellion in 1925.[25]

Firat characterizes the Cibran tribe as one of the most powerful in Kurdistan and one of the most loyal to Abdulhamid II. The Hormek, on the other hand, were property owners, peasants who considered themselves nontribal and non-Kurdish, belonging to a subdivision of Turkmen. Even given the fact that Firat was writing in 1948 and taking into consideration his desire and eagerness to portray the Hormek as non-Kurdish (in fact, throughout his book Firat makes the case that the Kurds are of Turkic origin and that it was Abdulhamid's policies and the Hamidiye that forced many of the people of eastern Anatolia to consider themselves Kurds), he indicates graphically the enmity created by the Hamidiye. The Cibrans were the leaders and administrators of Muş and Varto; they were commanders of Hamidiye Regiments, gendarmes, and police. Hormek requests to government offices were usually rejected. Their possessions, land, and lives were in constant jeopardy; they were the hated Alevis or Kızılbaş. The Hamidiye commanders confiscated the land of the Alevis and the non-Hamidiye tribes. Every Hamidiye commander became a *derebey* (large landowner), similar to the emirates that had existed until 1847. Every grievance and feud was settled in favor of the Hamidiye tribes. After clashes with the Cibrans and rejection of all their complaints to the government authorities (most of whom seemed to be Cibrans), the Hormek and other Alevis and non-Hamidiye tribes began to oppose the government. This opposition continued until the Sheikh Said rebellion.

The Cibrans were responsible for killing Ibrahim Talu, the venerated leader of the Hormek, in October 1894, a grisly murder the Hormek and Talu's family were never to forget. Ibrahim Talu's son Zeynel became a relentless foe of the Cibrans for the next twelve years; he was killed in 1906. The commander of the second Cibran Hamidiye Regiment, responsible for tracking down and killing Zeynel, was Halid Beg Cibran, who was to become one of the principal leaders of the Sheikh Said rebellion. The Alevi tribes of the Dersim-Tunceli region were not to forget Halid Beg's actions. They did not join him in his fight against the Kemalists in 1925. The Alevi tribes, even those that spoke the Zaza dialect like the Cibrano, did not join the Sheikh Said rebellion. Indeed, some Alevi tribes even fought against Sheikh Said in defense of the new Turkish republic.[26] The Alevis saw no reason to support a rebellion led by a Sunni Nakş-bandi sheikh who was the commander of many tribes that had participated in the Hamidiye, at whose hands they had suffered so much. When a consciousness of Kurdish nationalism began to be felt in the community, it was largely a Sunni affair. The Alevis felt little loss with the abolition of the caliphate. After all, it was the caliph, Sultan Abdulhamid II, who had created the Hamidiye, the source of so many of their grievances, hardships, and woes.

The Hamidiye Regiments were an important stage in the emergence of Kurdish nationalism from 1891 to 1914, serving as a fulcrum of Kurdish power for over two decades. There had not been such a concentration of Kurdish power and authority since 1847. From 1895 to 1914, the Kurds had 50,000 men, perhaps considerably more, under arms, most of whom were located in eastern Anatolia (five regiments were stationed in Syria). Some of the regiments fought in the Balkan wars, where they experienced contemporary warfare before the outbreak of World War I. The Kurds and their officers were exposed not only to Turkish nationalism, but to Balkan nationalism. While the research on this topic is scarce, the Kurds, especially the officers who had been trained in the schools established by Abdulhamid, became aware of the international politics that had contributed to the Balkan wars. The nationalism of the Balkan people must have seemed familiar to them as it had to Turkish officers before them. They also must have come to understand the thinking of their fellow Turkish officers as well as Arab officers. It certainly would not be incongruous for an educated Kurdish officer to identify with Turkish nationalism and find it similar to his own nationalistic thoughts and feelings. The Hamidiye gave an opportunity for the Kurds to experience and attempt to fathom the wider world. The provision of the decrees creating the Hamidiye provided for schools for the officers of the regiments. Children of the tribal leaders would be allowed to attend military school, a development that was to have far-reaching effects. For the first time, there was a cadre of Kurds educated in the contemporary curriculum obtaining in Istanbul. The Kurds were exposed to the same education as their fellow Turkish and Arab officers at a time when many innovations were being made in the curriculum. Many of the educational reforms were secular in nature.[27]

Abdulhamid's policies, implemented via the Hamidiye, also allowed the Kurds to oppose the bureaucracy of the Porte and their counterparts in the provinces more forcefully. Kurds looked upon the bureaucrats as implementing reforms that favored the creation of an Armenian state. Those Ottoman bureaucrats, willing or not, seemed to be the instruments of the European and Christian powers who advocated the reforms. Such a situation must have contributed to the Kurdish sense that they had to take matters into their own hands. The Hamidiye gave them this opportunity, with an Islamic touch. It is not just that Abdulhamid II was such a staunch Muslim or the Kurds so enamored of the caliphate; after all, they had not proven particularly beholden to it at times in the past. Abdulhamid's policies of Islamic unity allowed for some concession to Kurdish power and authority. It is difficult to speculate what his policy would have been if he had ruled for another twenty years. It is unlikely he would have supported the creation of an independent Kurdish state, especially with the absence of the Armenians. Given the evolution of Turkish nationalism, he probably would not even have supported autonomy for the Kurds.

In fact, the sultan himself began to change his policies in the late 1890s. Part of this shift may have been that the Hamidiye could consolidate many of the Kurdish tribes that had been fragmented since 1847.[28] The critics, even the Kurdish ones, are quick to point out that this meant a resurrection of the *derebeys* of the first part of the century. But these observations seemed to be a bit wide of the mark. The *derebeys* had existed in a non-nationalist polity, but this was decidedly not the case in 1900, let alone by 1914. While it is true that most of the Hamidiye leaders did not have the vision of Sheikh Ubaydallah, neither were their circumstances as propitious. The Hamidiye leaders did not have the political power of the emirs; they were not Bedir Khans or Muhammad Paşas. But this is not paradoxical. Nationalist ideas are more parochial and narrow than the more universal ideas of sultan, caliph, shah, or hereditary prince. They are also more antagonistic and fractious. If the ideas that emerged along with the development of the Hamidiye had been allowed to continue, it is unlikely that they would have evolved along nationalist lines. It is no irony that the Pan-Islamic policies of Abdulhamid II contributed to a stronger sense of Kurdish nationalism. Such ideas are usually ubiquitous when polities are in decline or having difficulty. In these circumstances, minority groups can develop their own polities without denying their allegiance to the symbol or symbols of their shared polity, whether caliph, sultan, king, or emperor. It was the policies of Abdulhamid II and the symbols of the caliphate that the Turkish nationalists opposed.

The creation of the Hamidiye also meant an internal shift of power in Kurdistan that led to a reduction of the power of the sheikhs. Sheikh Ubaydallah's movement had indicated the strength of the combined power of a religious-political leader. No one would be more aware of this than Sultan Abdulhamid II. Among the several reasons for creating the Hamidiye was the desire to reduce the power of the sheikhs. Tribal leaders would be more easily controlled; their jurisdiction would be in much smaller areas. They also would be less tempted to make cross-border appeals or invasions into other countries. A movement such as Ubaydallah's into Iran well might have resulted in the introduction of European or Russian forces, the last thing Abdulhamid wanted at this juncture. It is true that the rebellion of 1925 was led by a sheikh, but it was much more permeated and supported by nationalist ideas and by the nationalists themselves than Sheikh Ubaydallah ever hoped or, indeed, probably would have wanted. The interval between Sheikh Ubaydallah and Sheikh Said was led by secular leaders, a necessary intermezzo in the evolution of Kurdish nationalism. It was also recognition by the organizers of Sheikh Said's rebellion of the strengths of tribal societies and the weakness of the emerging nationalist slogans and appeals unless expressed in religious symbols and language by a man of religion with an impeccable and popular reputation.

Many scholars of late nineteenth century and early twentieth century Ottoman history are of the opinion that Abdulhamid's policies were a failure. The proof is that his regime was toppled by the Young Turks. Scholars of Kurdish history and nationalism usually consider this period a backward step in the evolution of a state structure because it is marked by tribal rule and the ruthless plunder and oppression by the Hamidiye against non-Hamidiye, especially the Alevi tribes. In addition, the Hamidiye suppressed and curtailed the emergence of the artisan and merchant class—a potential middle class, the usual bearer of nationalism. But it must be remembered that a substantial number of these classes in eastern Anatolia were Turkish. An increase in their power would hardly have benefited the development of Kurdish nationalism.

The tragedy from the Kurdish point of view was that the Hamidiye era plunged emergent nationalism into the vicious maelstrom of tribal politics. The question to be asked is: would Kurdish nationalism have been stronger in the wake of World War I if the Hamidiye had not existed? Kurdish nationalist historians and Marxist historians make a case that it would have been stronger, but I have tried to demonstrate that this is not the case. The Hamidiye era was a necessary interlude in emergent Kurdish nationalism, marking the third stage in its evolution. It contributed to feelings of solidarity among Sunni Kurds and offered leadership opportunities to many young Kurdish men. The Hamidiye also provided many Kurds with knowledge of military technology and equipment and the capabilities to use it.

Kurdish Nationalism from 1908 to 1924

The Young Turk revolution of 1908, beginning the third stage of Kurdish nationalism, led immediately to the public establishment of Kurdish nationalist organizations, especially in the capital city of Istanbul. The first one was the Kürt Terraki ve Teavun Cemiyeti (Kurdish Society for Progress and Mutual Aid), sometimes called Kürdistan Taali ve Terraki Cemiyeti (Society for the Rise and Progress of Kurdistan).[29] The society included some of the most illustrious sons of famous Kurdish families. The leadership of nationalist organizations also indicated that sons of former Kurdish emirs had sought and obtained educations while the tribal leaders were commanding the Hamidiye. Among the founders of the society were Emir Emin Ali Bedir Khan, Sheikh Abdul Qadir of Nehri, son of Sheikh Ubaydallah, General Muhammad Şerif Paşa, and Müşir Dhu al-Kifl Paşa, a roll call of Kurdish illuminaries, among whom the Bedir Kahns predominated. The society established a cultural affiliate, Kürt Neşri Maarif Cemiyeti (Society for the Propagation of Kurdish Education) that published a magazine, *Kürdistan*, that was a continuation of the same newspaper that had been published by Sureya Beg Bedir Khan in Cairo. In Istanbul he remained its principal contributor. The society also built a school for the Kurdish population in Istanbul, which in 1908 numbered about 30,000. The school was attended by Sayyid Kurdi or Nursi, who subsequently became an influential Kurdish Islamic leader and the exponent of Nuruculuk.[30]

Kürdistan Taali ve Terraki was shut down in 1909 by the Young Turks, who saw no advantage in allowing Kurds to organize. A second organization, Hevi-i-Kürt Cemiyeti (Kurdish Hope Society), was founded in 1912. The establishment of a second organization was indicative of the rivalry and differences among the Kurds of Istanbul. The Hevi was an organization of Kurdish students (some of whom came from the Hamidiye schools established by Abdulhamid II). According to van Bruinessen, its members were "sons of urban, Ottomanized notables. They belonged to the same social stratum as most Young Turks; their romantic nationalism paralleled that of the Turkish nationalists. . . ." This is one of the reasons that a number of Kurdish nationalists were among the founders and supporters of the Committee for Union and Progress (Ittihad ve Terraki Cemiyeti) such as Işak Sukuti, Abdullah Cevdet, Abdurrahman Bedir Khan, Hikmet Baban, Ismail Hakkı Baban, and Suleyman Nazif.[31] Ziya Gökalp, one of the leading contributors to Turkish nationalism, was a Kurd from Diyarbakır. But like the founders of Kürdistan Taali ve Terraki Cemiyeti, they were quite divorced from their people in eastern Anatolia, who were still traditional and religious and whose idea of nationalism was still tied to the caliphate, especially as that office had been exercised by Abdulhamid II. The officers and leaders of the Hamidiye were not yet sufficiently willing to cooperate with their citified brethren. The catalyst of World War I was needed to bring about that cooperation. Experiencing the common calamities of the war helped to bring the "Western" intellectuals and the eastern tribesmen and sheikhs together. In a way, World War I had an impact on Kurdish nationalism similar to that of the Hamidiye era. Although World War I was much shorter than the decade and a half of the Hamidiye era, its immense impact on the Ottoman Empire and the devastation wreaked in Kurdistan forced the "Westerners" and "Easterners" closer together and enabled more cooperation after the war.

By 1908, the idea of Kurdish nationalism had become better known and had grown, even if it did not follow the path hoped by the Kurdish nationalists, romantic and otherwise, in Istanbul. In Kurdistan the nationalist ideas found their way into the *tarikat*s and *tekkiye*s, where the sheikhs became their ardent supporters. Wadie Jwaideh thinks this

was a development of great significance in the history of Kurdish nationalism. For a number of reasons, the importance of the *takiyah*s as centers for the dissemination of nationalist ideas can scarcely be exaggerated. The ideas emanating from these focal points found ready and wide acceptance among the Kurds, for they bore the stamp of authority of the shaykhs. Moreover, the religious character and influence of the shaykhs gave the *takiyah*s relative immunity from interference and harassment by the authorities [the importance of this was clearly demonstrated in the Iranian revolution in the 1980s]. The shaykhs, who as a class

represented an important segment of the Kurdish elite, were ardent nationalists. Unlike the largely Turkified urban Kurdish
elite, they were closely associated with the Kurdish masses, and
identified themselves with them. Furthermore, both by training
and conviction they stood for the traditional Islamic state as
opposed to the modern secular state envisaged by the Young
Turks.[32]

The attitude and position of the sheikhs can be understood from a
petition they submitted to the Young Turk government soon after it
came to power. Sheikhs Abdulsalam Barzan and Nur Muhammad of
Dohuk delivered the petition, which consisted of the following
seven points:

(1) Adopt Kurdish administration in five Kurdish *kazas* (administrative districts).

(2) Adopt Kurdish as the language of instruction in the Kurdish
areas.

(3) The appointment of Kurdish-speaking *kaymakams* and *müdirs*
(both administrative officials) as well as other officials.

(4) Administration of law and justice should be according to the
Şeriyet (Shari'a).

(5) The positions of *kadi* (religious judge) and *müfti* (canon law
lawyer responsible for delivering formal legal opinions) to be filled
by adherents of the Şafii school of law.

(6) Taxes to be levied in accordance with the Şeriyet.

(7) Taxes collected for the exemption from labor service to remain
in effect, provided they were set aside for the repair and maintenance
of roads in the five Kurdish *kazas*.

As Jwaideh has emphasized, numbers 1, 2, 3, and 7 were expres-
sions of Kurdish nationalism; 4, 5, and 6 reflected religious views.
The fifth point, however, points out the subtlety of the sheikhs'
position, for the appointment of *kadis* and *müftis* of the Şafii school,
to which the majority of Kurds belong, "was tantamount to demanding the recognition of the paramountcy of the rite. This, of course,"
would have meant the establishment of a Kurdish national church."
This was the historical pattern that had been followed by the Greek
Orthodox peoples of the Balkans. But events were not to turn out as
propitiously for the Kurds as for the Balkan peoples; the Kurds were
confronted with a Turkish nationalism much stronger than their
own that eventually advocated dismantling of the religious institutions that supported the sheikhs. As the petition makes clear, many
of the sheikhs had nationalist goals, but they could not be pursued
without religious institutions and government tolerance. When the

sheikhs realized that the Young Turk government was antagonistic, they staged constant rebellions from 1908 through the war and after the armistice.[33]

In Istanbul Kurdish nationalists joined the opposition parties such as the Hürriyet ve Itilaf Firkası (Freedom and Accord party). One of the leaders of this party was Mevlanzade Rifat, the publisher of the *Serbesti* (Freedom) newspaper that printed articles by Kurdish nationalists such as Kamuran Bedir Khan. In 1914, Celadet Bedir Khan wrote an article that was printed by the *Serbesti* press. Rawanduzlu Fanizadeler, another Kurdish nationalist, was the general secretary of the Freedom and Accord party. Utilizing his position, he was able to gather a group of 150 Kurdish nationalists around him. Abdullah Cevdet and Ibrahim Temo created the Osmanlı Demokrat Firkası (Ottoman Democratic party), which also offered opposition in Parliament. Another Kurdish nationalist, Lutfi Fikri, was active against the Committee of Union and Progress. In 1910, he began the Mütedil Hürriyetperver Firkası (Moderate Freedom party) and also published for a time the newspaper *Tanzimat* (Reform).[34] With the outbreak of the war in 1914, however, Kurdish nationalists' activities, whether in support of or in opposition to the government or the Committee of Union and Progress, had to be subordinated to the patriotic cause of defending the homeland.

Throughout the war, Kurdistan was engulfed in the war zones. The theater of operations extended from Sarıkamiş, in the north, to Khaniqin in the south, to Erzincan in the west. It is difficult to determine how many Kurds participated in the war as soldiers; the numbers in different accounts vary widely. Muhammad Zaki states that the Eleventh Army headquartered at Elazığ (Mamuretülaziz) and the Twelfth Army at Mosul were made up entirely of Kurds. The majority of the officers and soldiers of the Ninth Army at Erzurum and the Tenth Army at Sivas were also Kurds. The Kurds also contributed 135 squadrons of reserve cavalry and a number of frontier units and numerous gendarmes. Zaki estimates that the Kurds suffered 300,000 casualties, which would imply that well over half a million Kurds served in the war; that would seem to be high. The Kurds did sustain heavy losses in battles against the Russian forces. In 1916, the Sixtieth and Sixty-first Corps in the Hınıs and Pasınler fronts suffered heavy casualties in one battle; there were several such battles. On 15 July 1916, the Ottoman (Kurdish) forces fought another major engagement with the Russians. Şerif Firat does not give casualty figures, but they must have been heavy—the battle resulted in a Russian retreat.[35] The number of Kurds that perished from famine, disease, and cold was probably greater than the losses sustained in the war against the Russians and in the civil war with the Armenians.

It is difficult to determine the population of the Kurds in the Ottoman Empire, let alone in Turkey or in eastern Anatolia. The debate concerning the number of Armenians who perished in World War I, however, has made statistics, whatever their reliability, available. The statistics for the Kurdish population in eastern Anatolia compiled by the Armenian patriarchate were Erzurum, 75,000; Van, 72,000; Bitlis, 77,000; Mamuretülaziz or Harput (present-day Elazığ), 95,000; Diyarbakır, 95,000; Sivas, 50,000—a total of 464,000 or 16.3 percent of the total population of the six eastern *vilayets* (provinces). Turks represented 25.4 percent, and Armenians 38.9 percent. The patriarchate, however, did not include the Kızılbaş (140,000), Zazas (77,000), or Yezidis (37,000) in the Kurdish figures. If we leave out the Yezidis, since they are not usually considered Kurds, but include the Kızılbaş and Zazas figures, we come up with the sum of 681,000 Kurds as compared to 666,000 Turks or 1,018,000 Armenians.[36] Thus, by the patriarchate figures the Kurdish and Turkish populations were about equal.

Justin McCarthy in a recent work based on Ottoman population censuses and other population statistics for the years 1911 and 1912, adjusted in accordance with accepted demographic calculations, gives only the figures for Muslims in the *vilayets* and does not give separate figures for Turks and Kurds. His figures for the Muslim population of the six eastern *vilayets* are: Erzurum, 804,388; Van, 313,322; Bitlis, 408,703; Mamuretülaziz, 564,164; Diyarbakır, 598,985; Sivas, 1,196,300—a total of 3,885,862 Muslims. If we leave out Sivas, which the Kurds did not claim, the total figure for Muslims in the remaining five *vilayets* would be 2,689,562, at least half of whom were probably Kurdish. Based on the patriarchate figures of 1912, Hovannisian believes that "there were at least as many Moslems as Christians." McCarthy concludes from his research that "all Anatolian provinces had overwhelming Muslim majorities, not simply pluralities. . . ."[37] He calculates that if all Anatolian Armenians had immigrated to the six *vilayets*, Muslims still would have outnumbered Armenians more than 2.5 to 1. If the Kurds were roughly half of the Muslim population, then they would have had a ratio of 1.25 to 1 for the Armenians. If the *vilayet* of Sivas is dropped from these calculations, the ratio percentage would be even greater— and this is after all Anatolian Armenians had immigrated to the six *vilayets* in question.

McCarthy calculates the devastating effect that World War I had

Table 1. *Population of the Six Eastern Vilayets of Anatolia in 1912 and 1922*

	Population in 1912	Actual Population in 1922	Difference
Erzurum	804,388	555,693	248,695
Van	313,322	119,155	194,167
Bitlis	408,703	238,955	169,748
Mamuretülaziz	564,164	474,854	89,310
Diyarbakır	598,985	440,942	158,043
Sivas	1,196,300	1,015,887	180,413
Total			1,040,376

on the Muslim population, again using just the statistics from the six *vilayets* (see table 1). Thus, 41.9 percent of the 2.5 million Muslims who died in the period of World War I died in the six *vilayets* of eastern Anatolia or, put in other terms, 7.6 percent of the total Muslim population. The Kurds were at least half of the 7.6 percent or 500,000. In 1919, after an extensive tour through Diyarbakır *vilayet,* Captain Noel, a British agent of whom more will be said later, estimated that the prewar population was 994,000, of which 750,000 were Kurdish and 3,000 Turkish. His postwar estimate was a total population of 648,500—a loss of 345,500. He estimated the postwar Kurdish population at 600,000 and the Turks at 2,500—a wartime loss of 150,500, of which 150,000 were Kurdish and only 500 Turkish.[38] Given McCarthy's calculations, Noel's figures seem quite high for the total population of Diyarbakır *vilayet:* high for the Kurdish and absurdly low for the Turkish. Noel's figures are all the more interesting in that he was the main British agent in Kurdistan, both in Anatolia and in Iraq, from 1919 to 1922. His figures and information played an important role in British policy toward Turkey and the Kurds during this period.

There is another set of figures for the eastern provinces for 1931. Two British consuls, Roberts and Ravensdale, traveled through the areas under discussion from 26 June to 11 July 1931 and gave the following figures: Erzurum, 300,000; Van, 80,000; Kars, 208,000; Malatya, 300,000; Elazığ (Mamuretülaziz), 200,000; and Iğdır, 104,000. Roberts and Ravensdale gave no figures for Diyarbakır or Sivas. Also, the *vilayet* structure had been changed by 1931; it is difficult to make comparisons since the new *vilayets* overlapped with the older six *vilayets*. But the figures are substantially lower than those given by McCarthy. These figures for the capitals of the *vilayets* and the towns and villages through which Roberts and Ravensdale passed are also shockingly low. For example, they recorded the following figures: Malatya, 20,000; Harput, 12,000–15,000; Bitlis, 12,000; Erciş, 3,000; Van, 5,000; Karaköse, 3,000–4,000; Kars, 12,000; and Erzurum, 25,000. Roberts and Ravensdale's account is similar to Alex K. Helms's report on the same provinces in 1929. He recorded these figures: Elazığ (Elaziz), 13,000; Diyarbakır, 30,000; Malatya, 14,000; Sivas, 29,000; and Giresun, 8,000. A few months after Helms's journey, W. S. Edmonds, another British consul, reported the following statistics: Gaziantep, 15,000–20,000; Urfa, 20,000; Bitlis, 5,000; and Muş, 3,000.[39] The figures given by the British consuls and officials suggest postwar population figures lower than those of McCarthy. But until McCarthy's figures are challenged or proven wrong, they provide a reasonable assessment of the great destruction wrought in eastern Anatolia on the Muslim and Kurdish populations; it only pales in comparison with the destruction of the Armenians.

It was suggested above that probably more than 500,000 Kurds died in Turkey proper during World War I. When one adds to this figure the deaths of Kurds in Iraq, Syria, Iran, and Russia, it is likely the total deaths among the Kurdish population neared the 1 million mark. Muhammad Amin Zaki and Wadie Jwaideh give detailed accounts of the destruction in northern Iraq. Zaki states that 300,000 Kurds were casualties of the war. A Kurdish source suggests that 700,000 Kurds were forced to evacuate their places of residence. Basil Nikitine, a Russian consul who was present in the area during the war, attests to the same terrible conditions and death in Kurdistan in Iran.[40]

The armistice between the allies and Ottomans was signed on 31 October 1918. This event was to mark a resurgence in Kurdish nationalist activity. The Kürt Terraki ve Teavun Cemiyeti (Kurdish Society for Progress and Mutual Aid) was reactivated in 1918 as the Kürdistan Taali Cemiyeti (Society for the Rise of Kurdistan). Unlike its predecessor, which had consisted largely of educated and urban nationalists, the new organization also included members from the tribes. Van Bruinessen has given a list of the members of the society, notable because of its indication of the new direction of Kurdish nationalism after World War I. The officers included as president, Sayyid Abdul Qadir, the son of the famous Ubaydallah; as first vice-president, General Fuad Paşa of Sulaymaniya; as secretary-general, Hamdi Paşa, a retired member of the general staff; and as treasurer,

Sayyid Abdullah, a son of Abdul Qadir. The military committee consisted of Miralay (Colonel) Halid Beg from Dersim, head of the Istanbul police; Mehmet Ali Bedir Khan, a retired colonel; and Mehmet Emin Beg of Sulaymaniya, a retired lieutenant colonel. Among the religious officials were Kweca Ali Efendi and Şefik Efendi from Ervas. Other members were Babanzade Şukri Beg, editor-in-chief of the newspaper *Tercüman*; Babanzade Fuad Beg; Fethullah, a trader; and Şukri Mehmet, a professor of medicine. Other members also included Alişan Beg of the Koçgiri region in Dersim, which was to stage a rebellion in 1920. The Hevi-i Kürt Cemiyeti (Kurdish Hope Society) was also revived and it subsequently merged with a faction at the Kürt Taali Cemiyeti composed of younger and more radical members to form the Kürt Teskilati-i Içtima'i Cemiyeti (Kurdish Social Organization Society). According to van Bruinessen, the split occurred when Sayyid Abdul Qadir, and possibly the Bedir Khans, "publicly declared that his aim was not an independent Kurdistan" but rather a limited form of autonomy. Many of the Bedir Khans joined with the young nationalists. The Kurdish Social Organization Society seems to have been effective due to support from the Kurdish population in Istanbul. The members of the society were instrumental in forming the Ciwata Azadiya Kurd (Society for Kurdish Freedom), which was later renamed Ciwata Kweseriya Kurd (Society for Kurdish Independence).[41] It was this organization that was to play an important role in the Sheikh Said rebellion.

Wadie Jwaideh states that almost immediately after the armistice a recrudescence of Kurdish nationalist activities took place. This was not only because of the efforts of the Kurds but also because of active Turkish support. The British wanted to use Kurds against the Turks and promised the Kurds a form of autonomy within a Turkish-dominated state under the suzerainty of the sultan-caliph, who would, of course, be a Turk. As we shall see, the Turks continued to offer a limited autonomy to the Kurds right up to the signing of the Treaty of Lausanne on 24 July 1923. Turkish promises in this respect increased after Şerif Paşa, the Kurdish representative at Versailles, signed an agreement with Boghas Nubar, the Armenian representative, on 20 November 1919 in Paris that stated the Kurds would support Armenian independence and that the Armenians would support Kurdish independence. Both parties agreed to leave the settlement of boundaries to the Peace Conference.[42] This development demonstrated that some Kurdish nationalists were not opposed to Armenian independence aspirations. It may well have been that some Kurdish nationalists felt less threatened by the Armenians in the wake of their deportation and massacre in the eastern provinces, where an independent Kurdish state would be established. They may also have felt some remorse over their own role, a major one. Another faction of the Kurdish nationalists was Pan-Islamic. It worked in cooperation with the Turkish groups that were actively anti-British. But the primary goal of the Pan-Islamic group was to prevent the creation of an Armenian state.

As early as January 1919, members of the Committee of Union and Progress were reportedly in Harput urging the Kurds to demand independence at the peace conference in Versailles. The leader of this movement was Ali Ihsan Paşa, former commander of the Ottoman Sixth Army. He was one of the Ottoman negotiators who had signed the armistice of Mudros, although he strongly disagreed with the terms. The activities in which he engaged were directed against the British action, especially the policy in Iraq. The British had occupied Mosul on 7 November 1918. This event increased Ottoman fears of further British expansion. Turkish support of Kurdish activities was part of a policy to deter British expansionism and support for an independent Armenia. The British were sure that Ali Ihsan did not favor an independent Kurdistan. Turkish support was meant as an embarrassment and impediment to Allied plans. It was an effective policy, but inherently risky. After the Greek occupation of Izmir in May 1919, the Greek killing of Turks was blamed on the British; the Kurds were apprehensive that a British-supported Armenian army in eastern Anatolia would take revenge for their role in the Armenian massacres just as the Armenians in the Russian army had done earlier. As a result, the Kurds supported the Turkish effort, which allowed them to get rid of the remaining Armenians; given the circumstances, the Turks could not allow this and risk international intervention. In June 1919, the Turkish-Kurdish Clubs that were supporting Kurdish nationalist activities were abolished.

The activities of the Committee of Union and Progress members in supporting Kurdish nationalist agitation confirm its role in leading resistance both before and after the commencement of Mustafa Kemal's resistance movement. Stanford Shaw and Ezel Shaw have made the observations that the CUP initiated resistance and was organized within the Ministry of Foreign Affairs. Erik Jan Zürcher's recent work demonstrates just how active the secret underground network of the CUP (Karakol) and the Special Organization (Teşkilat-i Mahsusa) were. He states that it is possible Mustafa Kemal went to Anatolia at the behest of Karakol. Mustafa Kemal's resistance campaign began in regions heavily Kurdish, probably with the blessing of the CUP.[43] Mustafa Kemal's resistance movement coincided with the CUP's activities in southeast Anatolia in support of Kurdish resistance to the British and Armenians.

The dilemma of the Kurds from the armistice of Mudros (31 October 1918) to the Treaty of Sèvres (10 August 1920) centered on the question of autonomy or independence. The agreement between Şerif Paşa and Boghas Nubai of 20 November 1919 confronted the Kurds with the necessity of declaring for a policy of autonomy or independence. We have seen that the Turkish reaction to the 20 November agreement was to promise autonomy to the Kurds. Some Kurdish nationalists wanted independence, some, such as Emin Bedir Khan, wanted separation from Turkey but recognition of the sultan as caliph. Bedir Khan wanted the self-determination principles of President Wilson to be implemented in Kurdistan. Sayyid Abdul Qadir Khan seemed to straddle the fence. His inability to take a strong position for independence, or calculated decision as some historians would have it, led to the split mentioned above in the Kürt Taali Cemiyeti (Society for the Rise of Kurdistan). In February and March 1920, Abdul Qadir made several statements to newspapers that he favored autonomy and supported Şerif Paşa's efforts at Versailles. Emin Bedir Khan and the intellectuals of the Society for the Rise of Kurdistan dismissed Abdul Qadir from his post as president after his statements. A historian of the Kurdish nationalist movement has written that the difference between Emin Ali Bedir Khan and Sayyid Abdul Qadir is that the latter preferred the autonomy of a *unified Kurdistan* to a fragmented Kurdistan.[44] Abdul Qadir hoped, apparently with the aid of Great Britain, to achieve a unified Kurdistan when circumstances made that possible.

It is ironic that the Treaty of Sèvres provided for an independent Kurdistan, but not a unified one—large parts of Kurdistan were to remain in Iraq and Iran.[45] The goal of nationalists who were striving for a unified Kurdistan resulted in their lack of support for those Kurds who advocated independence, even as a region of Turkey. It is further ironic that those nationalists who advocated a unified Kurdistan sought the support of Great Britain, whose occupation of Iraq and influence in Iran had made it clear by the signing of the Treaty of Sèvres that there was to be no unified Kurdistan. Thus, those nationalists who favored an independent Kurdistan were forced to seek that independence in Turkey proper. After 10 August 1920, however, it was clear that they would be challenged by an exuberant nationalist Turkish movement. The question from August 1920 to the middle of 1921 was to what extent the British would support a Kurdish independence movement in Turkey. The evidence, as discussed in chapter 3, is that great Britain was not willing to support a Kurdish independence movement in Turkey in the face of the rising strength of Turkish nationalist forces. But British policy until the middle of 1921 was to encourage the Kurds to think that they would support independence efforts. During this period, the British supported these efforts in Turkey with the conviction they would not result in an independent state but that the Kurds would be useful in obtaining concessions from the Turkish nationalist movement favorable to the British, especially along the Iraqi-Turkish border. In short, those Kurdish nationalists who favored a unified Kurdistan through autonomy were confronted by a British policy that supported autonomy only in Iraq and not a unified Kurdistan. The unfolding events after the Treaty of Sèvres were to demonstrate how badly the autonomists had miscalculated. Not only did the autonomists lose power and influence, but the core of the Kurdish nationalist movement itself moved to Anatolia, from which the next battles would be waged.

2. Kurdish Nationalism: From Sèvres to Said

THIS CHAPTER discusses the developments of Kurdish nationalism from the Treaty of Sèvres (signed 10 August 1920) to the outbreak of Sheikh Said's rebellion in February 1925, the fourth stage of Kurdish nationalism. The dilemma of Kurdish nationalism in Anatolia became clear immediately after the armistice of Mudros. In the Dersim area, the old conflicts between the Sunni and Shiʻi and Hamidiye and non-Hamidiye tribes once again resurfaced. In early summer of 1919, when Mustafa Kemal issued his proclamations for defense of the homeland against foreign invaders, Şerif Firat claims that none of the former Hamidiye Regiments or their members wanted to join the fight; he states that they had secretly agreed to support the idea of Kurdish nationalism and independence under the leadership of Miralay (Colonel) Halid Beg Cibran. This was the same Halid Beg who had become commander of the second Hamidiye Regiment in 1892 and who had led the assault on Zeynel Talu Hormekli, the son of Ibrahim Talu, in 1906.

Van Bruinessen suggests that Firat is wrong in stating that only Alevi units responded to the call of Mustafa Kemal to defend the homeland. His Kurdish informants state that all tribal units, former Hamidiye or not, joined the nationalist forces. The intensity of the Kurdish tribal regiments' attacks on the Russians and Armenians seems to indicate quite extensive Kurdish participation.[1] It was also thought to be in the interest of the Kurds to get rid of the remaining Armenians. It would then be easier to implement article 64 of the Treaty of Sèvres. One must keep in mind that van Bruinessen's Kurdish nationalist informants would find it desirable to indicate that Kurdish units, whether Sunni or Shiʻi, Hamidiye or non-Hamidiye, participated fully with the Turkish nationalist forces to push the Russians and Armenians back to the Caucasus. Firat's account, even if it is inaccurate, indicates the intertribal and interreligious conflict. He states that Halid Beg himself, in spite of being a colonel in the regular Ottoman army, not just a Hamidiye commander, did not participate in the campaign and even wired Kazım Karabekir, the Ottoman commander of the Army's First Caucasian Corps, not to accept the Alevi tribal units for fear of their treachery on the battlefront![2]

Most accounts of these events indicate, however, that Halid Beg Cibran not only participated but also distinguished himself in the eastern Anatolian campaigns of 1918. In fact, it seems that it was during these very campaigns that he realized that evacuation of the last Armenians meant that the Kurds would now be face to face with Turkish nationalism. There would be no buffer and no more bluff. In this regard, van Bruinessen records the following story: "on the day [he does not give the date] of the final victory over the Armenians, when every one else was merrymaking, Halid Beg looked very sad and sat brooding silently in his tent. Mehdi [Sheikh Said's brother] sat down with him and inquired what was the reason of Halid's black mood. After some insisting, the colonel told Mehdi the thought that had entered his mind and did not leave him at rest: 'This day we have whetted the sword that will one day cut our own throats!'"[3] If this is true, it indicates several things about Kurdish nationalism in 1918–1919. First, it shows that a Kurdish nationalist leader like Halid Beg Cibran was rather late in seeing the danger presented by Turkish nationalism and conversely seeing the advantage for the Kurds of having an Armenian presence in eastern Anatolia, especially with the small number of Armenians that remained after the massacres of 1915. The reason for the delayed appreciation can be traced to the hostility and virtual civil war between the Kurds and Armenians since 1878. Second, the appeal of Muslim solidarity, which meant cooperation with Ottoman and Turkish nationalist forces, obviously had a strong hold even on men like Halid Beg Cibran.

In 1919, men such as Halid Beg were in positions of governmental authority in the towns of the Dersim region and used their authority and some coercion to organize the tribes for rebellion against the nationalist government. It was in 1920 that Halid Beg and likeminded men began to make propaganda against the Kemalists, especially among the sheikhs and *hocas* (religious teachers). The Kurdish leaders began to wear Kurdish clothes, to speak Kurdish, and to circulate well-known Kurdish poems among the tribes. Throughout 1920, Halid Beg gathered supporters as well as detractors. After the Treaty of Sèvres, according to Firat, Halid Beg was in contact with the Kürt Taali Cemiyeti during the summer and fall of 1920 and with Sayyid Abdul Qadir. If this is true, it indicates that there was a greater amount of contact between the Kürt Taali Cemiyeti and the Kurds of Istanbul than previously thought. This cooperation seems to have existed prior to the establishment of the Ciwata Kweseriya Kurd (Society for Kurdish Independence) or Azadi as it was popularly known in Erzurum in 1921.[4] Throughout the fall of 1920, Halid Beg Cibran visited and organized the tribes in the areas of Varto, Bulanık, Malazgird, Hınıo, Karlıova, Solhan, Çapakçur, areas that were subsequently to participate in Sheikh Said's rebellion. He talked with the sheikhs, *hocas*, and heads of mosques as well as village heads (*muhtars*). He did not have much success among Alevi tribes. When exhortation proved insufficient to convince the Alevis of the merits of Kurdish nationalism, force was sometimes used.[5] By the late summer of 1920, the Kemalists became increasingly suspicious of Halid Beg's activities; in August 1920, he was assigned other duties in Erzurum.

While Halid Beg Cibran was biding his time in Erzurum, a Kurdish rebellion broke out in the Dersim (present-day Tunceli) region in November 1920. It is often called the Koçgiri rebellion after the tribe that played a major role in it. The main account of the rebellion was written by Nuri Dersimi, who was apparently sent back to the region from which he hailed as a representative of the activist section of the Kürt Taali Cemiyeti (Society for the Rise of Kurdistan). Dersimi was the son of a large landlord (*ağa*) and was well connected to local elites. Dersimi seems to have played a role in instigating the rebellion, although its exact nature is unclear. The origins of the rebellion indicate that the Society for the Rise of Kurdistan was eager to move after the Treaty of Sèvres and to implement articles 62 and 64. It also suggests that there was cooperation between the Society for the Rise of Kurdistan and its branches in Anatolia. The rebellion broke out less than three months after the signing of the Treaty of Sèvres.

Dersimi and a companion, Koçgirili Mustafa Paşa, had come to Istanbul immediately after the armistice of Mudros. Upon arriving in Istanbul, the two young Kurds learned that Sayyid Abdul Qadir supported autonomy, a position with which they strongly disagreed. In October 1920, Dersimi left for Ümraniye, the largest town among the Koçgiri tribes, and began to set up branches of the Society for the Rise of Kurdistan. These efforts caught the eye of Mustafa Kemal; in early September 1919, he apparently talked with Alişan Beg, one of the Kurdish organizers in Sivas. Alişan Beg, the son of Koçgirili Mustafa Paşa, the main leader of the Koçgiri tribes, told Mustafa Kemal that the Kurds were working for an autonomous Kurdistan, as proclaimed in President Wilson's Fourteen Points. Mustafa Kemal replied that the principles of President Wilson were worthless for the peoples of the East (apparently referring to all the peoples, not just the Kurds) and suggested that the Kurds should cooperate with his nationalist representatives in the Dersim region. Mustafa Kemal added further that it was a pity that Sayyid Abdul Qadir was an instrument of the Ferid Paşa government in Istanbul and a servant of the British. He also stated that he had information that the British spy, Captain Noel, in the company of some Bedir Khans, and members of the Cemil Paşa family in cooperation with the *vali* of Elaziz were planning to attack the Kemalist forces in Sivas. He added that at the Erzurum congress (23 July–7 August 1919) all of Kurdistan had promised to support him and, furthermore, that the Ferid Paşa government would not be able to fulfill the Sèvres Treaty or the Wilson principle for Kurdistan.[6]

It seems that it was Mustafa Kemal's harsh response that made it necessary for the young Kurds to cut their communication with the Society for the Rise of Kurdistan in Istanbul and to attempt a rebellion. It also became clear to the young Kurds that Mustafa Kemal was succeeding in drawing some Kurds to his side. By this time, the Kemalists were able to offer jobs as well as bribes to influential Kurds to join their cause. In spite of nationalist gains, the young Kurdish organizers were so successful that, although the Kurdish members of the Grand National Assembly informed the Allied powers that they would never separate from the Kemalists, the young Kurds continued to organize the tribes with the goal of obtaining an independent Kurdistan in spite of the fact that some Kurds supported the Kemalists. During the first months of 1920, organizational meetings were held with the purpose of coordinating the efforts with the Kurds of Diyarbakır, Van, Bitlis, and other areas. The connections of the sheikhs of the Huseyin Aptal brotherhood (*tekke*), where the meetings were held, with the Kurds of those regions played an instrumental role.[7]

By the summer of 1920, Dersimi estimated that the Kurds could muster a force of 45,000 in the western Dersim and another 45,000 in the eastern Dersim. The eastern and northern regions of the *vilayet* of Sivas were under their control. By July and August 1920, the Kurds were attacking Turkish ammunition shipments and police stations; some Turkish prisoners were taken. In order to defuse the rising unrest, the Kemalist government appointed Kurds such as Koçgiri tribal chief Alişan Beg to the position of governor (*kaymakam*) of Refahiye and his brother Haydar as mayor of Ümraniye. Some of the Kurdish activists wanted to proclaim the independence of Kurdistan publicly. As the Kurds advanced their political position, they continued to attack Turkish ammunition shipments and depots the Turks were stockpiling for use against potential Kurdish unrest. On 20 October, the Kurds seized a large arms shipment. Alişan Beg Koçgiri, using his position as governor of the Refahiye district (*ilce*), was successful in rallying more tribes to support the rebellion. Alişan Beg and other tribal leaders went as far as Hozat (Tunceli) to rally the tribes that were lukewarm to the independence movement. The tribal leaders held a parley at Çemişkezek, declaring their support for a declaration of Kurdish independence.

On 15 November 1920, after a meeting of the Kurdish leaders, they addressed the following declaration to the Kemalist government in Ankara, demanding a response by 24 November.

(1) The Ankara government should state whether or not it accepted officially the promise of Kurdish autonomy as agreed to by the sultan's government in Istanbul.

(2) The Ankara government should inform the leaders of the Dersim who wrote the declaration of their attitude toward the administration of an autonomous Kurdistan.

(3) All of the Kurdish prisoners in jail at Elaziz, Malatya, Sivas, and Erzincan should be freed.

(4) Turkish officials must be withdrawn from all areas with a Kurdish majority.

(5) The Turkish military forces sent to the Koçgiri region should be withdrawn.

The Ankara government sent a commission from Elaziz to Dersim to consider the demands, but the commission members were driven away. The Kurds then sent on 25 November (Tesrin Sani) a telegraph to Ankara stating that if an independent Kurdistan was not established in the *vilayet* of Diyarbakır, Elaziz, Van, and Bitlis as stipulated in the Treaty of Sèvres, the tribal chiefs of western Dersim would take armed action.[8] Ankara responded that it was in agreement with the demands, in an apparent effort to buy time. At the same time, it reinforced government troops in Sivas. The Turks had the additional advantage of the late season. Snow had fallen heavily in the Dersim region and it was impossible for other tribes to aid the Koçgiri. The other tribal leaders thought the rebellion should be delayed until late spring 1921, when the following program was to be implemented.

The Kurdish revolution would first be proclaimed in the Dersim. The Kurdish flag would be raised in Hozat (Tunceli). The Kurdish national forces would advance from the direction of Erzurum,

Elaziz, and Malatya toward Sivas and would demand the official recognition of Kurdistan's independence by the Ankara government. It was thought that Ankara would accept this demand because it was backed by armed force. The postponement of the movement to spring, of course, gave the Kemalists an opportunity to surround the area, to circumscribe the spread of unrest, and to coopt certain tribal leaders. The Kemalists continued to state they would have no difficulty in meeting Kurdish demands. The governor of Elaziz personally came to the district of Pertek and told Meco Ağa, recently appointed as a member of Parliament, that Mustafa Kemal supported the Kurdish demands. Important Kurdish leaders accepted the inveiglements of Ankara.[9] In addition to Meco Ağa, Mustafa Diyab Ağa, Ahmet Ramizi, and Major (Binbaşı) Hasan Hayri were appointed to Parliament by Mustafa Kemal. In spite of the opportunistic actions of these men, Dersimi is of the opinion that they still harbored and defended Kurdish spiritual and national convictions. Moreover, throughout the spring of 1921, most of the Dersim was under Kurdish control and nationalist activities continued. Sayyid Riza, a religious leader, had assumed administrative control. The Kurdish deputies in Ankara informed him that they hoped to obtain Kurdish rights by peaceful means. Dersimi states that the deputies made these statements either because they needed an excuse to cover up their opportunistic acts or because they had fallen so deeply into the clutches of Turkish deception that they were unable to distinguish what their own motives were.

Mustafa Kemal recommended to Alişan Beg that either he come to Ankara or accept a position as a high government official in Sivas. He also promised that a Kurdish assistant governor (*mütessarıf*) would be sent to the Dersim. Sayyid Riza and Alişan Beg responded that they wanted an independent (*bağımsız*) Kurdish administration and certainly did not want any of the Kurdish deputies in Ankara as governors in the Dersim region. In late 1920, Mustafa Kemal ordered the arrest of Nuri Dersimi on the charge that he had armed 1,200 Kurdish miners from Dersim at the Balya mine. Dersimi states that upon hearing of the order for his arrest, he resigned his position and began to organize the Kurdish tribes full-time. However, on 20 December 1920, Dersimi was arrested. Even in prison, differences between the Kurds and Turks were evident. The difficulty of organizing the Kurds became clearer to Dersimi when the state prosecutor, one Mustafa, whispered in his ear that in spite of his position, he, too, was a Kurd! Upon release from prison, the *vali* of Sivas, Reşit Bey, tried to persuade Dersimi to advise the Kurds of Dersim to remain loyal to the Ankara government at a time when it was threatened by foreign invaders. He also stated that Mustafa Kemal had ordered that Dersimi be given some land (*çiftlik*) in accordance with the Settlement Law (Iskan Kanunu).[10]

Clashes between the Kemalists and the Kurds began as early as January 1921. On 15 February, a Turkish regiment marched on Ümraniye. Given these circumstances, the tribes wanted to rise immediately; but the leaders of the Kurdish movement wanted to wait a few months to assure greater tribal participation. The Kurds thought the Ankara government planned to wait for the end of winter. When the roads to Dersim were open, the Kemalists would then strive to coopt the Kurdish revolutionaries one by one and to destroy the Kurdish organizations; without firing a shot, they would arrest some of the nationalists and deport others in order to isolate Dersim and prevent the revolt from spreading. The Turks demanded the unconditional surrender of the Kurds—if not, their villages would be destroyed.

Fighting between the Kurds and Turks increased. In March 1921, a major clash occurred in Ümraniye; the Kurds executed the Turkish commander and raised the Kurdish flag in the center of town. Turkish weapons, including machine guns, fell to the Kurds in addition to 1,000 horses and all of the mules. The Kurds let the Turkish officers and soldiers go, apparently without killing any of them. The Kurdish and Circassian officers among the Turkish forces joined the Kurds.[11] It seems that it was these events of 1921 in Dersim that caused the Koçgiri rebellion and forced the Ankara government to take stronger measures against the Kurds. The events of March also encouraged other Kurds to join the victors' bandwagon. Other tribes in Erzincan and Malatya were requested to send help, but because of weather conditions they said they were unable to do so. The Kurds even thought of asking the French in Urfa and Gaziantep for help, but the younger Kurdish nationalists rejected asking for help from foreigners. They would face the Turks alone. Women and children carried ammunition and food to the fighters. On 8 March, Kurdish forces, crossing the snow-covered Munzur mountains, captured Kemaha, arresting the large Kurdish landowners, whom they viewed as collaborating with the Turks.

On 11 March 1921, spurred on by their victories, the Kurds sent a telegram to Ankara stating that they wanted to establish a *vilayet* staffed by Kurds out of the areas they occupied. The Kemalists responded by sending a commission headed by Şefik Bitlisi, himself a Kurd, who stated that Ankara wanted to settle matters peacefully. But even as Şefik Bitlisi parleyed with the rebels, the Turks reinforced their troops in the area. On 15 March, the Ankara government declared martial law (the first of many such declarations) in the *vilayet*s of Elaziz, Erzincan, and Sivas. In response to Turkish overtures to stop the rebellion, the Kurds telegraphed Ankara that they knew the Turkish government wanted to deport them, just as it had the Armenians, and that they would continue to fight in defense of their nationalist cause. The Kurds had calculated that the Turks would have to be cautious because they would have to withdraw forces from the battlefronts with the Greeks, where ferocious fighting was taking place. It seems that the Kurds thought that the Turks could not fight the Greeks and Kurds at the same time. What the Turks did in spring 1921 was to take precautions that the rebellion would not spread—and they attempted to undermine support for the rebellion among the Kurds themselves. This method was very effective. The Turks also turned the Circassian regiment, commanded by Topal Osman and known for their barbarity, loose on the Kurds. These regiments committed many atrocities and the Kurds responded in kind. As the Turks mounted their offensive, other tribes decided not to join the rebellion and some withdrew. The rebels received no encouragement from the Kurdish deputies in Ankara. By April 1921, the Koçgiri Kurdish rebellion was pretty well crushed by the Kemalists. Both the Turks and the Kurds seem to have mobilized considerably less than 10,000 troops.[12] These numbers were much smaller than the forces employed in the Sheikh Said rebellion.

I have described the Koçgiri rebellion at some length because there are no accounts in any language other than Turkish and only two such works.[13] Also, the rebellion is very important for the developments of post–World War I Kurdish nationalism—especially in indicating the strengths and weaknesses of Kurdish nationalism after the Treaty of Sèvres. The main reason for the rebellion seems to have been that the Kurds wanted to use the stipulations of articles 62 and 64 of the Treaty of Sèvres to increase their autonomy within Anatolia. They wished to take advantage of the fledgling Kemalist government, which had only declared its National Pact (Misak-i Milli) one year before the rebellion. In spring 1921, the Kemalists were locked in battle with the Greeks; as mentioned above, the Kurds wanted to take advantage of the situation. The Kurds also were in a good position to receive international support for their activities and even aid from the French, British, or Greeks. Although the Kurds were in contact with all three, there is no evidence that they received support from any of them. It is likely that all three countries were delighted by the difficulties of the Turkish nationalists, much more formidable opponents than the Kurds.

The Koçgiri rebellion also demonstrated convincingly the weaknesses of the Kurdish nationalist movement; the leaders themselves became aware of these when they addressed the reasons for their failure. One reason was the lack of European support; the second offered was that the tribal nature of Kurdish society did not provide the necessary unity for a war of independence. The lack of a middle class also necessitated that the tribal chiefs assume the leadership for a nationalist rebellion, but they could easily be coopted by the enemy. Third, the religious and sectarian differences among the Kurds created mistrust that, because of the lack of an enlightened group, was hard to remove. Dersimi states that the young Kurdish organizers agitated for independence, while the leaders of the rebellion asked only for autonomy. In their 11 March telegraph to Ankara, they had asked only for an autonomous *vilayet* comprised of the area they then occupied.[14]

The self-criticism of the rebellion's leaders is well founded. Many of the tribal leaders, as has been pointed out, were easily coopted by the Kemalists, who gave them jobs, appointments, land, or, in some cases, bribes. The Kemalists had the vast lands and properties of the Armenians to distribute and the abundant patronage of a new and expanding government at their disposal. They made strong appeals for Muslim solidarity against the infidels who were attacking the homeland. In addition, many Kurds were probably unconvinced of the inherent strength of their nationalism. Much of the leadership for the organization of the rebellion had come from Istanbul, a rather distant place. The rebellion had demonstrated, however, that cooperation between the Kurdish nationalist societies and the tribal leaders and the sheikhs was possible. It also demonstrated that the struggle for Kurdish independence or even autonomy had shifted to the provinces, where it was to remain. The first Kurdish nationalist organization not established in a foreign city or in Istanbul was begun in Erzurum in 1921.

It is unclear from the accounts of the rebellion whether any of the participating tribes had also been part of the Hamidiye Regiments or the tribal regiments created during World War I. There does not seem to have been much participation. Most of the Hamidiye Regiments had been created from tribes that lived further east and south. This deprived the Koçgiri rebellion of much military experience. It took place closer to Ankara than the Sheikh Said rebellion and thus was more accessible, albeit over difficult terrain, to Turkish forces. Even though the Turks were engaged in a bitter war with the Greeks and in fact launched their second offensive against the Greeks on 23 March 1921 at the same time that they were engaged in quashing the Koçgiri rebellion, moving five or six thousand soldiers was a small matter after the great mobilizational efforts to fight the Greeks. The proximity of the region of the rebellion to areas largely populated by Turks also meant that the Kurds were more amenable to Turkish authority and more accessible to Turkish patronage. In spite of the weakness of Kurdish tribal society, the tribal leaders played the most important role in the rebellion. The sheikhs' role was much less significant than the one they were to play in Sheikh Said's rebellion. As pointed out above, however, the *tekke*s did play an important role, especially Huseyin Aptal. It may well be that the Kurdish nationalists learned important lessons from this: the sheikhs were more reliable than the chiefs as leaders of rebellion and their supratribal connections were an absolute necessity in creating extensive unity; also, the sheikhs were less easily coopted by the Turkish government and were more nationalistic than the chiefs. All three of these factors were taken into account in 1925.

Dersimi states that religious and creedal differences among the Kurds contributed to the failure of the rebellion. This implies that there were conflicts between the Sunnis and Alevis. These undoubtedly occurred, but both Sunni and Alevi tribes participated in the rebellion, unlike the Sheikh Said rebellion, in which only Sunni tribes participated. While it is unclear from Dersimi's account, it may well be that the Sunnis did not participate as enthusiastically as the Alevis. Van Bruinessen writes that "most Sunni Kurds saw at the time only an Alevi rising in it; they saw no reason to spontaneously support it."[15] This may be one reason for the reversal of roles in 1925. Both Kurmanci and Zaza speakers participated in the rebellion, unlike 1925, when it was largely Zaza speakers who rebelled. Whatever role the religious and language differences played in the Koçgiri rebellion in 1921, they were less important than in the 1925 rebellion. This, of course, could also be a weakness: the Sunni/Nakşbandi/Zaza-led rebellion may have been stronger and more unified because of language and religious homogeneity. The area of the rebellion was more confined than in 1925. The fact that the rebellion occurred in the dead of winter prevented help from outside even if it had been forthcoming. In addition, the winter of 1920 seems to have been even more severe than usual in the Dersim region. The season and the weather must have contributed to dampening the spirits of already lukewarm nationalists. The unpredictable elements—in addition to poor interregional organization, lack of communication, city-rural cleavages, and intellectual-tribal differences—were bound to make the rebellion short-lived.

Another reason for the failure of the rebellion was the overwhelming superiority of Turkish military power and organization and the

extensive patronage, land, and resources at the command of the Ankara government. In addition to all of the resources of an expanding
state, the fact is that many Kurds, in the region of the rebellion and
outside of it, supported Mustafa Kemal for many reasons. According
to van Bruinessen and his informants, many *ağas* knew Mustafa
Kemal personally. Some made his acquaintance when he was commander of the Sixteenth Army Corps at Diyarbakır in 1916. His
leadership had contributed to the retreat of the Russian army and
the destruction of the idea of an Armenian state in eastern Anatolia.
He was the symbol of the defense of the homeland (*vatan*) against
foreign and infidel invaders. He had invited prominent Kurds, including Kurdish nationalists, to the Erzurum congress (23 July–7
August 1919) and to the Sivas congress (4–11 September 1919). He
promised that Kurds would have equal rights with Turks. Kurds predominated in the Erzurum congress. A representative committee
(Heyet-i Temsiliye) was chosen, consisting of nine members (at least
three were Kurds): Haci Musa Beg (Mutki), Sedallah Efendi (Bitlis),
and Fewzi Efendi (a Nakşbandi sheikh from Erzurum).[16]

It would not be exaggerating, I think, to say that, without the support of the Kurds, it is quite possible that the Turkish nationalist
movement would not have been as successful as it was. To put it another way, if the Kurds had actively and militarily challenged the
Kemalists at Erzurum, it would have seriously retarded the Turkish
nationalist movement and its successes against the Russian and Allied forces and the Armenians. One of the ironies of Kurdish history
in Turkey is that the Turkish nationalist military and governmental
challenge to the Istanbul government and to the occupying forces
began in areas that Kurdistan nationalists claimed as part of the
homeland they wanted to establish. Instead, they aided the Turkish
nationalist forces, which prevented its realization. Even a more
moderate view must recognize that the Turkish nationalist revolution began in the area where Turkish and Kurdish populations overlapped. As the Koçgiri rebellion demonstrates, this turned out to
be an advantage to the Turks. Furthermore, the staging of a rebellion when the Turkish nationalists were locked in a life-and-death
struggle with the Greeks made it easy for the Turkish nationalists to
depict Kurdish demands for independence or even autonomy as trea-
sonous. A substantial number of Kurds agreed with the Turks on
this issue. It was not just for opportunistic reasons that some Kurds
supported Ankara.

But patronage certainly helped the Turks. As mentioned above,
four Kurds from the Dersim region alone were appointed members
of Parliament. Mustafa Kemal suggested to Alişan Beg, the chief of

the Koçgiri tribes, that he be a candidate for the Grand National Assembly. Ismail Beşikçi, a Turkish scholar of (alleged) Kurdish origin, maintains that throughout the years 1919–1921 the relations of the Kemalist forces—and Mustafa Kemal in particular—with the Kurdish chiefs and large landowners were better than those of the Kurdish nationalist organizations. This was clear during the Koçgiri rebellion. Among the reasons for this is that the Kurdish chiefs, *ağa*s, and urban notables knew they would need the support of the Ankara government to lay legal claim to the land and properties of the Armenians. This is another example, perhaps ironic, of how the destruction of the Armenians, in which the Kurds so enthusiastically and viciously participated, contributed to the defeat of Kurdish nationalism in Anatolia. As Halid Beg Cibran had speculated in his tent on the day of the defeat of the Armenians, their removal had left the Kurds face to face with the Turks. More than that, it left the Kurdish tribal leaders, landowners, and urban elites dependent on the Turks once the nationalists had consolidated their power. But how could the Kurds have guessed this, when no one, not even the Turkish nationalist leaders themselves, dreamed of such success? Ismail Beşikçi states that the religious emphasis of the Kemalist forces during the years 1919–1922 was important in securing the support of the Kurds. He believes that Mustafa Kemal must have written many more letters to Kurdish leaders than the seven that are incorporated into the documents (*vesikalar*) section of Mustafa Kemal's Great Speech (*Nutuk*). He states that many families reportedly received such letters.[17]

The seven letters incorporated into volume III of Mustafa Kemal's Great Speech provide good examples of Mustafa Kemal's tactics in dealing with Kurdish leaders.[18] His letter to Sheikh Ziyaettin Efendi of Narşin (Nurşin) of 13 August 1919 (document 52, p. 942–943) is instructive. Mustafa Kemal thanked the sheikh for his support in World War I and for his loyalty to the sultan and caliph, offering his heartfelt respect for this behavior. He stated, however, that it was now public knowledge that the same sultan and caliph wanted to make a gift of the eastern *vilayet*s to the Armenians. The government in Istanbul was completely incapable of defending the country. He also informed the sheikh of the creation of the Erzurum congress (which had been concluded just six days before) and stated that a Sivas congress would soon meet. He asked the sheikh to give greetings from him to all of the patriots of the area.

Mustafa Kemal also wrote a letter to Haci Musa Beg, the tribal chief of the Mutki (Modki) who, as was mentioned above, was chosen as a member of the Representative Committee at the Erzurum congress. This letter (document 47, p. 937–939) was written on 10 August 1919, just three days after the conclusion of the Erzurum congress. He thanked the chief for his and his family's services and sacrifices to the state and nation, especially his aid to the army in the region of Bitlis and Mutki. He told the chief that their enemies wanted to partition the land and to make an Armenia from the antient land of their ancestors. The weakness of the government in Istanbul was allowing this to take place; Mustafa Kemal thought it necessary to rectify this sorry situation. He mentioned how Haci Musa Beg had been elected a member of the Representative Committee along with Mustafa Kemal and "our brother the Hero of the Hamidiye" (*Hamidiye kahramanı*), Rauf (Orbay) Bey. If the circumstances warranted it, Mustafa Kemal would ask for Haci Mustafa's aid. After the conclusion of the Sivas congress, Mustafa Kemal said that he would meet with the chief in Erzurum and would inform him by telegraph of the time. Mustafa Kemal recognized that this would be a hardship for Haci Musa, but he was sure that the chief would be willing to make this sacrifice for the nation. This letter and the declarations issued by the leaders of the Koçgiri rebellion are good indications why most of the influential sheikhs and chiefs did not support Kurdish nationalist claims; most did not even support autonomy, especially if the demands for autonomy were challenged by the Turks.

The Koçgiri rebellion, however, did affect the policy of the government in Ankara and seems to have contributed to the first effort by the new nationalist government to deal with the "Kurdish question." Sometime in October 1921, the Grand National Assembly had sent a parliamentary committee to investigate the causes of the Koçgiri rebellion. Among the members of the Assembly Committee were Yusuf Isset Paşa (Bolu), Rağib Bey (Amasya), and Hakkı Hamid Bey (Sinop). The committee was headed by Safvet Bey, the former nationalist commander of Istanbul, who had initially opposed the Kemalists; for some reason it was thought that his credibility would be greater with the Kurds. Diyab Beg, deputy from Dersim, recommended that Safvet head the committee. While I was unable to find a report of the committee, a British intelligence source in the sultan's government, on the basis of a telegraph received from Ankara on 21 October 1921, stated that Ankara's intentions toward the Kurds were as follows: "For the present no punitive expedition will be sent against the rebels, but every effort will be made to win over the leaders of the tribes with presents and other peaceful means, until the treaty with Persia has been concluded and approved. A favourable opportunity will have to be awaited, because it will be necessary to send a force sufficiently powerful to deal with 40,000 horsemen operating in very difficult country. Under the present circumstances the Commission for National Defence considers that a punitive expedition would meet with certain defeat."[19] The same intelligence report indicated that the treaty with Iran mentioned in the telegraph contained a clause stipulating that the Iranian government would undertake to prevent the Kurds from Iran from helping their brothers across the frontier. Along with a copy of the report on the causes of the Koçgiri rebellion, the commission also drew up a proposed law concerning the administration of Kurdistan. The proposed law came up for debate in the Grand National Assembly, probably sometime in early February.

In the meantime, another special commission had drawn up a proposed law concerning the administration of Kurdistan. The proposed law was then sent to the commission that had investigated the Koçgiri rebellion. Sometime, apparently, in early February 1922, the draft law came up for debate in the Grand National Assembly. Five members voted against the motion to consider it. In addition to the three members of the Koçgiri Commission, Salih Efendi (Erzurum) and Selaheddin Bey (Mersin) voted against debate of the draft law. The motion, however, was accepted by the majority and it was decided that there should be a secret debate on 10 February. The members of the National Defense party (Müdafaa Milliye Cemiyeti) and the Defense of Rights party (Müdafaa-i Hukuk Cemiyeti) favored the draft law; sixty-five members opposed it. Salih Efendi opened the debate by saying that the Kurdish question could not be solved by such superficial measures as were embodied in the proposed draft law. He stated that if the agitation led by Koçgiri Mustafa Paşa, who had moved to the leadership of the Koçgiri and Dersim Kurds, was to be calmed, the Kurds taken to prison during the Koçgiri rebellion of spring 1921 would have to be released. He pleaded that in the interests of the country the recommendations of the Commission of Inquiry should be given practical expression in the draft law. Although he knew that Cevad Paşa, the responsible commander, had taken certain measures, "when the country was at war with the Greeks, it would not be easy to deal with the situation in that manner." Salih Bey stated further that the Koçgiri rebellions were due to the tyranny of the administration and the attitude of the Ankara government toward the caliphate. He was of the opinion that "the use of violence would only aggravate the situation. It was nonsense to say that there was no revolt in Kurdistan, for one had no need of a guide when the village could be plainly seen." Salih Efendi concluded that the rebellion was being supported by the Emir Faysal and the British, "and in the interests of the country the matter should be dealt with without using violence." Some of the Kurdish deputies opposed the draft law and strongly supported Salih Efendi. But the vast majority, 373 to 64, favored the draft law. If there were still approximately 72 Kurdish deputies in the Grand National Assembly, it seems that most of them opposed it.

It is not difficult to see why most of the Kurdish deputies opposed the draft law. Although article I (of the British report) of the draft law stated that the Grand National Assembly would undertake "to establish an autonomous administration for the Kurdish nation in harmony with their national customs," article II stated that "a Governor-General may be chosen by the dignitaries of the nation, together with an Assistant Governor-General and an inspector, who may be Turks or Kurds as the Grand National Assembly may decide." But article III stipulated that the Grand National Assembly would also choose a governor-general. At the end of three years (article IV), a new governor-general would be named "by the (Kurdish) National Assembly." Although the Grand National Assembly was to decide whether the assistant governor-general would be a Turk or a Kurd (article V), he was to be elected directly by the Kurdish National Assembly. The nomination of the governor-general, the assistant governor-general, and the inspector all had to be submitted for approval to Ankara.

Article VI stated that the administrative area of Kurdistan would be formed in the east from the provinces of Van, Bitlis, Diyarbakır, and the Sancak (district) of Dersim along with certain other *kazas* and *nahiyes* (lesser administrative districts). This clause made D. A. Osborne at the Foreign Office think that such words were the equivalent of a Kurdish national home such as had been established in Palestine for the Jews. Article XV stipulated that only Turkish could be employed in the Kurdish National Assembly and in administration. The Kurdish language would, however, be used in the schools. In addition, the Grand National Assembly had the right to oversee most of the budgetary concerns of the "Autonomous Administration." The proposed draft law is an interesting document in that it is the only one of its kind that is available (see appendix II).

It is obvious that the Kurdistan question was tied to the question of the caliphate and some of the deputies' opposition to the Kemaalists. Some obviously saw the Kurdish support for the caliphate as additional leverage against Mustafa Kemal, to whom opposition was growing in the spring of 1922. Salih Efendi's speech also indicates a genuine belief that the Kurds should be dealt with by other than forceful means. It also shows that the Kurdish deputies, in spite of their support for the Kemalist government and in spite of the fact that not one had spoken out about the harshness with which the Koçgiri rebellion had been suppressed, obviously felt that they could obtain more than the draft law offered as far as Kurdish rights and aspirations were concerned. This suggests that even the Kurdish deputies in Parliament were hopeful of obtaining greater autonomy than promised by the "administrative area of Kurdistan." On the other hand, it indicates that the Turks, at least those in the Grand National Assembly, did not favor a deliberately harsh and necessarily violent policy toward the Kurds. The proposed draft law makes it clear, however, that Turks, of whatever political persuasion, did not remotely consider independence or even autonomy in any meaningful sense of that term. At the most, it seems the Turks would consider greater authority for the Kurds in defined administrative areas and in circumscribed geographical areas. One must keep in mind, however, that what in retrospect seems a liberal policy, especially in comparison to what subsequently developed, was the idea of deputies and not the close advisers of Mustafa Kemal, who determined policy. That such a draft law was even discussed in the Grand National Assembly attests to the relative freedom of that body to discuss the Kurdish question so publicly. Later it would be more difficult and unpopular to do so, especially after the Treaty of Lausanne (24 July 1923). It was also a means to keep the support of the Kurds at one of the most challenging times of the young Turkish state. Kurdish nationalist activity experienced a resurgence after the Treaty of Lausanne, which was to lead directly to the outbreak of the Sheikh Said rebellion. After the treaty, which made no mention of an independent Kurdistan or Armenia, the Kurds had no choice but to attempt to achieve greater rights through the use of armed force.

The Establishment of the Azadi

The Kurdish nationalist organization that was responsible for events leading to Sheikh Said's rebellion was the Ciwata Azadi Kurd (Society for Kurdish Freedom), later named Ciwata Kweseriya Kurd (Society for Kurdish Independence) and called Azadi for short. Van Bruinessen states that the Azadi was founded in 1923, but reports from Kurdish soldiers who precipitated the mutiny at Beyt Şebab on 4 September 1924 told British intelligence that the organization was founded in Erzurum in 1921.[20] There is virtually no information on the Azadi, since it was an organization begun in Anatolia and very secretive. Van Bruinessen is the first scholar to stress its importance.

The five deserters from whom British intelligence gained most information were Ali Zaki Ibn Wali, Ismail Hakkı Efendi Ibn Muhammad Ali (Mosul), Ihsan Beg Ibn Nuri Beg (Bitlis), Tewfik Efendi Ibn Hasan (Mardin), and Ahmet Rassim Efendi Ibn Mikdal (Can). All of them were officers serving in the Turkish Army's Eighteenth Regiment of the Seventh Army's Second Division. Ihsan Nuri, Tewfik Hasan, and Ahmet Rassim Efendi were the sources for the information regarding the Azadi.[21] The first two were captains and the latter a second lieutenant. If the Azadi had been founded in 1921 and not 1923, it would mean that the Koçgiri rebellion and its consequences and the continued unrest in the Dersim region might have influenced its creation more than the political developments between 1921 and 1923.

According to these Kurdish officers, the creation of the Azadi was the result of several factors.[22] It should be pointed out that British intelligence took considerable pains to check the Kurdish officers' version of how and why the Azadi was established; their information turned out to be very accurate. The Kurds said the Azadi was founded in 1921 in Erzurum by Miralay (Colonel) Halid Beg Cibran, former commander of the garrison at Erzurum. Other branches and subsections were formed under the control of the initiating branch. The number of sections and their leaders was kept secret and the Kurdish officers claimed that they had no knowledge of how many branches existed. They did know that branches existed at Diyarbakır, Siirt, Istanbul, Dersim, Bitlis, Kars, Hınıs, Muş, Erzincan, Malazgird, Harput, and Van. The Kurds thought that Siirt had five branches, Bitlis two, and Van seven, including that of Beyt Şebab, for a total of twenty-three branches. Halid Beg Cibran (Erzurum); Cemil Paşa Ekrem Beg (Diyarbakır); Kör Huseyin Paşa, militia commander of the Haydaran tribe (head of the Menazgird branch); Halid Beg of the Hasanan tribe (head of the Varto branch); Yusuf Ziya Beg (head of the Bitlis branch); Haci Musa Beg (Muş, chief of the Mutki and Kwite tribe); Beyt Haji Bayram (Şernak tribe); Ayub Beg (Mardin, from the Milan tribe); Faris Isa Ibrahim Ağa (near Mardin, from the Dakuri tribe); Mahmud Beg Ibn Ibrahim Paşa (Milli tribe); and Simko, the well-known leader of the Şernak, were mentioned.

A longer report concerning the Azadi and the Beyt Şebab mutiny was received by the Colonial Office on 27 November. This report gives more detailed information than the 8 November report regarding the members of the Azadi, although the list is not complete.[23] In addition to names in the 8 November report, it mentions seven more for Erzurum: Abdul Rahim, a lawyer (Istanbul) and Sayyid Abdul Qadir (head of the Istanbul branch); Taşgird (no name given); Raşid

Efendi (Hınıs); along with Rusti Efendi (head); Muş (no names); Haci Hasan, Haci Dursun Ağa, and one Abdurrahman (Bitlis). The latter was from the Şernak tribe and at the time was in prison in Siirt. Van had six members in addition to Mulla Abdulmacid Efendi (head). There were three more members in Jezira (Cezire), two in Mardin, five in Diyarbakır in addition to Cemil Paşa (head), and also branches in Harput. The information in the two reports suggested that there were twenty-three branches of the Azadi, and this was only a partial list. Many of the leaders were officers in the Turkish army and many of the tribal members had been commanders in the Hamidiye. (See appendix III for a complete list of Azadi members as of September 1924 and appendix IV for a list of Kurdish officers who deserted to the British in Iraq after the mutiny of Beyt Şebab.)

The Kurdish officers were certain that "all tribes would support it [Azadi] for reasons of nationalism and religion." Names of tribal leaders who would support Azadi in addition to heads of branches were provided. The tribes included many of those in the areas of Bitlis, Van, Mardin, and the Şernak areas. The officers estimated the tribes had 5,000 rifles in the areas of Malazgird, Bitlis, and Muş. The Azadi had been actively supporting tribal rebellion in the same areas since August 1924. As a result, no Turkish force of under 200 could safely travel from Muş to Bitlis. The Bohtan tribes of the Şernak area were estimated to be able to raise 2,000 to 3,000 fighting men. The Kurdish officers also supplied the British with a list of military officers, mostly captains and lieutenants, from the Seventh Army who were members of Azadi (see appendix III). It can be seen that, as a result of the establishment of the Azadi organization in 1921, the Kurds would be much better prepared in 1925 when they rebelled against the Kemalists than they had been in the 1921 rebellion of the Koçgiri.

The Kurdish officers also gave eleven political reasons for their increased preparations for armed revolt (as rendered by British intelligence). The list is important because it is one of only two or three available sources that state Kurdish grievances and demands prior to the Sheikh Said rebellion:

(1) A new law regarding minorities already applied to Christians; it is Turkish Government intention to transplant all the Kurdish population of the Eastern Vilayets to Western Anatolia, replacing them with refugees and others of Turkish race, thereby removing the break in the broad Turanian ribbon which stretches from the Mediterranean across Anatolia, the Caucasus, and Trans-Caspia to Turkestan. (Ac-

cording to the informants many of the more enlightened Kurds have already been deported from Eastern Anatolia and replaced by Turkish refugees as the preliminary step in the gradual establishment of a Turkish majority.)

(2) The abolition of the Caliphate by the Turkish Government, which has broken one of the few remaining bonds between the Turks and Kurds.

(3) Limitation of language to Turkish in the law courts and schools and prohibition of Kurdish being taught in the latter. These measures are stated to have rendered education among Kurds practically nonexistent, a state of affairs which is favored by the Turks. The latter have also closed down religious institutions which were the only remaining source of education for the Kurdish race. (Notwithstanding the above repressive steps an education tax is still levied throughout Kurdistan.)

(4) The word "Kurdistan" was omitted from all educational books and Turkish geographical names are gradually being substituted for Kurdish throughout the country.

(5) The senior government officials in Turkish Kurdistan, i.e. Valis and Mutasarrifs, are practically without exception Turks and Kaimmakams about half Turk and half Kurd. Although the majority of the minor officials are Kurdish, the Turks are extremely careful as to whom they employ and exclude all suspected Kurdish nationalists. (The Kurds consider Turkish Kurdistan as embracing the Vilayets of Erzurum, Erzincan, Bitlis, Van, Diyarbekir, and Harput to which list the Vilayet of Hakkari should doubtless be added.)

(6) General absence of benefit from Government from any of the taxes paid, though these are not infrequently demanded more than once a year. No justice in the courts could be attained except through bribery.

(7) Government interference in election of deputies to the Turkish National Assembly from the Kurdish Vilayets, resulting in almost all Deputies being "elected" by Turkish Government orders and not in accordance with the free vote of the people.

(8) Turkish policy of setting one Kurdish tribe continually against another to prevent racial unity and consequent power of resistance to Government exactions.

(9) Military raids on Kurdish Villages, commandeering of animals, and corruption connected with receipts and payments for supplies requisitioned.

(10) Abuse and ill-treatment of Kurdish rank and file in the army
and the habit of selecting them for rough and unpleasant
duties.
(11) Attempts by Turkish Government to exploit Kurdish min-
eral wealth with the aid of German capital.[24]

The Turks were very much aware of the Azadi and its activities
and were doing everything in their power to suppress it. They hoped
to accomplish this by transferring or dismissing any of their own
officials not considered reliable and by severely punishing any Kurds
who were thought to be members of Azadi. An example of the former was the transfer of Zahni Bey, a native of Erzurum and *vali* of
Bitlis. He was succeeded by Kazım (Karabekir) Paşa, commander of
the Second Division.

The Azadi had three main objectives, at least in late November of
1924, as expressed by the Kurdish officers: to deliver the Kurds from
Turkish oppression; to give Kurds freedom and opportunity to develop their country; and to obtain British assistance, realizing that
Kurdistan could not stand alone. The Kurds claimed that the Soviet
Union had offered to help but that they had refused, still hoping that
the British would assist their cause. To achieve this goal, Kurdish
officers had been appointed to establish ties of friendship with Great
Britain and secure its support. Kurds were in Baghdad and in touch
with a number of tribal chiefs and important centers of organization
from the mouth of the Khabur River to Erzurum. These Azadi members had full authority, provided that Great Britain assured its aid, to
create revolutionary movements that could be directed by the British. Movements had already been started to obtain this objective
north of Siirt. The officers assured the British intelligence officials
that they could guarantee that the remaining parts of Kurdistan
would join in similar movements.

In order to support these goals, the Kurdish officers made three
requests: that a British officer accompany Kurdish officers from
Baghdad to the frontier zones where the movements would be instigated; that the Kurds be allowed to publish newspapers in Mosul as
a means of foiling Turkish propaganda and encouraging the revolutionary idea of Kurdistan; and that the Kurds be allowed to establish
a center in Zako that would allow them to keep in close touch with
the tribal chiefs of the Goyan, Solopi, and Şernak tribes through
whom the Azadi could send newspapers into the heart of "their
country." The Azadi had four chief hopes that their goals could be
realized, if certain things materialized: they needed to be assisted by
Great Britain with money and arms and have assurance that Great

Britain would stand behind them if they were successful; they believed that they could create a rebellion in the name of Kurdistan that would be supported "to a man" (this turned out to be a great miscalculation);[25] the Azadi wanted to instigate small uprisings throughout Kurdistan so that foreign powers could see the genuineness of their purpose, attested by the fact that they claimed fifty percent of the officers in the Turkish army were Kurds; above all, if the British supported the rebellion, it should start in the Şernak area for three reasons: the tribes were the most reliable; the region was the most easily defended; and the Şernak were the closest to British forces in Iraq.

The Azadi Kurdish officers also had their fears, chief of which was that the Turks would mobilize a strong force against them on the excuse that it was intended against Mosul, but which would actually be used for the suppression of the Kurdish movement. This fear was subsequently realized. The officers' second major fear was that the Turks would arrest and kill participating Kurdish officers and that the rebellion would commence before the time was ripe. This fear, also to be realized shortly, compelled the Azadi to press for immediate assistance from the British.

The Kurdish officers' fear that Turkish officials would arrest or kill Kurdish officers known to be active in Azadi was well founded. The length to which Turkish intelligence went to discredit Ihsan Nuri and the other deserters from the 4 September Beyt Şebab mutiny is an example of the profound Turkish concern with Azadi's activities. Ihsan Nuri was one of the three main informants for British intelligence regarding the origins and aims of the Azadi and the main instigator of the mutiny at Beyt Şebab. He was to become a prominent leader in the Sheikh Said rebellion and one of the leaders of the Kurdish rebellions in 1928 to 1930.

Ihsan Nuri became a member of the Hevi Society in 1908,[26] graduating from the Military College in Istanbul in 1910. In 1919, he rebelled against his Turkish officers (for reasons not mentioned in the intelligence reports) at Gallipoli, arresting his commanding officers among others and taking command himself for two months. He was court-martialed for these actions and transferred to Bitlis. Before proceeding to Bitlis, Ihsan Nuri apparently joined the Society for the Rise of Kurdistan and received instructions to work on behalf of the Kurdish movements in Bitlis, Siirt, and Diyarbakır. He led the mutiny at Beyt Şebab on 4 September 1924 on the order of Yusuf Ziya Beg of Bitlis. The British intelligence reports never mentioned the Azadi movement by that name. They did not seem to distinguish between one Kurdish nationalist organization and another, generally just stating that so-and-so belonged to the Kurdish national movement, as though that were the name of an organization.

The British went to great lengths to determine whether any of the deserters from Beyt Şebab were spies, as the Turks attempted to imply through misleading cipher codes.[27] On 1 January and on 7 January 1925, Turkish intelligence sent two incriminating letters that it intended British intelligence to intercept, implicating Ihsan Nuri as a spy. The British determined this after deciphering the letters and examining them closely. They dismissed the evidence in the captured letters as a clumsy Turkish counterintelligence effort. The Special Services Office (SSO) captain who wrote the report concluded that the charges made against Ihsan Nuri were false for three reasons: the Turks frequently sent such incriminating letters, intending that they should be captured; they wrote the letters in cipher to make them more realistic; and the Turks intended that the mail bag should fall into the hands of the British at the very time when the officers who participated in the Beyt Şebab mutiny were being court-martialed. Why not try to get the British to punish Ihsan Nuri since the Turks could not? (See appendix V for the letter from Turkish intelligence to Ihsan Nuri to implicate him as a spy to the British.)

According to van Bruinessen and his informants, the Azadi convened its first congress in 1924, although the date is not clear.[28] Sheikh Said, who was to lead the rebellion of 1925, was a leading Nakşbandi sheikh. He also was related by marriage to Halid Beg Cibran. His contemporaries state that he was a fervent nationalist. He had been invited to the congress because of his great influence among the Sunni Zaza-speaking tribes northeast of Diyarbakır. The former Hamidiye tribal commanders were also present at the congress. They seemed to be less enthusiastic about the rebellion than sheikhs such as Said, but they were persuaded of its necessity by Sheikh Said himself. This is evidence of the sheikh's early support and leadership of the planned rebellion. The first Azadi congress made two important decisions. First, it determined that a general rebellion would take place, at which time a declaration of independence would be made. Second, it decided that foreign assistance would be needed. Both the Soviet Union and Great Britain were to be contacted. Neither said it would support the rebellion, but neither said it would oppose it. The Kurds seemed ready to ignite the rebellion on their own.

Van Bruinessen states the Azadi's first congress was held in 1924. But it is important to determine just when it was held because of its influential role in planning the Sheikh Said rebellion of February 1925 and the Beyt Şebab mutiny of the night of 3–4 September 1924.

A Turkish-Kurdish congress had taken place in the first part of August 1924. In fact, the congress had opened in Diyarbakır on 1 August.[29] At the Diyarbakır congress, the Turkish government had promised to consider and to rectify six demands by the Kurds: (1) a special form of administration should be established in designated areas of Kurdish majority; (2) the Turkish government would provide a loan to the Kurds (the amount is not stipulated in the documents); (3) a general amnesty was to be declared for the Kurds in prison; (4) there would be no conscription in Kurdistan for a period of five years; (5) the Turkish government would restore the Shariʿa (Şeriyet) courts and all the arms confiscated in the country; and (6) certain specified obnoxious Turkish military officers and officials would be removed from their positions in Kurdistan. In return for Turkish fulfillment of these demands, the Kurds were to support the Turkish government's position and tactics with regard to the Mosul question.

It is possible that the first Azadi congress took place after the Turkish-Kurdish congress of 1 August in Diyarbakır. If this is so, it would imply that the Kurds were unhappy or not hopeful that the Turks would fulfill the agreements made at Diyarbakır. In the weeks after the Diyarbakır congress, there was again a large-scale rebellion in the Dersim region among the Koçgiri tribes. Cevad Paşa, the inspector-general of the Sivas army, was given complete authority to quell the rebellion. It may have been the Turkish government's response to the Koçgiri uprisings that prevented or impeded any fulfillment of the Diyarbakır Accords. On the other hand, it seems likely that the Turkish government never had any intention of fulfilling the agreements made at Diyarbakır. Many Kurdish leaders had gathered for the congress at Diyarbakır and would have been available for a meeting either before or after the 1 August congress. If the Azadi congress took place before the Turkish-Kurdish congress at Diyarbakır, then it would mean that it, too, had no intention of adhering to the agreements made there. Turkish intelligence would have been aware of this; hence it is possible that the Turks called for the meeting at Diyarbakır and met some Kurdish demands simply to buy time, to distract and to mollify Kurdish leaders, to obtain some Kurdish support and military help against the British along the Turkish-Iraqi border, and to prevent Kurdish aid from reaching the Kurds in Koçgiri. Exactly one month after the conclusion of the Turkish-Kurdish congress in Diyarbakır, a total of some 500 Kurdish officers and soldiers rebelled at Beyt Şebab, a small town about twenty kilometers north of the Iraqi border. As mentioned above, the rebellion was instigated by Ihsan Nuri and his fellow officers by the order of Yusuf Ziya, a leading member of the Azadi from Bitlis and a former member of the Grand National Assembly.

According to the Kurdish officers who deserted to Mosul, the rebellion at Beyt Şebab was carried out to foil Turkish plans to increase suppression of the Kurds and at the same time to position their forces to better pressure the British forces in Iraq, many of whom were Assyrian levies and Indian troops. In order to execute this plan, the Turks had seven major objectives; (1) to fortify their already formidable positions before the fall of snow; (2) to establish ammunition dumps, depots, and so forth; (3) to begin the construction of roads; (4) to create and post detachments under the guise of Kurdish tribes that would establish communication with Sheikh Mahmud, the Kurdish leader in Iraq, in order to consolidate their control of the hill country skirting the Mosul plain; (5) after obtaining the above objectives, to occupy the areas of Kirkuk and Sulaymaniya, from which they would be in a good position to menace Mosul; (6) to make preparations to bring Kurdish tribes down from the north to preach rebellion against the British to the southern tribes in Iraq (in compensation, they would allow the northern tribes to loot Christian villages—stirring up religious zeal and *jihad* against the British would also dampen any hopes of support for the Kurds from the British); and (7) to garrison themselves in Kirkuk and Sulaymaniya to await the results of the Mosul negotiations and by their presence to compel the League of Nations to give a verdict in their favor.[30] In such fashion, speculated the Kurds, the Turks hoped to extinguish forever the hopes of the Kurdish people for independence and deliverance from their oppression. The Kurdish officers who were members of the Azadi told British intelligence that they thought fifty percent of the officers and soldiers of the Seventh Army in Diyarbakır were Kurdish and they hoped for support from them. In addition, they thought that as many as twenty percent of the Turkish officers and soldiers were in sympathy with Kurdish aspirations.

With this much political support, the leaders of the Azadi decided to stage a rebellion at Beyt Şebab the night of 3–4 September 1924. The mutiny had three principal objectives: to prevent Kurdish tribes from coming into hostile contact with the British forces in Iraq; to prevent the concentration of Turkish forces in the Assyrian hills; and to weaken the morale of the Turkish army. The Kurds hoped that the achievement of these three-pronged objectives at Beyt Şebab would draw Turkish attention to the Kurdish movement in the whole of the Bitlis-Van-Diyarbakır region and make the Turks cease their operations in the south.

In an indication of things to come, the mutiny at Beyt Şebab was carried out before the Azadi leaders could coordinate their efforts with the tribal leaders. As a result, the tribes failed to rise. The Turkish officer commanding the garrison at Beyt Şebab learned of the intended mutiny and immediately started arresting suspected participants. The principal leaders, as we have seen above, were forced to flee to Iraq. The net result was that three companies of one battalion and one company of another deserted en masse: a total of 500 officers and soldiers. They buried the breechblocks of four mountain guns and took thirteen automatic rifles with them when they fled.[31] The Kurds were adamant that time was of the essence: action had to be taken within the next three months, because the Turks were thoroughly aware of the extent and organization of the Kurdish nationalist movement, especially the Azadi. The Kurds thought that the Turks would concentrate great force against them in the next few weeks in order to suppress organized opposition. The garrisons were relatively small in September and October and the rebellion had to begin before reinforcements arrived.

The British intelligence officers assessed the Kurds' plans and hopes as somewhat visionary, but they were impressed that the officers sought no employment in the British-Iraqi army and wanted to return as quickly as possible to Kurdistan north of Iraq to carry out the rebellion. The British were not sanguine about the ability of the Kurds to organize on the level that the Kurdish officers planned. They were impressed, however, by the ability of the Azadi to instigate a mutiny of half a Turkish regiment. In the Beyt Şebab mutiny, the British saw the strengthening of a policy that they were to follow for over three decades. They realized that the Azadi would be a very powerful weapon against Turkey in case of war. But even in peace it would be very useful. The silent threat of encouragement to Kurdish nationalism, noted an SSO captain, could be a by no means negligible diplomatic factor. The threat of Kurdish nationalism had been of considerable value during the past years and had been more effective on account of the considerable Kurdish population within Iraq's borders. The Kurdish informants repeatedly mentioned the Azadi support for their actions. Sayyid Taha's support of rebellion in Iraq was to be the signal for more rebellion north of the border. It was clear to British intelligence and to British officials who had some sympathy for the Kurds that generous treatment of Kurds in Iraq and emigrant Kurds and encouragement of their national sensibilities, if they could be reduced to practical terms, "would repay themselves over and over again. Such a policy would go far towards providing a friendly population over the border along the whole northern frontier and northern third of the eastern frontier with Iran, and would furnish the Iraq government with a weapon against the Turks in diplomacy and in potential war."[32] In the rebellion of Beyt Şebab, British intelligence in Iraq had seen quite clearly a more coherent definition of a policy that Great Britain had been following for some time.

3. The Second Time Around: British Policy toward the Kurds from Mudros to Lausanne

THE BRITISH government's policy of utilizing the Kurds as a diplomatic, political, and military instrument against the Turks was considered and realized sometime before the mutiny at Beyt Şebab in September 1924. British policies toward the Kurds, however, underwent many changes during the five years from 31 October 1918 (the armistice of Mudros) to 24 July 1923 (the Treaty of Lausanne).[1] Writing a detailed history of British policies toward the Kurds during this period would necessitate in many ways rewriting much of post–World War I history, a task that cannot be undertaken here. But an understanding of British policies toward the Kurds within the broad strategy of British imperial and Middle Eastern politics in the post–World War I Middle East is vital to understand the reasons for the Sheikh Said rebellion in 1925.

For the two years between the armistice of Mudros and the signing of the Treaty of Sèvres (10 August 1920), British policy toward the Kurds consisted largely of supporting small autonomous units or princedoms in areas of Kurdistan, especially in Iraq, after Great Britain became the mandatory power on 25 April 1920. Assumption of the mandate for Iraq meant that British policies toward the Kurds would be intimately tied to its Sharifian-Hashemite policies in the Middle East and its wider imperial interests, particularly in India. Its mandatory status in Iraq also made Great Britain a neighbor of Turkey and Iran, two countries that had Kurdish populations larger than Iraq's. The bulk of this population was also contiguous with the border areas of Iraq.

British policy during 1919 could well be called the Noel policy. Edward William Charles Noel was a British intelligence agent who was active in attempting to ascertain the viability of a policy that supported an independent Kurdish state or, at least, a viable autonomy for the Kurds. If either were to be achieved, it would be under the aegis of the British. Noel was often called the "Second Lawrence," usually disparagingly, by officials in the Colonial Office concerned with the Middle East. These officials were as uncertain about the depth of Kurdish nationalism as Noel was convinced of its strength. Colonial Office officials were not sure a "Kurd Revolt" would improve the British position in the Middle East, especially with Turkey after the Kemalist victories throughout 1921. Noel, however, remained faithful to the cause of a Kurdish independence movement throughout his service there, which lasted through 1922.[2] He preached the genuineness of Kurdish nationalism in his dispatches to the Colonial, Foreign, and India offices. He was attached to the India Office, which had primary responsibility for Mesopotamia until the creation of the Middle East Department in spring 1921.

Noel made extensive journeys in Kurdistan both north and south of the armistice lines. During the months of June, July, and August 1919, he reported extensively on the situation in Diyarbakır, Maraş, Polatlı, Malatya, Harput, and Aleppo. Noel was made aware of the great interest that Turkish officials took in his movements by Kurdish *valis* (governors) in the eastern provinces of Anatolia. In the last chapter it was noted that Mustafa Kemal himself thought that Noel was trying to incite the Kurds to attack the Sivas congress.[3] Noel was received hospitably by the Kurds along his route, as were the members of the Bedir Khan family he took with him: Sayyid Muin, a son-in-law of Sayyid Abdul Qadir and son of Emin Ali Bedir Khan, and Sayyid Ibrahim, a notable from Dersim. The support of the Bedir Khans, and especially Sayyid Abdul Qadir, for Noel's mission is an indication of the relationship, although at times stormy, between the Bedir Khans and the British right up to the time of Sheikh Said's rebellion. Noel's mission to the Kurdish areas did not result in an organization similar to the South Kurdish Confederation he had organized under Sheikh Mahmud of Sulaymaniya, Arbil, and Rawanduz in early 1919.[4] One of the reasons the British did not pursue a North Kurdish Confederation at the time was that the South Kurdish Confederation turned out to be a fiasco: Sheikh Mahmud really did want an independent Kurdish state and the British were forced to quash him with military force in June 1919. Perhaps this made the British government less supportive than Noel realized during his sojourn of June, July, and August among the Kurds in Turkey. Sheikh Mahmud's revolt also indicated to British officials the difficulties, and the danger, of pursuing a policy of supporting a unified Kurdish state.

As noted in chapter 2, article 62 of the Treaty of Sèvres had called for "a scheme of local autonomy for the predominantly Kurdish areas lying east of the Euphrates, south of the southern boundary of Armenia . . . and north of the frontier of Turkey with Syria and Mesopotamia." By 1920, it seemed highly unlikely that the British would push for the fulfillment of article 62. There would be no North Kurdish Confederation or *cordon sanitaire*, as Major Noel envisioned. The reason was the growing strength of the Turkish nationalist forces. After 1920, British concern was concentrated largely in Iraq and not against Turkish forces north of the Iraq-Turkish border. The contradictory, undefined, and unarticulated policies pursued by the British toward the Kurds are illustrated by a combined meeting of Foreign, Colonial, War, Air Ministry, and India Office officials held on 13 April 1920. Even though the Cairo conference had discussed the future of Kurdistan on 15 March, narrowing policy toward the Kurds, the memorandum had still not reached many or most of the officials who attended the combined meeting at the Foreign Office on 13 April. The War Office was represented by W. H. Gribbon, John Tilley, and E. Forbes Adams; L. Oliphant represented the Foreign Office; Hugh Trenchard, air chief marshall of the RAF, and J. A. Chamier represented the Air Ministry. John Shuckburgh of the India Office, soon to be appointed head of the Middle East Department in the Colonial Office, also attended. Lord Curzon, foreign secretary, presided.[5]

The members first reviewed the proposals of their previous three or four meetings held during the latter part of 1919 and early 1920. Three proposals had been made and discussed: a fringe of autonomous Kurdish states should be formed around the borders of the Mosul *vilayet;* the French proposed that Kurdistan should be divided into British and French spheres of influence; and the British should cut themselves loose altogether from Kurdistan and confine themselves to the river districts. By April 1920, the British concluded that they were in a position to cut off Kurdistan, including northern Kurdistan, but they had been unable to find anyone to set up an autonomous state in that part of the country. Colonel Arnold Wilson, acting civil commissioner for the Persian Gulf, had made indignant protests against any British abandonment of southern Kurdistan. If this were done, Wilson argued, it would be detrimental to British influence in Iran and put it at risk in Mesopotamia. Curzon disagreed with Wilson. The committee discussed the proposal. Nuri Paşa, an official in the Iraqi government and future prime minister—it was pointed out to the committee—had suggested that the Kurds of southern Kurdistan would be quite willing to accept the suzerainty of Şerif Abdullah, son of Şerif Huseyin, as the head of an Arab government in Baghdad. Nuri Paşa had suggested the idea that the intervention or appointment of Abdullah might extricate the British from all their troubles. John Shuckburgh intervened at this point and said he thought that it had been Colonel Lawrence who had supported the idea of Abdullah going to Mesopotamia. In order to resolve the indecision of whether to move in the direction of proposal 1 or 2, Robert Vansittart of the Foreign Office submitted a draft report that would not sever Kurdistan "straight off" but left the problem to be solved in the course of the next year. Vansittart's proposal was accepted by the committee and subsequently became articles 62, 63, and 64 of the Treaty of Sèvres.[6]

Edwin Montagu, secretary of state for India, stated that he was in favor of an independent Kurdistan if it could be arranged. He suggested that the way to do this would be to make a treaty with some party in Turkey that would sign it without compulsion, in which case they might give up Kurdistan willingly. Curzon was emphatic, however, that Britain did not want Turkey to be left in a position of strength against Armenia. He stated that the peace conference, at which he was the principal British representative, was contemplating the expulsion of the Turks from Armenia. Curzon responded to Edwin Montagu's preferences for an independent Kurdistan by stating that if the British established a quasi-autonomous Kurdish state with British administration, the French might be tempted to establish a similar state with French advisers in northern Kurdistan. It should be noted that Montagu's "independent state" was quickly translated by Curzon to "a quasi-autonomous Kurdish state with British administration." Curzon's terminology, however, was what was meant subsequently by the word "independence" whenever it was used. In order to obviate French demands, Curzon revealed that he had told Philippe Berthelot, French foreign ministry official at the Quai d'Orsay, that Britain would abandon southern Kurdistan. Curzon was apprehensive that, if Britain changed its position, it would reawaken opposition at the San Remo peace negotiations then in process (the San Remo agreements were made public on 5 May 1920).

The discussion then shifted to the proposals, referred to as the Air Scheme, that would allow the air force to become the dominant military presence in Mesopotamia.[7] General Radcliffe of the army was of the opinion that the proposals showed great promise and would result in the reduction of Britain's military commitment. It is important to understand that if the Air Scheme was to work as well as its proponents thought it would as of April 1920, these views would be reflected in the depth of British commitment to Iraq. The greater the commitment, the greater the desire to include southern Kurdistan in the new state. The avid proponents of the Air Scheme were among the staunchest supporters of a "Greater Iraq." One of the exceptions was Winston Churchill, who was strongly in favor of the Air Scheme, but who, until late 1921, still favored a quasi-autonomous Kurdish state or states as a *cordon sanitaire* north of Iraq.

Lord Curzon said he had read the Air Staff's scheme and "was rather nervous about it," because an aviator would necessarily be a young man and not the best person to deal with tribesmen. Air Marshal Trenchard explained that an aviator would have no more to say about policy than a subaltern commanding an infantry company. He was convinced that the air force could undertake the control of Mesopotamia and Kurdistan if the policy followed the lines suggested by Montagu.[8] Trenchard's remarks are the first indication that the air force was confident that it could pursue a "forward policy" in Iraq, which very much militated against the establishment of an independent or autonomous Kurdistan. But, in 1920, the British wanted the northeast mountains as a frontier to control the valleys below. It is interesting to note that the very mechanics of implementing the Air Scheme that would work against an independent or autonomous Kurdistan were being discussed and partially implemented in 1920 when the Treaty of Sèvres advocated such a policy! It is commonly assumed that the major reason for the abrogation of the Treaty of Sèvres was the great success of the Kemalist forces. There can be no question of that. But the implementation of the Air Scheme and all that it implied and foreshadowed, although it was not fully recognized by many British officials at the time, also worked strongly against any meaningful implementation of articles 62, 63, and 64 of the Treaty of Sèvres. It is a good example of technology influencing politics and, as it turned out, history.

Trenchard tried to lessen Curzon's fears of Air Ministry political power by stating that the civilian officer would remain at his post and call up the air force as required. It was not proposed to set up airfields except along the main lines of communications. Native rulers would be employed as far as possible. If a town or village became rebellious, it could be dealt with more easily from the air than the ground. The expense would be greatly reduced by having no line of communications. Lord Curzon did not buy Trenchard's arguments. He pointed out that experience in the past had shown that the mere presence of British officials, however "wonderful their influence was," was not sufficient without the presence of some kind of force on the spot. Curzon did not like the idea of force being summoned solely for the purpose of destruction. Trenchard replied that the Air Scheme contemplated the use of a militia or levies, the latter composed largely of Assyrians. Ground forces had traditionally been used to control these nearly inaccessible mountain areas.

General Radcliffe then suggested that, in view of the possibility of the Air Scheme being accepted, it would be a pity to leave the area under an emir. He thought the government should consider the India Office's suggestion (apparently from Edwin Montagu) of October 1919 that Mosul, Baghdad, and Basra should form a Mesopotamian state with an Arab cabinet under Sir Percy Cox, the high commissioner. Radcliffe did not include southern Kurdistan in this suggestion. This suggestion is indicative of the army and air commanders' advocacy of direct British control and of the Air Ministry's confidence in being able to accomplish this cheaply. It was the great expense of direct rule that had helped push the British to "indirect" rule in previous decades. Now the effective and inexpensive use of air power would reduce the need for indirect rule. The implementation of this policy in Iraq was unique and experimental. Its successful or unsuccessful implementation would help to determine British imperial policies not only in Iraq, but in the entire Middle East and, indeed, globally. An independent or autonomous Kurdistan was one of the first casualties of this new imperial policy.

The Air Scheme policy in Iraq and in Kurdistan was to be one of the first examples of harnessing air power to the imperial policies of Great Britain throughout its possessions in non-Western areas and the Third World. It allowed Great Britain to pursue a "forward policy" in some areas and to consolidate its power in other areas even as it retreated in still other parts of the world. Kurdistan was the first testing ground of this great postwar experiment. While the great import that the Air Scheme was to have on future imperial policies was not appreciated fully by all nine officials at the 13 April 1920 meeting, its potential was clearly recognized. The differences between the civilian and military officials and heads of ministries was clearly in evidence. Curzon represented the old guard; Radcliffe and Trenchard the new.

Hubert Young of the Foreign Office staff stated that the British should make clear that their intention was to set up an independent state in southern Kurdistan that could later opt to join either Mesopotamia or northern Kurdistan, if the latter succeeded in establishing its autonomy. Curzon again interpolated that the French would possibly lay claim to commercial concessions in "any purely independent state," although it was true that the French economic sphere had hitherto been restricted to Cilica. The meeting was concluded with the following agreement: Britain regarded southern Kurdistan as part of Mesopotamia and northern Kurdistan should be treated as discussed in the proposals submitted by Robert Vansittart, which were to be incorporated into the Treaty of Sèvres as articles 62, 63, and 64. British policy toward the Kurds as discussed in the 13 April 1920 meeting was in this fashion embodied in the Treaty of Sèvres signed 10 August 1920.

The next detailed discussion of British policy was held in Cairo, Egypt, 12–30 March 1921.[9] The Cairo conference, as it was officially known, represented an attempt by the British to arrest the drift of British policy that had occurred in 1920 and continued to characterize policy in early 1921. The newly created Middle East Department had drawn up a memorandum in London that it submitted to the political committee for Kurdistan, which consisted of Winston Churchill (chair), Sir Percy Cox, Miss Gertrude Bell, Cox's secretary, and Colonel T. E. Lawrence. Major Hubert Young and Major E. W. C. Noel were consulting members. Major R. D. Babcock was secretary of the political committee on Kurdistan. The memorandum of the Middle East Department stated:

> We are strongly of opinion that purely Kurdish areas should not be included in the Arab state of Mesopotamia, but that the principles of Kurdish unity and nationality should be promoted as far as possible by H.M.G. The extent of the area within which it will be possible for H.M.G. to carry out this policy must necessarily depend upon the final terms of the peace settlement with Turkey. Whatever the extent of this area may be, we consider that not only control by H.M.G. will be facilitated if there were some form of central Kurdish Organization to which a British adviser could be attached. This adviser would be under the orders of the H.C. [High Commissioner] for Mesopotamia and would report through him to H.M.G.[10]

At a meeting of the political committee on 15 March 1921, Sir Percy Cox took issue with the Middle East Department's memorandum. He stated that the Kurds were predominant in Kirkuk, Sulaymaniya, and the districts north of Mosul that formed an integral part of Iraq. Cox was contradicted by Hubert Young, who proposed that a Kurdish state be established without delay and that it be put under the direct control of the high commissioner, not part of, or responsible to, the Iraqi government. Young was supported by Major Noel, who thought that the Kurds would prefer "home rule" and might be useful as a buffer state against both Turkish pressure "from without and Iraqi anti-British movements from within." Winston Churchill agreed with the sentiments of Young and Noel. The secretary of colonies thought that a future ruler of Iraq with the power of an Arab army behind him "would ignore Kurdish sentiment and oppress the Kurdish minority."[11] The committee concluded its meeting by adopting the recommendation of Hubert Young to keep Kurdistan separate from Iraq. The members who supported this position tried to mollify Cox by stipulating that this arrangement be maintained until such time as a representative body of Kurdish opinion might opt for inclusion in Iraq.

Of the seven members of the political committee on Kurdistan, four favored a Kurdish entity separate from Iraq: Churchill, Young, Noel, and Lawrence; Cox and Bell were opposed. Babcock, the secretary, did not enter into the discussion. Thus, as of 1 May 1921, most of the members of the Middle East Department and the two members representing the department in Cairo wanted "Southern Kurdistan" separate from Iraq, although responsible to the high commissioner for Iraq. The Middle East Department had the strong backing of the secretary of colonies, Winston Churchill.

An amazing policy reversal was to occur in the course of the next few months: the Middle East Department and Churchill's policy was rejected in favor of Cox's. Cox himself was the instrument of this reversal. He may have been influenced by his perception that the Iraqis did not want an independent Kurdistan and the difficulty that he would have as high commissioner in finding a sufficiently tame Kurdish leader for the independent entity. The first indication that the majority position at Cairo was in jeopardy occurred less than two weeks after the conclusion of the Cairo conference. In an intelligence report from Mesopotamia dated 15 May, Reader Bullard, one of the most perceptive members of the Middle East Department, thought he saw the emergence of "a policy for Kurdistan." He believed that the intelligence report, which Cox had undoubtedly seen before it was sent to the Colonial Office, gave the impression that "it was desired to leave as little as possible of Mesopotamia outside the control of the Baghdad government,"[12] although the proposals were not complete. For example, the report did not state whether the British sub-mutassarif (assistant governor) in charge of the Zako-Dohuk area would be under the mutassarif of Mosul or the Ministry of Interior (i.e., the Baghdad government). Also, noted Bullard, the districts of Arbil and Sulaymaniya were not promised autonomy in fiscal matters.

What Bullard had deciphered from the 15 May intelligence report was made clear by Cox in a dispatch to Churchill on 2 June.[13] Cox stated that when he left Cairo he had "intimated that in view of pertinent clause [64] in Treaty of Sèvres" he "should continue to administer Kurdish districts and that, in reply, Council of State [Iraq] found it necessary to object to an arrangement which they thought ultimately would lead to excision of Kurdistan from Iraq." He had then convened a meeting of Kurdish experts after which it was "unanimously decided that best solution from all points of view would be to retain Kurdistan as one integral part of Iraq *for financial and fiscal purposes* but for the H.C. to administer them directly through Kurdish and British officials on *such a basis of local auton-* omy as would satisfy Home Rule Idea" (emphasis added). One might gather from Cox's proposal that article 64 of the Treaty of Sèvres implied, at the most, home rule. All Kurdish areas, with the exception of Sulaymaniya, preferred, stated Cox, to be an "integral part of Iraq." He was sure it would be possible to satisfy both the League of Nations and the Kurdish districts that his policy was the best solution and he "trusted" that Churchill would agree with him. Young and Shuckburgh in minutes on Cox's dispatch noted that Cox did not make it clear whether the Kurdish areas were to come under the Arab government. If this was to be the case, it would be a mistake which it would be very difficult to undo. Emir Faysal, now ensconced as king of Iraq, would be embarrassed, they thought, if he found Kurdish elements in his Council of State or his National Assembly. Churchill also was not aware of the rapidly shifting policy, because a few days earlier he had instructed the Middle East Department "to take up the question of getting Major Noel back to Kurdistan." Cox was not happy when he learned this.

Exactly one week later, on 9 June, Churchill answered Cox. He stated that Cox's proposals appeared to follow the policy decided upon at Cairo and approved them "on the assumption that they do not entail Kurdish representation in National Assembly or Council of State, or the submission of Kurdish budget to either of those bodies or to an Arab minister. So long as the temporary inclusion of Kurdish area in Iraq is dependent solely upon presence of British H.C., and so long as British officials form the only link between the two countries he shall be in a strong position to deal with any future Arab ruler whose Arab advisers may persuade him to attempt interference in Kurdish affairs." [14] In spite of Cox's 2 June dispatch, in his answer Churchill used the phrase "two countries," indicating that he was still thinking of a Kurdistan separate from Iraq. Differences between Churchill and Cox began to appear on smaller issues, which were part of each man's larger policy formation. In his 9 June response to Cox, Churchill again recommended the services of Major Noel. Cox was slow to respond to this suggestion. The matter of Noel was also connected with that of Sheikh Mahmud of Sulaymaniya, who had been imprisoned in India after his rebellion in July 1921, made possible, as mentioned in the last chapter, by the support of Noel and the British. Cox responded that the only alternative to Sheikh Mahmud's detention, "it would seem," was to release him on parole. Churchill queried Cox about Mahmud on 21 April; Cox did not respond until 8 June, nearly two months later. Churchill was outraged by Cox's answer and its tardiness, exclaiming, "A great deal more trouble has got to be taken to meet wishes which I express in these matters."

While Churchill was peeved at Cox's attitude toward Sheikh Mahmud and Major Noel, he did not seem aware, at least to what extent, Cox was opposing their return and using their absence to integrate administratively the Kurdish areas of southern Kurdistan into the Iraqi state. The strength of the policies of the official on the spot over that of the one in the distant capital was beginning to emerge. Coxian persistence was beginning to dominate Churchillian persuasion: more was to come.

Cox was willing to use other events to advance his policies. By June, he was fully informed of the Koçgiri rebellion in the Dersim area and sent telegrams to the Colonial Office regarding the possibility of Kurdish unrest in Anatolia against the Kemalist government in Ankara. On 13 June, Churchill asked Cox for details of his view of "our making more capital out of Kurdish Nationalists towards Turkish nationalism." Churchill reiterated that he was still in favor of the policy of setting up a Kurdish buffer between Arabs and Turks as contemplated at Cairo: "I consider that from this policy we ought not be deflected either by Arab pressure or by any other cause." The Koçgiri rebellion, however, provided a weapon in Cox's growing arsenal. Cox's small victories over Churchill with regard to Sheikh Mahmud, Major Noel, and the opportunity provided by the Koçgiri rebellion, in addition to his ability to implement a forward administrative system in Iraq, emboldened him to state his position less ambiguously on 21 June in a response to Churchill's 9 June dispatch. Cox stated that two alternatives were mooted at the Cairo conference: that Kurdish districts should be retained as part of Iraq; and that Kurdish districts should be encouraged to separate, stating flatly, "Generally balance of opinion was in favour of former."[15] He then repeated measures that he had taken as discussed in his 2 June dispatch, adding, "I appreciate considerations however which now incline you rather in direction of alternative no. two."

Cox said that while proceeding on lines of alternative 1 he realized that the British program must be more attractive than any alternative that the Turks might offer and must be broad enough to satisfy the more ambitious Kurdish nationalists. He anticipated that little change would be required to bring alternative 1 into line with number 2, the policy favored by Churchill and the Middle East Department. Cox proceeded to make arguments for the first alternative—that Kurdish districts should be retained as part of Iraq. He discussed what he considered to be the four areas of Kurdish Iraq and argued that for economic, military, communication, and political reasons two areas should be included in Iraq. The first area was north of the two Zab rivers and the second centered on Arbil, between the two Zabs. The third area in the mountainous region between the Zabs and west of Arbil was not under his administrative control and the Turks were contesting it. In the fourth area of Sulaymaniya, Cox thought, however, that Churchill's wishes could be met exactly, as he indicated in his dispatch of 2 June. He suggested that the third area could be joined to the first two areas along lines suggested in alternative 2. He would administer the newly created compact province "and not through an Arab minister." Happily, thought Cox, the "new province" would be able to be self supporting from the first.[16]

The high commissioner stated he *was not taking action* pending a reply from Churchill "in order that there may be no misunderstanding." Cox wanted to hear definitely from Churchill that policy alternative 2 that Kurdish districts "should be encouraged to separate is the policy that he now wished to follow." On 26 June, in a Group Meeting (officials from the concerned ministries), with minutes by John Shuckburgh, much of Cox's dispatch was disputed. Hubert Young and T. E. Lawrence stated that Sir Percy's recollection of the "balance of opinion" at the Cairo conference was faulty. The general consensus at Cairo had favored the second of the policies quoted by Cox, the policy "to which the Department has always inclined and it forms the basis of the draft telegraph now submitted. This position was supported by Major E. B. Soane, who had recently been political officer in Sulaymaniya, and by Captain Stephen Longrigg, who was assistant political officer in Kirkuk but now in London. The Middle East Department thought none of Sir Percy's advisers could speak with the authority of these two men."

On the very same day, 21 June, that Cox sent dispatch no. 201 described above, he also sent another telegraph in response to Churchill's query of 13 June about the possibility of using Kurdish nationalists against Turkish nationalism. He reminded Churchill that "the active stimulation of Kurdish revolt was carefully considered" in the fall of 1920. But it had then been decided that, if support of Kurdish rebellion was to be successful, three conditions would have to be fulfilled: Jazirat Ibn Umar (Cezire) would have to be occupied temporarily; the Kurds would have to be provided with arms; and the British had to guarantee that the Kurds would not be handed over to the French after being liberated. Condition 2 was negated by the secretary of state for India on 18 January 1921 and conditions 1 and 3 appeared diplomatically impossible. Cox stated that, given the undeveloped situation in Iraq, a commitment to Kurdish rebellion against the Kemalists would involve the British in a moral commitment "which hereafter may become embarrassing." However, if such a policy were adopted, Cox would try to implement it.[17]

It was at this juncture in April, May, and June of 1921 that the British became aware that the Kurds and Greeks were also in contact. The British high commissioner in Istanbul, Sir Horace Rumbold, informed Curzon on 11 May 1921 that he had received information to that effect, but he thought that it would be difficult for Kurdish leaders to enter into relations with the Greeks because of "religious and racial sentiments." He did not think that Mustafa Kurdi Paşa of Sulaymaniya or Kurd Hakkı Beg would be of much use to instigate Kurds against Turks.[18] A few weeks later, however, Rumbold had more information on the Kurdish-Greek relationship. On 25 May 1921, Emin Ali Beg and his son, Celadet Beg, visited the political officer at the British Embassy in Istanbul and told him that the Society for the Rise of Kurdistan was in touch with Greek representatives, who were favorably disposed to a Kurdish movement against the Kemalists, and that the Greeks would, without any formal cooperation, promote the interests of both Greece and the Kurdish nationalists; Emin Ali replied that he could not pursue such a relationship without British sanction. He wanted to know if he or other Kurds would be allowed to go to Mosul and if the British would allow a Kurdish nationalist organization to operate publicly from British occupied territory. Ryan, the political officer, replied that the British could not support a rising in Kurdistan or Kurdish relations with the Greeks for the purpose of a Greek-supported Kurdish rebellion against the Kemalists.

The idea that the Greeks should support the Kurdish nationalists had first been suggested to Venizelos, the Greek leader, by the Greek high commissioner in Istanbul, Kanellopoulos, who was in contact with Emin Ali Beg Bedir Khan and his brother Hamid Beg. Venizelos had apparently instructed Kanellopoulos to secure the cooperation of the British. These proposals were made in 1919 and 1920, but little was done. Early in 1921 (the month is not specified), the Greek high commissioner sent a Kurd, Hamdi Cavuş, to Kurdistan. He was introduced to one Votsis, a Greek church official in Amasya. Nothing is known to have resulted from this meeting. In the meanwhile, Emin Ali and Hamid Beg approached Votsis with a proposal to cooperate with the Greeks. The Kurds would use the Kurdish prisoners captured by the Greek army. Emin Ali Beg wanted the Kurdish prisoners separated from the Turkish prisoners and given favorable treatment with the idea that they would subsequently be sent to Anatolia as propagandists. This scheme was referred to General Papoulos, one of the leading Greek commanders, who acted on the suggestions as far as the prisoners were concerned, but apparently did nothing else. In October 1921, Emin Ali Beg and Abdurrahman went to Egypt with funds provided by the Greek high commissioner. Emin Ali Beg's son, who knew Greek, drew up proclamations in Kurdish in collaboration with the Greeks, which were to be dropped by airplane over the Turkish armed forces.[19] I found no evidence that this did in fact occur.

Also during this period, in spite of Horace Rumbold's poor opinion of him, Kurd Mustafa Paşa was also in contact with the Greeks and Armenians. In February and March 1921, Kurd Mustafa had been in close touch with the Armenia National Democrat party (Dashnaktsuthiun), which the Armenian patriarch of Istanbul supported, as did the Greek high commissioner before he left for Kurdistan around July 1921.

British intelligence was of the opinion that Mevlanzade Rifat "and other Kurdish leaders were known to be making common cause with the Greeks in exchange for financial support." Kurd Mustafa Paşa arrived on 12 July in Damascus, then went to Mosul and Sulaymaniya with the aim of stirring up the Kurdish tribes against the Kemalists. It was speculated that he had had a hand in recent Kurdish revolts and maybe an indirect influence on the Koçgiri rebellion, but since his movements were restricted to southeast Kurdistan it was believed that he had not played a role in instigating the rebellion. The British had no doubt that secret organizations of the Greeks existed in Konya and Kurdistan. Furthermore, it was known that the Greeks had helped to foster and incite the Konya rising a few months previously and had played a role in keeping that area in a perpetual state of unrest. The British believed that the Greeks "have also taken administration of the movement for autonomy in Kurdistan to foment a definite outbreak to weaken the military position of Kemalists in Anatolia" and that "the Kurdish Party [apparently with reference to the Kürt Taali Cemiyeti] in Constantinople had been taken over by Greek authorities owing to the absence of funds at the disposal of the Kurdish leaders."[20] Ryan stated, however, that the British had no objection to Bedir Khan or members of the Bedir Khan family going to Mosul. His advice to Emin Bedir Khan was in keeping with British policy of not actively supporting Kurdish rebellion in parts of Anatolia away from the Iraqi border area, but instead encouraging Kurdish nationalism with the impression that in the right circumstances, the British might support active rebellion. In April 1921, the British had supported the journey of Emin's brother Abdurrahman to Beirut in order for him to confer with the French over division of the area that the Kurds wanted for their state.[21]

The London conference (21 February–12 March 1921), which had been called by the British to seek some kind of accommodation with the Turkish nationalists, failed when the Ankara representative, Bekir Sami, refused to negotiate while the representative of the sultan's government was present. He also refused the Allied demand to make the Treaty of Sèvres the basis of negotiations. The failure of the conference resulted in greater British activity in support of Kurdish nationalist groups. Also, by the middle of May, the British were aware of the agreement between France and the Kemalists from which Curzon thought that the French would be "unable to withdraw."[22] The possibility of an agreement between the French and the Turkish nationalists heightened British interests to pursue accommodation with the government in Ankara.

As early as May, Shuckburgh indicated that "as a last resort" Churchill would make some concessions to the Turks with regard to southern Kurdistan, but for the moment he did not approve of negotiation with the Kemalists.[23] Curzon agreed with Churchill. As of May 1921, the secretary of colonies and foreign secretary were in accord that there should be no negotiations with the Turks. The result was more encouragement to the Kurdish nationalists. Churchill did broach the idea that Faysal might be used to probe the possibility of negotiations with Mustafa Kemal. On 24 May, Shuckburgh informed the Foreign Office that Churchill was aware that article 3 of the draft mandate gave control of foreign affairs to Britain, but Churchill suggested that to allow Faysal to negotiate with a de facto government not officially recognized by Great Britain would involve no serious breach of that principle. If an arrangement agreed to by the Kemalists was subsequently disavowed by a "constitutional" Turkish government, such a disavowal would not directly affect the credibility of Britain, which would be free to take up negotiations *de integro* with the Turkish government. On 31 May, Curzon agreed with Churchill that in certain circumstances Faysal might "on his own initiative" undertake negotiations with Ankara. On 14 June, Churchill wrote Cox that perhaps Faysal could open negotiations with Ankara.[24] Thus, internal memoranda indicated that as early as May 1921 the British position was softening toward the Kemalist government. This was based upon the belief that negotiations would be to the benefit of British policy in Iraq and in the Middle East as a whole and reflected the assumption of the Cairo conference that Britain would be dealing with a "friendly Turkey." Even as the Turks fought fiercely against the Greeks throughout the summer of 1921 until their successful repulsion of the Greeks at the battle of the Sakarya (21 August–13 September), they also sought to stimulate the Kurds against any westward push from Yerevan by the Armenians, as well as to impede the British advance in northern Iraq. These rapidly changing circumstances, especially the nonmaterialization of a friendly Turkey, were now undoing the assumptions of the Cairo conference. It was also becoming clear from the Churchill-Cox correspondence that there was no agreement as to policy toward the Kurds.

On 24 June, Churchill responded to Cox's telegram of 21 June (no. 201). Churchill stated immediately that "I carried away from Cairo rather a different impression of the balance of opinion there with regard to our Kurdish policy."[25] He said that Cox had not made a clear-cut distinction between that part of Mesopotamia that he should control directly "whatever its ultimate fate may be and that part which should eventually come under Iraq." Churchill stated that Cox had said nothing of area (group) two in his dispatch, which would include Arbil and Kirkuk, and reminded Cox that in his dispatch of 25 May he had recommended that the Kirkuk area be excluded from Iraq. He said he "had in mind the picture of a buffer state ethnologically composed of non-Arab elements and interposed between Iraq and Turkey." Churchill, relying on the advice of two Kurdish experts, Captains Soane and Longrigg, wrote that the boundary line between the areas controlled by Cox and the Iraqi government should be "the ethnological limit of purely Arab areas than that of purely Kurdish areas."[26] The towns of Arbil, Kifri, and Kirkuk were in no sense Arab; when British garrisons withdrew from these towns, Churchill did not want them replaced with officers of the Arab army. His policy stipulated no Arab units and that the frontier force had to consist of Turcomans, Kurds, and Assyrians. In part three of this dispatch, Churchill defined the boundaries of his non-Arab province, which was to consist of three divisions, rather than Cox's four.

Before Churchill had received Cox's reply to his 24 June dispatch, he wrote Cox with regard to his 13 May telegram stating that he was not contemplating "the encouragement of a Kurdish revolt *outside*

Mesopotamia" (emphasis added) but "encouraging it in Kurdish areas within our sphere of Kurdish nationalism." For these purposes, Churchill again recommended Major Noel, in case "Kemalist policy necessitated our resorting to Kurdish propaganda or other measures." On 21 June, before he had received Churchill's telegram, Cox wrote Churchill that "the deliberations at Cairo were based on the assumption of a friendly Turkey. This can no longer be assumed." He went on to describe Turkey's hostile attitude, exemplified by the reported arrival of a Kemalist officer and thirty-seven men in Rawanduz. Cox said that, in light of this action, the policy of military reduction decided on at the Cairo conference could no longer be followed. From a political point of view, he suggested that the only weapon the British had "to combat a possible campaign of Turco-Bolshevism from Angora and perhaps from Teheran will be a solid block of Arab Nationalism and our policy must be to foster that to the utmost and give it all material support we can." The minutes on Cox's telegram indicate that it was a report of "a very corrupt telegram" that had been the background for Sir Percy Cox's proposals (21 June telegram) with regard to Kurdistan and the modification of the Cairo program of military reduction.[27]

Cox's proposals of June very much put in jeopardy the Cairo conference position on Kurdistan. How could southern Kurdistan be kept separate from Iraq if the British or, indeed, even Cox pursued a policy of Arab nationalism? Cox had added two new weapons to his growing arsenal against Churchill, the Middle East Department, and the Colonial Office: the purported increase of Turkish hostility and Arab nationalism. Over the next several months, he was to be a strong advocate of using the Kurds against the Kemalists.

By August, Cox still had not answered Churchill's telegram of 24 June. He now included constant reports of Turkish acts of hostility in his telegrams. On 26 August, he gave a long account of their actions and the organization of Kurds against the Turks in the frontier regions with Turkey and Iran, especially those efforts of Abdurrahman of the Şernak and Ismail Simko Ağa of the Şikak. Simko Ağa and the Kurds of Iran were emboldened after the fall of Sayyid Ziaeddin's government in Teheran in May 1921. In August, Cox confirmed that Nihad and Muheddin Paşas, ex-Turkish officers of Kurdish origin, were organizing Kurdish tribes against the British. The Turkish-supported group had established itself in Goran and Dasht-i Harir. On 14 August, Nihad and Muheddin Paşas attacked Rania. From 14 to 21 August, the British air force attacked the same town, including night bombing raids. Incendiary bombs were used; many villages that had supported the Turkish detachment were destroyed.[28]

On 8 September, Churchill approved of Cox's proposal, "while refusing formal intercourse with Kurdish chiefs beyond our borders to use opportunities to ascertain their intentions and to take (?promptly) such action as may be necessary to ensure safety of frontiers of Iraq. It is impossible not to recognize that their quarrel with their present suzerain [Turkey] may break out but I shall carefully avoid any side of it. However circumspect our action we shall be accused of complicity."[79] As of 8 September 1921, Churchill apparently did not think support of Cox's policies as to raising the Kurds "to ensure safety of frontiers of Iraq" would affect or abrogate his policy suggestion of 24 June. Cox did not say where he thought the frontier of Iraq lay. He also used the indefinite term "frontier" rather than "boundary." Churchill was apparently willing to let Cox proceed in his "administrative" arrangements without a clear definition of what his intentions were.

Cox's intentions became clearer in his telegram to Churchill on 20 September. He informed Churchill on the status of the Kurdish districts: "You will understand? uncertain and it will be specifically raised again in connection with elections for Constitutional? Assembly." He stated that he had discussed the situation with King Faysal, who "was still not very clear as to real wishes and policy of His Majesty's Government . . . he was in difficulty as to what line to take." Faysal said he understood that the Kurds in Turkey were attempting to establish independence, just as were the Kurds in Iran; given that situation, "unless it was soon decided what was to be status of Kurdish districts in Iraq some if not all of them would certainly secede and join up with" the Kurds in Turkey and Iran.[30]

In his dispatch Cox informed Churchill that he had told Faysal the substance of what he and Churchill had discussed in their correspondence, specifically from 21 June to the present, indicating his disagreement with the Cairo conference majority recommendation and that he was in favor of incorporating Kurdish districts into Iraq. Faysal told Cox that

the question of Kurdistan had further aspect for him as King of Iraq which had probably not been fully considered by us. This was question of preponderance of Sunnis or Shiahs with special reference to question of constitutional (Assembly) shortly to be convoked. As we were aware there was already technical and numerical preponderance of Shiahs and excision of a large slice of Sunni districts of Iraq out of state and exclusion of their representatives from National Assembly would place Shiahs in a very strong position and filled him [Faysal] with misgiving. Personally he believed as long as they were assured of being administered by Kurdish officials and if necessary were allowed to deal with Iraq Government through High Commissioner (an arrangement which if necessary was quite acceptable to him) rather than resort to possible alternative of becoming part of mandated State under control of some European? state senate they [the Kurds] would prefer to be nominally under rule of Muhammadan King.

Cox concluded that Faysal's suggestion would be a "reasonable course for inclusion of Kurdish districts, their participation in National Assembly on condition of local autonomy, and special supervision by British officers and if necessary by? High Commissioner."[31] Five months after the Cairo conference, the balance of opinion had certainly shifted in Cox's favor. An important element in the shift was Faysal's joining Cox's ranks. The men on the spot in Baghdad were clearly outmaneuvering those in London.

As could be expected, the members of the Middle East Department responded to Cox's latest telegram with voluminous minutes. The perceptive Reader Bullard agreed with the gist of Cox's telegram and noted, "It is amusing to see Feisal relying on the Kurds, who certainly never asked him as allies against the Shi'ahs who were supposed to be in revolt last year precisely because they couldn't get Feisal. But no policy that works is really absurd! and the Kurds will always be able to break away if they wish." James Masteron-Smith, permanent under-secretary of state for colonies, stated it was "not surprising" that Faysal was in doubt about the real wishes and policy of Britain because "we have never succeeded in really making up our minds on this very difficult question of policy in Kurdistan." Masterton-Smith said in effect that there were two policies: "one Cox's; the other Churchill's." But he noted that for practical purposes, the two alternatives necessarily overlap one another to some extent: "even if Sir P. Cox dealt directly with Kurdistan, he could do so only through the machinery of the Dept. at Baghdad, unless his staff were duplicated at prohibitive expence."[32] Since one of the policies of the Cairo conference was to reduce British expenses in Iraq, opposition to Cox's and now Faysal's position would undo that part of the conference as well. Churchill's own under-secretary of state had struck a blow for his boss's opponent: part of London was joining Baghdad.

Churchill seemed to be giving way. On 3 October, he telegrammed Cox that he appreciated the force of his and Faysal's arguments and that he "was prepared to consider favourably the proposals contained in the last paragraph thereof subject to proviso that Kurds are not to be under Arabs *if they do not wish"* (emphasis added).[33] Since Cox had already indicated in his telegram of 21 June that two out of four of his defined districts wished to join Iraq, Churchill's response indicated acquiescence in Cox's position. Churchill's response of 3 October gave de facto authorization for Cox's plan to incorporate the Kurdish districts into Iraq. The majority decision of Cairo was undone. In addition, Churchill was unable to make a trip to Iraq as he had planned. If Cox had outmaneuvered Churchill, it seemed unlikely that Hubert Young, who was sent instead and who had advocated a separate Kurdish entity at Cairo, would be able to dissuade Cox from his policy. On 29 September, Cox wrote Churchill that, in spite of the Turkish nationalist smashing of the Greek offensive at Sakarya (21 August–2 September), the Turks were still leery of the Bolsheviks and that maybe "the time was ripe for Faysal to open negotiations with the Turks." Churchill replied, with Lord Curzon's approval, that Britain would welcome Faysal's attempts to initiate negotiations with Mustafa Kemal. On 18 October, Cox informed Churchill that the British air force was having good effect on Turkish garrisons in Rania and Rawanduz. The Turkish commander, Ali Şefik al-Misri, popularly known as Özdemir Paşa, had been forced to withdraw from Qala Diza on 17 October and Koi Sanjak was reoccupied (temporarily as it turned out).[34] (See appendix VI for Özdemir's proclamations to the Kurds.) The increasing audacity and effectiveness of the air bombing was another instrument in Cox's now nearly full quiver for the incorporation of the Kurdish districts into Iraq.

The above actions had been taken by the time Cox telegrammed Churchill on 25 October, informing him that he had briefed Faysal on their exchange of ideas. Cox and Young had met with Faysal on 24 October and explained that Britain's policy was now "encouragement of Arab Nationalism not Arab imperialism." Faysal was told that a friendly Kurdistan was vital as an important shield against Turkey and that friendship of Kurdistan with Iraq was necessary because markets for Kurdistan were in Iraq, as well as Kurdish access to the sea. The only obstacle to the implementation of this policy was the threat of Turkey, which had a twofold policy: reliance upon the community of religion to incite Kurds against British and reliance upon anti-Arab prejudice to incite the Kurds against the Arabs. Thus, it was recognized by Cox, Young, and Faysal that "unless a Moslem focus could be found for Kurdish nationalism, the policy of treating Kurdistan as purely British dependency while remaining the basis of (second) propaganda would encourage first"—that is, treating Kurdistan as a purely British dependency would reduce the Turks' ability to incite anti-Arab prejudice, but increase their ability to use Islamic propaganda against the British. On the other hand, if Iraq were to become an integral part of an Arab kingdom under a Muslim Arab king, the Turkish ability to incite anti-Islamic propaganda would be reduced, but the Turks' ability to incite anti-Arab prejudice among the Kurds would increase.[35]

When Faysal was posed with the two alternatives, he replied that, until he knew to what extent military responsibility rested with him or the British, he did not see how he could express any definite view. He then asked four questions of his own:

(1) Is Great Britain prepared to undertake to defend Kurdistan if attacked from outside and consequently to guarantee Iraq against attacks through Kurdistan, if so, for how long?

(2) Is Great Britain prepared to accept responsibility to prevent internal disorder in Kurdistan which might be a danger to Iraq, if so, for how long?

(3) Regarding the fact that some Kurdish communities had expressed preference for inclusion in Iraq, is it the intention of Great Britain to compel them to remain separate, if so, for how long?

(4) In the event of separation, what form of government does Great Britain propose to establish and with what ultimate end in view?[36]

On 28 October, Cox gave his comments to Churchill with regard to these questions. With respect to question 1, Cox told Churchill that the military forces were based on the assumption of a friendly Turkey. As a result, the level of forces was very low and no military operations could now be carried out. The only available means of offense were airplanes and gunboats, for which the levies (largely Assyrian and Kurdish) and the Arab army would have to give ground support. Cox, on the advice of his commanding general, thought that the situation might improve when the Air Scheme went into effect (which was to take place in October 1922, one year later). Cox advocated that with regard to question 1, Faysal should be informed of the transition stage of Britain's military capabilities and that, when the Air Ministry assumed control, Britain's position would be strengthened. As to question 2, Cox thought Faysal could be given an affirmative answer, on the assumption of a friendly Turkey. His third question could be answered to the effect that Great Britain would not compel any Kurdish area to separate from Iraq; Faysal would be informed when a *final decision* had been reached. As to Kurdistan policy, all Kurdish districts to be included would be able to reconsider their positions in light of what that decision was. In response to the fourth question, Cox recommended that Faysal be told that, in the event of separation, Great Britain would propose to establish a system of local autonomy under British supervision in the affected area. The objective would be to discourage Turkish propaganda and bring about eventual federation of Kurdistan with the Arab districts in a united Iraq. As usual, in his last paragraph, Cox again stated the policy that he had outlined first on 21 June.

Churchill responded to Cox's very important telegram of 25 October on 11 November. He emphasized immediately that it was not possible to authorize Faysal to open negotiations with Mustafa Kemal, "as other larger negotiations are already in train with a view to a general peace with Turkey." Churchill then told Cox that he should "maintain a firm posture on the frontier as the immediate Turkish effort was geared to the west and not toward Iraq" and said, "I deprecate any attempt at the present moment to encourage the Kurds."[37] This last remark was in reference to the suggestion by Cox in his 28 October telegram to incite and actively to support Kurdish nationalist objectives. Cox suggested in that telegram that the British support a Kurdish revolt in the interests of Greece in Anatolia as an alternative to direct negotiations should the latter fail.

In a "Very Special" portion attached to his 28 October telegram, Cox had made the following proposal: first he mentioned that Halil Beg Bedir Khan and five members of the Society for the Rise of Kurdistan were in Baghdad and the Kurdish Revolt for which they had been working for two years was about to break out. According to plans, the areas of Dersim, Diyarbakır, Bitlis, and Van, "whose population total five to six millions," were to rise simultaneously in rebellion. Halil Beg told Cox that the Kurds wanted the help of Noel, British guns, and other support.[38] In part three of his telegram, Cox made the following recommendations in support of instigating a Kurdish rebellion against the Turks in Anatolia to relieve the Greeks. The British should support a Kurdish rebellion if the Turks would not negotiate and if the French continued to be unsupportive of British policies in the Middle East. Second, Cox recommended, with regard to India, that only Khilafat fanatics would be offended by British support of the Kurds. Third, Cox thought that the Iraqis would not like the idea of Britain supporting the Greeks against the Turks, but the success of the revolt would make the defense of Iraq easier and the "far-sighted" among the Arabs could be induced to accept it. Fourth, stated Cox, the objections of the French to the revolt could be taken care of by promising them commercial privileges in Kurdistan. Fifth, if rebellion of the Kurds were to break out soon, as

Halil Beg Bedir Khan promised, and if the Kurds were defeated, it seemed likely that Turkey would demand territory all of the way to Kifri. Regarding the Arms Convention to which Britain was a signatory, Cox was of the opinion there would be no problem passing the arms through Iraq, just as the government of India had passed arms to Tibet. In any case, Great Britain was still at war with Turkey so it would not be a violation of international law to supply arms to the Kurds. Finally, Cox wrote that it was important that the British not "cold-shoulder" the Kurds: the threat of a Kurdish revolt in Anatolia might have a salutary effect on the Turks to negotiate. This was the first time since his 21 June dispatch that Cox had mentioned the possibility of instigating Kurdish rebellion *outside of the mandated territory*.[39] He obviously thought that increased Turkish activity on the frontier would threaten all of his administrative policies for incorporating the Kurdish districts into Iraq. It also fit into his earlier announced preference for encouraging Arab nationalism as a deterrent to Turkish nationalism.

On November 8, 9, and 10, the Middle East Department unanimously took issue with Cox's proposed Kurdish revolt. J. H. Hall was opposed because such a revolt would not, he thought, be popular in Iraq. He emphasized that it would be a failure and prejudice any further British attempts to negotiate with the Kemalists. The French had already anticipated the British and won all of the kudos with the signing of the Franklin-Bouillon Treaty of 20 October 1921. Furthermore, reasoned Hall, Faysal had already gotten in touch with the Kemalists in anticipation of British approval. British support of a Kurdish revolt in Anatolia would put Faysal in a very bad light, especially as armed support for such a rebellion would have to come via Iraq. Reader Bullard understood Cox's proposal as an alternative to direct negotiations, but he found his "Machiavellian" proposals distasteful. Furthermore, if the Greeks were not entirely opposed to negotiations, as Sir Ronald Lindsay in Istanbul indicated, Bullard stated emphatically that the British should have nothing to do with the Kurdish revolt project. Bullard reasoned that Cox's proposed revolt would only bring disaster to the Kurds and discredit Great Britain. He emphasized that there was no unity among the Kurds, and that it was probable that, instead of a concentrated simultaneous rising in parts of Turkey so widely separated as Van, Bitlis, Diyarbakır, and Dersim, there would be sporadic outbursts that would eventually be suppressed by the better-organized Turks just as at Bitlis in 1916 and recently at Şernak. And what effect would British participation have, asked Bullard? Either the Kurds would estimate British intentions accurately and therefore not act or they would act, not receive any genuine help, fail, and blame the British for their failure. Bullard was emphatic that the British should give no aid to Kurds outside the mandated territories.[40]

Colonel Meinertzhagen did not like Cox's proposal either. British policy was based on a friendly Turkey—here was a proposal to make Turkey Britain's eternal enemy, he wrote. So far Britain's hands were clean, and this policy should be continued. The colonel thought that stirring up revolt was seldom justified, even in war, and invariably reflected on the party behind the scenes. Meinertzhagen had little confidence that the Kurds were a homogeneous nationality in spite of the fact that Major Noel "would doubtless have us believe it, but Noel is one of the General Gordon type, a fanatical enthusiast, who is capable of leading the empire to disaster in order to fulfil his dreams." He strongly disagreed with Cox's proposal, even as an alternative to direct negotiations between Faysal and Ankara. He recognized that the French had scored a temporary success with Kemal at British expense, but he thought "the Turk has by no means lost his respect for us. If we forfeit this last vestige of hope, we shall sink in the Middle East to the same level as the Latin races."[41] When the minutes of Cox's proposal were completed, three out of the five active members of the Middle East Department were strongly of the opinion that Great Britain should not support a Kurdish revolt.

John Shuckburgh, head of the Middle East Department, wanted Winston Churchill to see Hall's, Bullard's, and Meinertzhagen's minutes as they related to "a question of high policy: whether the Kurds outside Iraq should be encouraged by us in their project of revolting against the Turks." But he noted that nothing could be done about the proposed Kurdish revolt until it was clear: "(1) that there was no prospect of a settlement between ourselves and the Kemalists; and (2) that the proposal to permit Faysal to negotiate directly with Mustafa Kemal was definitely ruled out." Masterton-Smith in his minute added, "Whatever may be the outcome of these two questions, I am entirely against giving the Kurds any encouragement to revolt against the Turks. Furthermore, if the revolt should fail, as it surely would, the British would find themselves with a swarm of Kurdish refugees on our hands to take the place of the Assyrians and Armenians whom we have just got rid of." By supporting such a plan, Shuckburgh thought the British would win the undying resentment of the Kurds and render the prospects of a settlement with the Turks hopelessly remote. Sir Percy Cox had to be told that the government could not "in any circumstances agree to action on the lines suggested by him."[42] On 11 November, Shuckburgh advised Churchill to negate any suggestion of support for Cox's proposal. Churchill did this in his telegram, quoted above, on the same day. For once, London was able to overrule Cox on a matter of high policy.

Once this policy had been decided, the presence of Major Noel and the Bedir Khans in Baghdad again became an issue between London and Baghdad. But now the positions were reversed from five months previously. At that time, Cox had been opposed to Noel and the Bedir Khans' mission because he had thought it would encumber his policy of incorporating the Kurdish districts into Iraq. It will be recalled that Noel and the Bedir Khans wanted a separate entity. By November, Cox wanted Noel and his Kurdish operatives in Baghdad—not to ensure that the Kurdish districts not be incorporated into Iraq, but to stir up Kurdish rebellion against the Turks in Anatolia. By November 1921, it is also quite possible, if I have interpreted the Churchill-Cox correspondence correctly, that Cox already realized he had achieved his objective of incorporating the Kurdish districts into Iraq.

During this time, the summer and fall of 1921, Sayyid Abdul Qadir was making representations to the British in Istanbul and through his emissaries in Baghdad. He pleaded with the British to support him and insisted that he would be able to raise all of northeastern Kurdistan, including Ismail Ağa Simko in Iran, to support him in rebellion against the Turks. Sayyid Abdul Qadir emphasized that the British must act quickly to create a buffer Kurdish state against the Bolshevik menace. Cox responded huffily on 23 November to Churchill, saying that, of course, Churchill had sources of information of which he was ignorant, but that he found it most difficult to accept the view that Iraq was not an immediate Turkish objective. He listed all of Turkey's recent hostile acts toward Iraq. In spite of these hostile acts, Cox agreed that it was not the proper time to give Kurds any encouragement, but hoped that they could be kept in play. In the meanwhile, Cox informed Churchill that Halil Beg Bedir Khan was leaving Iraq and that Rifat Beg, one of his associates, was also returning to Istanbul.[43]

On 1 December, Churchill wrote to Cox that he did not accept his suggestion that the Kurds should be kept in play or that "special instructions to this effect" should be sent to British representatives abroad. He informed Cox of the reasons why Great Britain could not support a Kurdish revolt outside the mandated territory, especially in cooperation with the Greeks. Most of Churchill's objections were those formulated by Bullard, Meinertzhagen, Shuckburgh, and Masterton-Smith, as described above, but not fully incorporated into Churchill's telegram of 11 November. Churchill concluded the telegram by saying, "We have not yet been able to liquidate all the promises given or alleged to have been given to the Arabs during the war. I am entirely opposed to creating similar difficulties with the Kurds."[44] By 1 December 1921, there was, then, unanimous disapproval of proposals such as Cox's to instigate Kurdish rebellion against the Turks outside of the British mandate in Iraq, whether in alliance with the Greeks or not. This did not mean that the Kurds would not be used in the undefined frontier area of the Mosul *vilayet*. The British were "to keep in with the Kurdish revolutionaries as a necessary precaution." This was a policy that Britain followed right up to the signing of the Turkey-Iraq Treaty of 5 June 1926.

Sir Percy Cox, however, was not to be informed just how decisively his Kurdish revolt scheme was to be rejected because the Middle East Department did not want to send too "stiff" a telegram to him because of the need for his cooperation on other decisions of London such as Faysal's status and the reduction of expenditures on levies. Winston Churchill agreed with the Middle East Department (i.e., Shuckburgh and Bullard) and suggested that in such a sensitive situation the best thing to do was to "abridge the telegrams from London to Baghdad by allowing considerable intervals to intervene when matters are not urgent. . . ." While Cox was informed of the decision to negate his proposal, he was not informed of the categorical rejection of it by the Colonial Office and the Middle East Department. As a result, Cox continued to "keep the Kurds in play" without the full realization that London had decided not to support them if they entered the game. The decision reached in November–December 1921 concerning British support of a Kurdish rebellion against the Turks outside its mandated territory was reiterated in March 1922 in what, as far as I know, was the last seriously considered proposal to incite the Kurds against the Turks. It was made by Colonel A. Rawlinson on 4 March 1922, and Colonial Office and Middle East Department officials wrote minutes through 17 March.[45]

Rawlinson was an intelligence and political agent of the British in the Middle East from 1918 to 1922. He was on duty in Turkey from October 1919 to November 1921, at which time he was released from prison by the nationalist Turkish forces and exchanged for Turkish prisoners interned by the British in Malta. Upon his return to Great Britain, he wrote several reports for Lord Curzon and Winston Churchill, respectively, foreign secretary and colonial secretary, as well as the director of military intelligence at the War Office. The report was written at the request of Winston Churchill. In the first part, Rawlinson posed three questions and then proceeded to answer them: (1) How far did the policy of the Allies contribute to the consolidation of Turkish nationalist power?; (2) What measure of success attended their defiance of the Allies' proposals?; and (3) What prospect did the Turkish nationalists consider themselves to have of realizing the terms of their "pact"? In response to question 1, Rawlinson stressed the uncertainty among the nationalist leaders of being able to "obtain the general support of their countrymen" despite their strengthened position after the Erzurum congress and the Sivas congress—he believed that until the spring of 1920 the Turkish nationalists still had much opposition. But, contended Rawlinson, this opposition had evaporated as a result of the Allied occupation of Constantinople (16 March 1920); Allied support for the Greek invasion of western Anatolia via Izmir (15 May 1919); the announcement of the Treaty of Sèvres (10 August 1920); and the Nationalist Peace Treaty with the Soviet Union (16 March 1921).[46]

In answering question 2 regarding the success of nationalist defiance to the Allied proposals for peace, Rawlinson stated that the Turks had been able to mobilize the entire Turkish (Osmanli) population; they had captured Kars and the Armenian forces (September 1920) and had begun vigorous military operations against the Greeks in western Turkey. In addition, the nationalist leadership had sent German-trained intelligence officers to establish regular connections via Kabul with revolutionary leaders in India, Iraq, Palestine, and Egypt. Rawlinson then posed his third question as to whether the above operations had met with "very considerable measure of success." He answered that: the nationalists were certainly confident that the Greek forces posed no threat to the nationalists; "under no circumstances will the Allies be prepared to undertake any military operation in Anatolia"; and, therefore, they had nothing to fear from the Allies' present policy, "but that the longer that policy continues the more certain they will be of obtaining their demands in full and they are therefore prepared to consider nothing less."

In Rawlinson's opinion, the nationalists' confidence would result in demands whose realization would lead to the creation of a confederation of all Muslims—Sunnis from the "Bosphorus to the Caspian including Daghistan with the ports of Batoum and Baku in Turkish hands, this being the avowed object of their eastern aims, as such a confederation would dominate the political position in the Near East." To prevent such an eventuality, Rawlinson thought it important to "consider whether a line of policy cannot be adopted by the Allies, or even by the British Government alone, which will tend to weaken the Nationalist position and so render them less truculent and more amenable to the consideration of reasonable propositions, so that by this means a way be opened to an eventual settlement." He stated that to achieve such ends and to be of any practical value such a policy should: not be antagonistic to Islam; be such as to inspire a dread of further development; not call for the employment of troops of any considerable expenditure; and be capable of being discontinued whenever desired. Rawlinson then suggested that a policy meeting the above four conditions could be implemented "owing to the disaffected and uncontrolled state of the Kurdish tribes in the Eastern Valayets." Furthermore, due to the mobilization of every available Turk on the eastern and western fronts, the Kurds were "left enormously in the majority in the eastern districts of Anatolia and all Turkish posts there being very weakly held are at the mercy of the local Kurds, being particularly vulnerable should Kurdish raids be carried out approximately simultaneously, say within the same month."

Rawlinson reported that the Kurdish chiefs were dissatisfied with their position and extremely antagonistic toward the Turks. He thought the chiefs could be induced to carry out raids for little money or arms; significantly, he mentioned machine guns. Each Kurdish chieftain would attack the Turkish posts and garrisons in his own district. Such raids would require little cooperation among the tribes, of which, said Rawlinson, the Kurds would be incapable in any case. He suggested this policy could be put into effect "by use of a fast British vessel, preferably a destroyer, in the Black Sea, which could call at night at various points on the Anatolian coast, land agents etc., and, standing out to sea during the day, the vessels would return at night in accordance with a prearranged system of fire signals from coast range. Such an undertaking would be inexpensive to organize and, even if not attended with entire success, it was a line of policy which the nationalists above all things dread, as they are well aware of their weakness in this direction." The success of such a policy would have a great impact on the nationalists, for "they also dread the great moral effect of such a policy, and the possible cutting off of their eastern from their western armies with the danger of dissensions amongst themselves, which by that means would be encouraged."[47] In Rawlinson's view, this policy had three advantages: there could be no question of any religious feeling being aroused; such a policy could be ended at any moment; and the undertaking could be carried out without any European publicity such as had attended the Franklin-Bouillon mission.

Rawlinson concluded his report by suggesting that the Kurdish tribes and/or chieftains to carry out the mission should be: Ayeeb

(Eyub) Paşa of the Olti district, who would be capable of taking Erzurum; Huseyin Paşa of Alaşgird, who would be capable of taking Kara Kilise or Bayezit; and the Dersim Kurds who were already in open insurrection and able, he thought, to take Erzincan at any moment. There were still others who could be made use of in Rawlinson's view: the Black Sea range was "in the hands of insurgent bands consisting of Pontine Greeks and deserters who could also be encouraged." He had confidence in the policy's success because he had "personally seen and conversed with the leading personalities in those tribes." Rawlinson was positive the policy's success would be "very effective in modifying the present attitudes of the nationalist Turkish government."

By 9 March, John Shuckburgh had distributed Rawlinson's report with his own minute attached to that of Reader Bullard, Richard Meinertzhagen, and T. E. Lawrence, who was still serving as an adviser on Arab affairs in the Middle East Department. After mentioning the salient points of Rawlinson's plan, Shuckburgh brought it to the attention of his subordinates that Sir Percy Cox had "more than once raised the question of utilizing the Kurds from the Iraq side, but we here [Colonial Office] have always strenuously opposed the suggestion." Shuckburgh mentioned that in Rawlinson's view the Kurdish chiefs accessible from Iraq would be of no use, since they did not have sufficient influence or following. Shuckburgh thought, however, that Rawlinson's proposals elicited the objection entertained at the Colonial Office to similar proposals by Sir Percy Cox.

T. E. Lawrence made his minute on the same day. His view was that such sporadic local movements would only call for "police work in prevention and will not gravely embarrass the Kemalists." In addition, suggested Lawrence, to foment a successful revolution would require foreign direction and experts such as "assisted the Hejaz operation during the war." Lawrence did not like the locations from which the revolt would spring. Olti and Alaşgird bordered Russia and would require Lenin's help; the Dersim region was impossible to reach except by the Euphrates Valley. Finally, Lawrence was of the opinion that it was madness to attempt to make a serious rebellion from the base of a single destroyer. In spite of his reservations, Lawrence did "believe a Kurdish movement is a possibility if such a power as ourselves is willing to provide the bases, or base, the arms, stores, instigating staff, & the money." The amount of money would be considerable because "the Arab Revolt, a fair parallel, under better circumstances, occupied some eight ships, fifty British officers, and £5,000,000 in money, and over £16,000,000 in stores." Lawrence concluded his minute by stating that if a Kurdish revolt was to be considered, it should be on the same scale as the Arab revolt. But its aftermath would create formidable difficulty with the Turks and Armenians. "I regard it as a desperate measure," he concluded.

Reader Bullard was more critical in his minute, stating that Rawlinson's proposals violated most of the conditions he laid down as essential; in some quarters it would be seen as antagonistic to Islam; heavy expenditure, such as mentioned by Lawrence, would be incurred; "and it could *not* be discontinued at will" (emphasis in original). Bullard had other criticisms: "Is it seriously proposed that we should stir up the Kurds against the Turks and then leave them to be massacred when we have secured the political advantage we desire? Hasn't Col. Rawlinson learnt from the fate of the Armenians, who were instigated by the Russians to revolt against the Turks and, later on, abandoned?" Furthermore, Bullard thought Rawlinson's proposal, to some extent, nullified those of Sir Percy Cox because the Kurds Cox wanted "to stir up are precisely those whom Col. Rawlinson thinks no good." Bullard was "totally opposed to our becoming involved in Turkish Kurdistan . . . even the Kurds of Iraq sit on the fence when a company of ragged Turkish infantry comes to Rawanduz." Bullard concluded his minute by stressing that as soon as a policy decision was made, Sir Percy Cox had to be told what should be done with Halil (Khalil) Beg Bedir Khan and Major Noel.

Meinertzhagen was curter. He appreciated, he said, the "desire of vengeance which must be indelibly stamped in Col. Rawlinson's heart," but he regarded "the scheme as immoral & mad. Any success would be but temporary & in the end it would rebound against us, as all such ventures in the past, including the Hejaz Revolt." It is interesting to note at this point that, in addition to Meinertzhagen, several other members of the Middle East Department, including Reader Bullard, considered the Arab revolt rather a failure—and this was in 1921–1922. In this respect, they ordinarily disagreed with T. E. Lawrence's proclivity to support more adventurous schemes of intrigue and rebellion.

On 15 March, a group council meeting of the concerned personnel met with Shuckburgh and rejected Rawlinson's plan in toto. Meinertzhagen also informed the group that it was the opinion of the director of intelligence at the War Office that "the Turkish Nationalists have the Kurds in their pocket & that to rely on them to any degree in embarrassing the Turks is to live in false hope." Furthermore, even if the Turks could be so embarrassed, the director of intelligence considered Rawlinson's method both "crude & unpractised." The same day Reader Bullard was again quick to remind

Shuckburgh "[Winston Churchill] must tell Sir P. Cox that as there is no prospect of adoption of Kurdish insurrection scheme in near future (if ever) it is unnecessary to retain either Noel or Khalil." On March 15, Shuckburgh recommended to Sir James Masterton-Smith that Rawlinson's proposals be dropped for the reasons discussed in the minutes and that Sir Percy Cox "be informed that as there is no likelihood of our adopting the policy of utilizing the trans-border Kurds there is no reason why he should keep Major Noel and Khalil at Baghdad any longer." On 15 March, Masterton-Smith approved Shuckburgh's recommendations in his minute; on 17 March, Winston Churchill initialed his approval.

Rawlinson's recommendations for instigating a Kurdish rebellion substantially north of the territory occupied by British forces in Iraq indicates how out of touch he was with the direction of British policy toward Turkey in early 1922. Although, as discussed earlier, various schemes had been floated to stir up the Kurds throughout 1920–1921, they had begun to be viewed with increasing skepticism by the middle of 1921. Rawlinson thought the Turkish nationalist forces could still be checked or intimidated sufficiently to withdraw from their stated objectives of the National Pact of 28 January 1920, especially those clauses that demanded national sovereignty and territorial integrity over Anatolia, western Thrace, and Istanbul. This meant Greek and British evacuation of those areas. The rejection of Rawlinson's scheme points out the rather dramatic evolution of British and Allied policy toward the nationalist government after the Treaty of Sèvres was signed on 10 August 1920. The year 1921 marked victories of the Turkish forces over the Greeks and crucially important nationalist agreements with France, Italy, the Soviet Union, the Ukraine, and Afghanistan. The most significant achievement was the Franklin-Bouillon Treaty of 20 October 1921. Ömer Kürkçüoğlu has labeled 1921 as the year of "softening" (*hisbî bir yumuşama*) of British policy toward the nationalists.[48] My contention here is that the noticeable softening of British policy toward the Turks was first revealed in the Churchill-Cox correspondence over their "battle" for Kurdistan.

As this correspondence makes clear, the British desire for peace with Turkey, on the best terms for itself, of course, subordinated Britain's Kurdish policy to this objective. It is not coincidental that, as the Colonial Office and Winston Churchill were rejecting Rawlinson's Kurdish revolt project, the British and Turks—Curzon and Yusuf Kemal, the Turkish foreign minister—were engaged in another London conference (16–19 March 1921). The conference failed due to demands that were unacceptable to the Turks, such as establishment of an Armenian state, removing Turkish troops from the Straits, letting Greeks remain in Izmir, and so forth, but the Turkish nationalist victory over the Greeks at Sakarya (21 August–13 September) ensured that there would indeed be negotiations. Even the Çanakkale crisis only temporarily delayed the momentum propelling both countries toward negotiations. On 11 October 1921, the armistice of Mudanya was signed; on 21 November, the Lausanne conference began. On 24 July 1923, the Treaty of Lausanne was signed. Kurdistan was not even mentioned. The reasons for articles 62, 63, and 64 of the Treaty of Sèvres had been, it seems, completely forgotten. Article 3 in the second paragraph of the Treaty of Lausanne had even relegated the question of the boundary between Turkey and Iraq to bilateral negotiations between Great Britain and Turkey, which were to reach a decision within nine months of the implementation of the treaty. During the period 20 August 1920 (Sèvres) to 24 July 1923 (Lausanne), British policy toward the Kurds had gone from the support of an independent state with defined borders to indecision as to how much of Kurdistan should be included within the state of Turkey and how much within the state of Iraq.

As the Churchill-Cox correspondence indicates, by late 1921 there was really no longer a supportable argument for a separate Kurdish entity within Iraq—Sir Percy Cox had seen to that. British support for Sheikh Mahmud in fall 1922 and early 1923 was simply an effort to use him and the Kurds against the strengthening of the Turkish position on the question of Mosul. When Mahmud was found to be dallying with the Turks, he was deposed by the British, for the second time. By the summer of 1923, when Iraq held elections for its Constituent Assembly, the Kurds were given no choice: they were incorporated into the new Iraqi state.[49] Some one and a half years after his 21 June 1921 telegram to Churchill, Cox had achieved the policy that he had outlined and announced in that correspondence.

The Cox-Churchill correspondence, especially from 21 June to 7 December 1921, was so important in defining British policy toward the Kurds that it is necessary to make some judgments as to why Cox prevailed over Churchill and the majority policy as expressed at the Cairo conference on 15 March 1921. The main reason for Cox's dominance of policy is that he was the man on the spot. This example gives credence to the view that officials on the peripheries of the British Empire were in a good position to pursue their own policies. The major reason for this is that they controlled or were able to determine the administrative districts, their frontiers, and, most significantly, the personnel to staff them. In a complex geographical and ethnic area such as northern Iraq, this allowed Cox much room for manipulation and maneuver, something he did brilliantly. The rapidly changing political scene in the Middle East and Turkey also gave great advantage to Cox: he was able at timely moments to utilize Kurdish nationalism or Arab nationalism or to stress the threat or to exaggerate Turkish hostility. He did all of this to marvelous advantage. He had achieved so much of his policy of integrating the Kurdish districts into Iraq that, by October 1921, he was bold enough to advocate a Kurdish revolt in alliance with the Greeks in Anatolia against the Turks. This was taking place while London had not completely abandoned the idea of a separate Kurdish entity in Iraq. By October 1921, the success of Cox's policy for Iraq threatened to influence British policy in the entire Middle East and to disrupt the evolving relationship between Turkey and Great Britain. Such was the diplomatic and political power of the periphery on the center of the empire.

Cox was fifty-seven years old and Churchill was forty-eight, so Cox did not have a great experience advantage over Churchill. By 1921, Churchill had already served as home secretary, minister of munitions, and secretary of war. By 1921, Cox had served nearly three decades in India, East Africa, and the Persian Gulf. In 1904, he had been appointed acting political resident of the Persian Gulf. He knew Persian and Arabic—and he also knew what he wanted in terms of what he had determined to be British interests in the Persian Gulf region. He pursued his goals in a consistent and singularly tenacious manner. Churchill, on the other hand, as colonial secretary, had responsibility for the entire British Empire. He also had to rely on advice from a Middle East Department that had just been organized and was feeling its way in terms of developing policy. The Middle East Department was confronted by Cox, who was an exemplary bureaucrat. He won the fight against Churchill in the battle over Kurdistan. The only major policy that Cox did not achieve was his project to raise the Kurds in rebellion in alliance with the Greeks against the Kemalists. This, wisely, was rejected by the Colonial Office and Winston Churchill. From spring 1921, then, to early 1922, this was the sole political and diplomatic victory of Churchill over Cox in the battle over Kurdistan.

Cox also had the great advantage of having the RAF in London and in Baghdad as his allies. Both Hugh Trenchard, air chief marshal, and Sir John Salmond, air officer commander in Iraq, favored a "forward policy" against the Turks in Iraq. The Air Ministry knew throughout 1921 that it was to replace the War Office as the main military force in Iraq and the officers commanding were eager to demonstrate that the Air Ministry could not only secure the peace but could also

·   expand it. The Air Ministry's and Cox's plans coincided. Ironically, the Air Scheme was strongly supported by Churchill, an advocacy that undermined the Kurdish policy he wanted to implement in 1921. In many ways, the majority opinion with regard to British policy toward the Kurds as expressed at the Cairo conference was unmade by the success, efforts, and effectiveness of the RAF. The successful link of the air force and those who controlled its technology would prove to be a formidable political weapon in the hands of those who advocated the expansion of empire. The union of air technology and the "forward firsters" was to provide effective spokesmen for the policies of the British Empire after World War I in certain parts of the world even as it retreated in other parts. In a way, the experience of Iraq from 1920 to 1923 was a victory of the advocates of the new air technology over the old naval technology. It is interesting that the older man, Cox, realized its advantages and employed it with great skill in pursuit of his objectives in Iraq. Churchill, of course, was a supporter of air power; as a former head of the Admiralty and war minister, he was more aware than most British officials of the importance of weapons technology, but maybe even he, at first, underestimated the great impact that air power would have on politics and diplomacy. The experience of Iraq from 1920 to 1923 seems to bear this out. But Churchill had worldwide responsibility as colonial secretary in 1922–1923 and therefore had to be more cautious than Cox. This was a demonstration that new weapons technology such as air power could be used much more effectively in the hands of a capable official in influencing policy at the periphery of empire than in the hands of the officials at the center of the imperial government. Truly, Iraq provided a good case study in the interrelationships among weapons technology, politics, and diplomacy. The first post–World War I experiment of this kind occurred in Iraq, and its great success was to continue to influence British imperial policies until the end of World War II. Sir Percy Cox, then, in a sense was riding the cresting waves of a new and innovative policy, one he used to his advantage. It enabled him to best the formidable bureaucratic and diplomatic skills of Winston Churchill.

There were other factors that influenced British policy toward the Kurds from mid-1921 to mid-1922, but the evolving perception that peace with Turkey was essential to British interests was the dominant one. After the Franklin-Bouillon Treaty on 20 October 1921, it was clear that Britain had fewer policy options against the Turks. By September 1922, during the Chanak (Çanakkale) crisis, Britain stood alone. It is true that Winston Churchill joined Lloyd George and those in favor of military action to defend the freedom of the Straits, but this display of military might or bluster seems to have been for temporary political advantage. Even if war had ensued, this did not substantially affect Churchill's position that peace negotiations with Turkey should continue apace, as displayed in his correspondence with Cox.[50] By the late fall of 1922, there was a constant need for a more hawkish public position as the road to Lausanne shortened.

The general impression given by the Cox-Churchill correspondence is that the British intention to negotiate and to recognize the Ankara government occurred earlier than some historians of this period suggest—that is, the British realized that they would have to negotiate with the Ankara government somewhat before the Mudanya negotiations in October 1922, even though Britain did not give de facto recognition to Ankara until the negotiations at Lausanne. British policy toward the Kurds indicates, however, that the British realized the need to negotiate with Ankara before the commencement of the Lausanne negotiations. The de facto recognition of Turkey at Lausanne was a negotiating strategy, not an expression of assessed political reality: that political assessment had occurred earlier, during the last six months of 1921. When Cox's policy triumphed over that of Churchill, it removed one of Britain's main levers in pursuing a policy of nonnegotiation and nonrecognition of Turkey. The territories gained by Turkey at Lausanne were, after all, territories Churchill had been willing to concede in December 1920.[51]

The British policy toward the Kurds after Lausanne was largely one of defining the boundary between Turkey and Iraq. The Air Ministry files, the intelligence reports of the Air Ministry that was responsible for intelligence on Turkey, and the Colonial Office records indicate that after Lausanne the British never thought that Turkey would use military force to secure the *vilayet* of Mosul. British intelligence agents, who apparently included a former minister in a cabinet of Mustafa Kemal's government during the period 1921–1924, also told British intelligence that Ankara never really thought of employing large military forces to secure Mosul. The Kurdish nationalists must have realized this as well, as suggested by increased Azadi mobilization after the Treaty of Lausanne. The Kurdish question after Lausanne, however, played an important role in internal Turkish politics and in international politics.

Air Ministry intelligence reports of 7 October 1924 and 21 January 1925 are particularly interesting in this regard because they seem to reflect the British impression of internal Turkish politics, which in turn influenced the Iraqi-Turkish frontier question and attitudes toward the Kurds. The source for the following discussion is a former cabinet minister during the years prior to 1925, although his name is not mentioned in the report. According to the former minister, in 1920 the Ankara government had resolved on a "pseudo-oriental" policy that was followed up to 10 October 1922. The main purpose of this policy was to take advantage of better relations with the Soviet Union that materialized in the Treaty of Friendship on 16 March 1921 and the Treaty of Kars, 13 October 1921, after the Turco-Armenian war, and the Turco-Ukrainian Treaty of 2 June 1922. After 10 October 1922, Ankara decided to follow an "occidental" policy by establishing closer relations with Japan and emphasizing Pan-Turanianism. Ismet İnönü was chosen to pursue this policy, which was followed after the Treaty of Lausanne until his resignation on 22 November 1924. He resigned because he was awaiting the solution of the question of Mosul and the Syrian frontier, so "he had to humor Russia up to that point."[52]

Regarding Mosul, Ankara remained convinced that it would not gain much. All that Ankara hoped for was a certain modification of the frontier line so that it could feel secure both militarily and economically. The non-Turkish races in the Mosul area fell outside of Ankara's occidental program. Ankara wanted Adana secure and had its heart set on Antakya (Antioch) and Iskenderun (Alexandretta), since it considered them Turkish towns with Turkish populations. The minister felt sure that this goal would be achieved.

After the resignation of Ismet İnönü on 22 November 1922, an attempt was made to turn back to the oriental policy. This, said the informant, was "the work of Fethi Bey [Okyar] and his colleagues." The informant stated that Fethi Okyar, Feyzi Bey, his minister of public works, and Esad Bey, minister of justice, were "rabid Russophiles" (one has to keep in mind that the informant undoubtedly had his own political agenda) and that within the People's party (Halk Firkası) there was a group of about thirty members, of whom the most prominent were Yunus Nadi, Ahmet Aghaiev, Yusuf Akçura, Sami Bey, and Mahmud Bey, who were strong supporters of the oriental policy. When Fethi Okyar came into power, all of the "true nationalists" were displeased. One of the reasons for this displeasure was the possibility of Pan-Islamic impulses being raised against Great Britain. The informant thought, unhappily, that it was Ismet İnönü himself who wanted Fethi Okyar to succeed him. The reason for this was that İnönü "knew" that the solution of the Mosul question "could not be a brilliant one for Turkey and he wanted Fethi in position to receive the brunt of the responsibility."[53]

Another important reason for İnönü's resignation seems not to have been foreign policy, but the fact that Mustafa Kemal was very worried about the revolt within the ranks of the People's party and the formation of the Progressive Republican party (Terrakkiperver Cumhuriyet Firkası), which occurred during the period 26 October– 9 November. Many of the new members of the Progressive party were also members of the Second Group, men such as Kazım Karabekir, Ali Fuad Cebesoy, Refet Bele, and Rauf Orbay, who were opposed to some of Mustafa Kemal's more secularist and dictatorial policies, but not necessarily his westward orientation, unlike Fethi Okyar, the new president of the Progressive Republican party. It seems Mustafa Kemal chose Fethi Bey to be prime minister because he thought he was more moderate than some of the other dissident members of the People's party. By making Fethi prime minister, Mustafa Kemal apparently intended to take the wind out of the sails of the Progressive Republican party. The informant thought that if Fethi Bey did not stop the disintegration of the People's party, Mustafa Kemal would turn to Recep Peker, the minister of the interior. In turn, the opposition, ensconced in the Progressive Republican party, thought that with Fethi as prime minister they would be able to develop a new party that could engage the People's party in an open contest for power.

Fethi Okyar, meanwhile, was eager to compromise with the Soviet Union, but he "was afraid of Mustafa Kemal and the nationalists."[54] According to the minister informant, Fethi Okyar wanted a "semi-oriental" and a "semi-occidental" policy. At the very moment that Okyar thought that he had discovered this formula, Recep Peker, the minister of the interior, resigned. This resignation had been arranged beforehand between himself and Ismet Inönü and the nationalists. Recep Peker's resignation was to be the signal of the first appearance of danger. As minister of the interior, he would be privy to information that would indicate changes in policy, although his resignation was premature due to the importance of the die-hard Kemalists. According to the informant, the basis of Fethi Okyar's policy was a proposal by the Soviet Union to Turkey to organize a Black Sea Basin Joint Naval and Air Fleet in which the two countries would be on equal terms. If the proposal was accepted, the Soviet Union would loan Turkey the money to implement it. In connection with the project, the Soviets proposed to Turkey that the two countries should combine to follow a single program and policy in the matter of the Dardanelles. If Turkey accepted the proposals, the Soviet Union would further propose that Turkey should associate itself with the Soviet Union in the elaboration of a special Russo-Turko Program for the administration of Transcaucasia with a view to becoming joint mandatories for the entire region. The two countries would bear an equal share of the revenues and expenses.

Upon hearing of these proposals, probably from Recep Peker, Mustafa Kemal and the nationalists were alarmed. Mustafa Kemal immediately organized a Ministry of the Marine and the portfolio was entrusted to Ihsan Bey, a deputy of Parliament from Cebel Bereket and a staunch nationalist and trusted supporter of Mustafa Kemal. Also, said the informant minister, "On the resignation of Recep, we forced Fethi to give the portfolio of Interior to Cemil Bey, who is one of our men."⁵⁵ Moreover, Fethi Okyar was obliged to make an exposé of his proposals before the Grand National Assembly, under the presidency of another staunch Kemalist, Hamdullah Subhi, and to the Central Committee of the People's party. The latter did not accept the "Russian Proposals" and Fethi was forced to promise that he would put forth a detailed account of the proposals within a month.

In the meanwhile, according to the informant, who was giving an insider's account of current events, Mustafa Kemal wanted to ride out the crisis until the return of Ismet Inönü, still "convalescing" on the island of Heybelli in the Sea of Marmara. The question was: would Inönü consent to accept office before the solution of the Mosul question? If he chose to prolong his convalescence, the situation, thought the source, could become dangerous. Mustafa Kemal sent a telegram to Inönü, received on 13 January 1924, which reportedly stated: "Do not be uneasy. The black project is arrested and postponed. The danger is dissipated. We now merely await the good news of your recovery." By 28 January 1925, it was reported that Kara Vassıf, head of the Constitutional Committee for the Progressive Republican party and the parliamentary opposition to the Kemalists, said that the party's relations with Inönü were good with respect to foreign affairs. One of the major reasons for the drawing together of the Progressives and the Kemalists was Fethi's "Russian policy."⁵⁶

Thirty-eight days (19 February 1921) after Mustafa Kemal telegraphed Ismet Inönü not to be "uneasy," he again telegraphed Inönü: "Come to Ankara by the first train. We expect you without fail."⁵⁷ British intelligence was of the opinion that Inönü had not expected such a call—he had verbally invited Dr. Emin Bey, prefect of Istanbul, at six o'clock the same evening to come to lunch with him at Halki the following day. On 21 February, one day after Inönü left for Ankara by train, British intelligence reported that there was still no official reason given for his recall but offered the opinion that there were three primary reasons: Turkey's relations with the Soviet Union and France; disarray of the People's party; and the rebellion of Sheikh Said in Kurdistan. In consideration of these reasons, Mustafa

Kemal wanted İnönü to assume the presidency of the Council of Ministers.

Turkey, in addition to the Black Sea Basin Project, had to consider that the Soviet Union had accorded Turkey a credit of 10,000,000 gold rubles for military purposes; the government had to consider French demands for French schools and rectification of the Turco-Syrian frontier. The People's party was in disagreement about Mosul, Italian immigration into western Anatolia, and Turco-Greek relations. The party was also in general disarray, disagreeing in particular as to what should be done with the Ankara public prosecutor's investigation of whether the 20,000 British pounds given to the Progressive party by Egyptian princess Kadria had come from the British. British intelligence was of the opinion that the Sheikh Said rebellion was due to the disregard of the Turkish government for the decisions for the Turkish-Kurdish congress that had taken place during the first part of August 1924. As of 2 March 1925, Ismet İnönü, it was reported, refused to replace Fethi Okyar as prime minister, in spite of demands that he do so, until the Mosul question was resolved. But in the meanwhile, he wanted Fethi to follow his advice. Mustafa Kemal "begged" Fethi to follow İnönü's advice and Fethi Bey agreed to do so.[58]

On 2 March 1925, British intelligence issued another report on the Sheikh Said rebellion, apparently based again on the former cabinet minister turned informer. The British intelligence source thought that Ankara "must execute promises it made to Kurdish chiefs at the time of the Diyarbekır Congress." The present government, he opined, had disregarded them. The informant was convinced that it was for this reason that the Kurds had revolted at this critical moment—on the eve of the solution of the Mosul question. In his opinion, foreign influence and the growth of reaction against the new regime were to be classed only "in the second rank of the contributing causes. I repeat and I have good reason to repeat that the principal causes of the revolt are: (1) that the present government has neglected to carry out the promises made to the Kurds by the previous cabinet; (2) that it has consistently disregarded the warning reports sent in by the Valis; (3) that it has omitted to take any sort of measures likely to tranquilise the Kurds and to induce them to submit to authority." The informant thought that Ankara would announce that its fulfillment of the Diyarbakır Agreements and that this would pacify the Kurds. He added:

> For the satisfaction of public opinion in Europe, since the government will not be able to admit its negligence, the explanation

that the revolt was due to foreign intrigue and the forces of reaction will serve very well for dissemination through the me-
dium of the press, of public speeches, etc. And by these means
we can smother or threaten all the centers of reaction and para-
lyse the intrigues both of the opposition and of the foreigner.
This explanation will also tend to ally the discontented elements
in Trebizond and other vilayets. But, at the same time we must
be ready with our military, police and administrative measures.[59]

In fact, the rebellion of Sheikh Said would be helpful in dealing
with other problems now faced by Turkey. "We [Turkey] must gain
time by putting forward as a pretext for the delay the Turkish government's inability at this juncture to take decisions on such matters
when all its attention and energies have to be devoted to dealing
with the Kurdish menace. But after the settlement of this affair,
which is closely linked with the Mosul question, it will be easy
enough to find an amicable solution in the case of the above mentioned matters."[60] The information provided to British intelligence
by the formerly highly placed official in the Ankara government
proved to be so accurate that it is tempting to think that it influenced British decisions about Turkish policies in general and particularly policies toward the Kurds. One of the seemingly few errors
in the judgment and prognostications of the informant minister was
his belief that in the wake of the Sheikh Said rebellion the government would announce its intention to fulfill the promises made to
the Kurds in Diyarbakır during the first part of August 1924. Turkey
did not make such an announcement.

4. Mobilization for Rebellion: From Beyt Şebab to Piran

THE BEYT Şebab (referred to as Bayt Ash-Shabab or Bayt Shabab by the British, present-day Beytüşşebap in Turkey) mutiny on 3–4 September 1924 hastened Azadi plans for revolt. The mutiny put the Turks on full alert as to just how well organized Azadi was. Over 500 officers and soldiers had taken part in the mutiny; throughout the autumn of 1924, courts-martial took place in Diyarbakır and Bitlis. In chapter 2, I indicated the extent to which Turkish intelligence went to implicate Ihsan Nuri, the leader of the Beyt Şebab mutiny, as a Turkish spy. At the end of the last chapter, it was stated that a former cabinet minister in the Turkish government, who was a major intelligence source for the British, thought that the Turkish government's noncompliance with the agreements of the Turco-Kurdish congress of the first of August 1924 had precipitated the movement toward rebellion, which helped precipitate the Beyt Şebab mutiny. Van Bruinessen, relying on his informant, Mela Hesen, states that preparations for the rebellion, however, continued throughout 1924.[1]

The caliphate was abolished on 3 March 1924. On 8 April, a National Law Court Organization Regulation (Mahkeme Teşkilati Kanunu) abolished the Şeriyet (Shariʿa) courts, retired their judges, and transferred their jurisdiction to the secular courts. On 3–4 September, the Beyt Şebab mutiny took place; on 29 October 1924, the Grand National Assembly accepted a new constitution and declared Turkey a republic. The constitution of October 1924 forbade the use of Kurdish in public places. Law number 1505 made it possible for the land of large landowners to be expropriated and given to Turkish speakers who were to be settled in Kurdistan. Şerif Firat states, interestingly, that it was the declaration on 29 October that Turkey would be a republic that greatly facilitated the Azadi's preparations for rebellion, rather than the abolition of the caliphate on 3 March or of the Şeriyet courts on 8 April. All of these events contributed to the ability of the Azadi to rally the sheikhs, *hocas*, and tribal leaders to their cause. The Azadi had decided at its first congress, held probably, as we have seen, sometime in the late summer or early fall of 1924, that it would be "doubly advantageous to give the coming revolt . . . a religious appearance."[2] This was to be the plan, not only to attract the Kurdish religious leaders, but also to take advantage of the conservative and religious opposition to Mustafa Kemal in hopes that the Grand National Assembly would not be unanimous in its opposition to the rising.[3] The Azadi "even attempted to establish contact with the exiled ex-sultan, Vahideddin." It was to take advantage of the above situation plus the great appeal and attraction and reputation of the sheikhs among the Kurdish population that "Azadi expressly had chosen shaikhs as the overt leaders of the revolt."[4]

Meanwhile, the Beyt Şebab mutiny continued to have repercussions. On 10 October, Yusuf Ziya was arrested in Erzurum and sent to the military war court in Bitlis, where he confessed to complicity in the mutiny and other nationalist activities. He allegedly implicated Halid Beg Cibran, Hasananlı Halid, Sheikh Said, and Haci Musa, chief of the Mutki. Haci Musa was arrested and then released in an attempt by the new vali, General Kazım Dirik, to drive a wedge between the tribal chiefs and nontribal leaders of Azadi, especially former officers in the Turkish army. This different treatment of the Kurdish nationalists indicates that the Turks were aware of the composition of the Azadi and had adopted a strategy for containing it. By releasing Haci Musa and Sheikh Nurşinlı Masum, head of the Nakşbandi *tarikat,* and Hızanlı Selahattin, Kazım Dirik hoped to dissuade the Kurdish tribes of the Muş, Bitlis, and Hızan areas, all of whom belonged to the Babakurdi tribal confederation, from participating in the rebellion. The general's tactics were successful. When Haci Musa was freed, his brother Nuh Beg delivered some seventy pack animals of ammunition and other goods to Kazım Dirik.[5] The divide-and-rule tactics of the Turks worked very well early in the unfolding of the rebellion. On 20 December 1924, Halid Beg Cibran was arrested and imprisoned in Bitlis. He and Yusuf Ziya Beg were later killed in the same prison. Kazım Dirik now wanted to arrest Hasananlı Halid and Sheikh Said. The former had already attacked Bitlis several times and raised the tribes in attempts to release Yusuf Ziya and Halid Beg Cibran from prison. Fear that the two might be liberated may have led to their execution. Hasananlı Halid was not captured and became one of the leaders of the rebellion.

Sheikh Said was also called to the military war court in Bitlis, but he pleaded that he was too old and too sick to travel that far and asked to give his testimony in Hınıs, which he did on 22 December 1924. Said testified that Yusuf Ziya wished to slander him because he had failed to loan him money. Şerif Firat claims that the governor (*kaymakam*) of Hınıs, Maksun Bey, was under the spiritual influence of Sheikh Said (possibly meaning that Maksun Bey belonged to the Nakşbandi *tarikat* that Sheikh Said headed) and he wired that Sheikh Said was a ninety-year-old (he was sixty) blessed saint who entertained no ambition and had no greed. When Sheikh Said returned from Hınıs, he received instructions from Halid Beg Cibran that the rebellion should begin immediately; Sheikh Said was to establish relations with Syria via Diyarbakır and the tribes should occupy all of the government centers in their own districts. Sheikh Said then informed Hasananlı Halid that he should attack Bitlis and free Halid Beg Cibran at the first opportunity. On 27 December 1924, Sheikh Said left the Hınıs area (Kolhisar) for the Çapakçür, Palu, Lice-Hani area. He did so in order to avoid arrest and to make preparation for the rebellion.[6] The sheikh would also be in the safe territory of the Zaza-speaking tribes, who were among his most fervent and loyal adherents (*murids*) just as they had been of his father and grandfathers before him. There were few government forces in these areas, which could easily be swept aside when the order for rebellion was given. Sheikh Said could use his tour to collect his annual fees, contributions, gifts, and other revenues that would be useful for buying weapons and supplies for the rebellion. He also used his January tour to coordinate the date of the rebellion, inform the men who should lead it, and rally the populace to his cause. Most importantly, the strategy, fronts, and allocation of forces had to be determined.

On 4 January 1925, in the village of Kırıkan, several important *ağa*s, sheikhs, and tribal chieftains, among whom was a former Hamidiye colonel, Selim Zırkanı, gathered to discuss strategy. Sheikh Said had not yet decided on rebellion, but it was at this point, early January, that his son Ali Rıza returned from Aleppo, where he had sold twenty herds of sheep, the proceeds of which were to be used for the rebellion. Ali Rıza had left for Aleppo sometime around the time of the arrest of Halid Beg Cibran and Yusuf Ziya and after Sheikh Said's own interrogation. After selling the sheep, Ali Rıza had gone to Ankara and Istanbul to consult with members of the Society for the Rise of Kurdistan and with Sayyid Abdul Qadir, although the latter was not, apparently, an official member of the Azadi. He also consulted with those people, Kurd and Turk, who were opposed to Mustafa Kemal. Ali Rıza informed Sheikh Said and his lieutenants that the people in Ankara and Istanbul thought that the rebellion would be more successful if the first uprisings took place near Diyarbakır. The sheikh's confidence was reinforced by the news that his

son brought and he immediately issued a *fetva* (religious decree)
that condemned the Ankara government and Mustafa Kemal for destroying religion and stated that it was lawful to rebel against such
sacrilege. On 4 January 1925, Sheikh Said wrote a letter to the Hormek and Lolan Alevi tribes, hoping to get them to join the rebellion,
but the tribes refused absolutely and stated that they would fight
against the rebellion.[7] Sheikh Said tried to compromise with the two
Alevi tribes. He wrote that Ankara would take away all religion. He
pleaded that the Alevis and Sunnis should cooperate to rescue their
honor and their religion. But the Alevis refused to accept his pleas
and actually fought with the government forces. This was the same
government against which they had rebelled since the beginning of
the Koçgiri rebellion in 1920.

The Alevis, it seems, did not want to aid in the creation of an independent Kurdistan, which would be Sunni-led. Many of the leaders
of the planned Sheikh Said rebellion were former Hamidiye commanders, who had harshly repressed the Hormek and Lolan, including Halid Beg Cibran, who had killed Zeynel, the son of Ibrahim
Talu, the famous leader of the Hormek. The Alevis thought they
would be better off in a secular Turkey, nominally Sunni, than in
a self-declared Sunni Kurdistan in which the Nakşbandi (Sunni)
tarikat would assume a major role. The Alevi rejection of his over-
ture greatly limited the potential area of rebellion. In spite of this
setback, the sheikh continued his mobilization throughout January.
On 6 January, he held a meeting in the village of Kanıreş in the district of Karlıova, where it was decided which forces would be used to
attack the Alevi tribes that did not join the rebellion. On 8 January, another meeting was held in the village of Melekan, where the
fronts and their commanders were assigned. The date for the rebellion, March, had already been set at an earlier meeting. Five
major fronts were to be established. The north/northeastern front
was under the command of Sheikh Abdullah of Melekan. Commanders of other sectors of this front were the sheikhs of Can, the
Hasanan tribes, Mehmet Ağa, Halile Kete, and Sheikh Said's son, Ali
Riza. The Harput front was to be commanded by Sheikh Şerif of
Gökdere. The Ergani front was to be commanded by Sheikh Said's
brother, Abdurrahim. The Diyarbakır front was to be led by Hakkı
Beg and the western by Emiri Faruk, both of whom were Zazas. The
Silvan (Farkın) front was to be commanded by Sheikh Şemseddin.
Sheikh Said was to be the supreme commander-in-chief.[8]

From the 6 January meeting until the outbreak of the rebellion on
8 February, Sheikh Said continued on his tour, mobilizing men and

selecting local leaders. He continued to issue *fetvas* and to give speeches denouncing the Ankara government and the godless policies of the Kemalists. The sheikh said that he had come to restore religion. On 12 January, Said was in Çapakçür; by 15 January, he was in Darahini, where he was received as a messiah. Here he took the title *emir al-mujahidin* (commander of the faithful and fighters for holy war). On 21 January, he was in Lice; on 25 January, he was in Hani (Hini), where he conferred with Sheikh Şerif, the appointed commander for the Harput front. It was decided in Hani that Sheikh Şerif would attack Elazığ when the rebellion began. On 5 February, Sheikh Said arrived in Piran with about one hundred armed men. It was here that the rebellion broke out on 8 February 1925.[9]

Participation in the Rebellion

The Kurdish tribes who participated in the rebellion were almost all from the Zaza-speaking Kurds of the mountainous areas of Lice-Hani-Çapakçür. The Zaza call their own language Dimili, which indicates a possible connection with Daylam in northern Iran. The Zaza dialect of Kurdish is closer to the dialect of the Gurani Kurdish speakers in the Sulaymaniya area of northern Iraq than to the Kurdish dialect of central Anatolia, which is largely Kurmanci. Of course, many of the Zaza and Kurmanci speakers speak both dialects, as many of their dwelling areas were closely intermingled.[10]

Van Bruinessen stresses that many of the Zaza-speaking population owned pieces of land and a few animals beyond tribal possession. Some of the tribes were in the process of detribalization. He suggests that this resulted in less difference between the chiefs and the tribesmen and "there were thus no conflicts of interest to make commoners refrain from participation at the demand of the Aghas." This may have resulted in closer solidarity among the Zaza than among some of the Kurmanci speakers and thus fuller participation in the rebellion. The dialect difference, however, was no barrier in the social relations between the two groups. Şerif Firat, a Kurdish author who gives one of the only two accounts of the Sheikh Said rebellion based on firsthand information, states that of the three major Kurdish tribal confederations in central and eastern Anatolia—Babakurdi, Kurmanci, and Zaza—many of the tribes belonging to the Babakurdi group who lived further to the east of the area in rebellion did not participate. The Kurmanci were divided into two confederations, the Mil and the Zil, of which only the former participated. Most of the Zil—Burukan, Milan, Hasanan, Hayderan, Semsi,

Epdoyi, Celali, Dakuri (Takori), Zirkan, Şadili, Ademan, Torular—
did not join Sheikh Said; in fact, many fought on the side of the
government.[11]

There was also participation by the Kurmanci-speaking Cibran
tribe and the Hasanan. Halid Beg Cibran was the first president of
the Azadi. Van Bruinessen mentions, however, that he could not determine whether the two tribes participated fully or not. Kasım Beg,
one of the Cibran chiefs, "reportedly" betrayed Sheikh Said when
the latter tried to escape to Iran when it had become clear the rebellion would not succeed. It does seem, however, that the Cibran tribe
largely supported the rebellion. Some tribes promised to join the revolt, but when it broke out they remained aloof, gave only token
support, or joined the Turks; examples are the Pençinaran, Reman,
and Reşkotan.[12]

As of 5 April 1925, the tribes of the Şernak, Jezira (Cezire), Siirt,
Midyat, and Mardin districts remained neutral. The tribes between
Van and Şernak—Mankuran, Godan, Bezdima, Alan, Jürgan (Cürgan),
Karısan—also did not participate in the rebellion. Three reasons
were given for their nonparticipation. First, the chiefs of the tribes
had been bribed by the Turks with large sums of money and promises of government posts after the rebellion had been quelled. Second, the Şernak district, in contrast to the Dersim region, was rich
in land and cattle and the tribes preferred the "security of peace to
the ravages of war." Third, the Şernak tribes were waiting for assistance from Great Britain and "presumably the remaining tribes
along the Iraq frontier are taking the lead from them." The fact that
the Şernak tribes did not participate in the rebellion greatly reduced
its potential scale. The Şernak area was of great importance because
of its proximity to Iraq and the reliability of its tribes. It was speculated that if Sheikh Said received no assistance from the Şernak
tribes, the possibilities of a sustained rebellion were not good; but
if the Şernak tribes did join the rebellion, then all of the neighbor-
ing tribes would join and the Turks would be hard put to suppress
rebellion simultaneously in so many areas where communication
and rapid movement of troops were almost an impossibility. Apparently, the leaders thought that if the Şernak joined the rebellion,
they would do so with the support of Great Britain. In this event, the
rebels hoped to capture Sivas. The informant for British intelligence,
apparently one of the officers who had defected after the mutiny at
Beyt Şebab, was certain as of April 1924 that offers of assistance
from Christians in Aleppo and Erzurum and from Armenians had
been firmly rejected. The reason he gave was that the rebels could
scarcely permit the assistance of infidels as long as they claimed

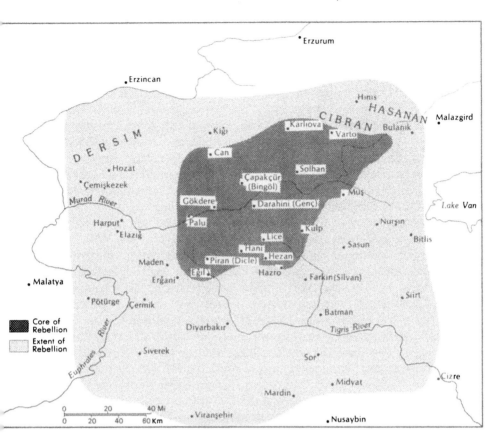

Map 1: The Core and Extent of the Sheikh Said Rebellion

to be fighting for the cause of their religion. In fact, it was reported that a Christian from Aleppo who was carrying papers with offers of assistance to Sheikh Said was caught by the Turks in Urfa and hanged. It was speculated, however, that offers of certain assistance from Great Britain "would outbalance even the strictest religious scruples."[13] Motivations for joining the revolt other than nationalism included the tendency of many of the tribesmen simply to follow their chiefs, sheikhs, or *ağa*s when ordered to do so. Some of the chiefs wanted to use the opportunity to settle old scores against other tribes and against government representatives.

For these reasons, the Alevi tribes, both Kurmanci- and Zaza-speaking, did not join the rebellion. This was a major setback for the rebels. The Alevi tribes of the Dersim had gained much experience

in fighting with the Kemalists since the Koçgiri rebellion in 1920–
1921, in which—it is important to emphasize—they had declared
nationalist goals. Sporadic revolts and low-level guerrilla warfare
continued, indeed, right up to the time of the Sheikh Said rebellion.
The Alevi nonparticipation, especially from the Hormek and Lolan,
meant that Turkish troops could pass through or around their areas
without challenge. The lack of support of the Alevis greatly nar-
rowed the area of operations for the rebels and correspondingly reduced the area that the Turks had to conquer, occupy, and pacify.[14]
The nonsupport of the Alevis meant that the Sheikh Said rebellion
was a Sunni-led rebellion against a Sunni state, which enhanced the
program of secularism that the Kemalists advocated.

The economy of the areas in which the rebellion occurred was
weak. World War I had caused much devastation; few Armenians
were left and trade was mostly in kind and by barter. Some of the
villages produced tobacco; what they did not use themselves, they
bartered for other goods.[15] Hunger was no stranger. Many young men
had been conscripted and killed in World War I and many others had
immigrated to the larger towns of western Anatolia to find work.
Many of the 30,000 Kurds in Istanbul were from the Zaza tribes and
villages. The scattered small villages and the lack of powerful landowners allowed for a modicum of participation among the peasant
landowners and local authorities. This situation permitted sheikhs
of the Nakşbandi order to assume a dominant role in settling disputes. The sheikhs of the area in which the rebellion occurred were
influential. Sheikh Said was the most powerful.

The nontribal Kurds occupying the plains around Diyarbakır also
did not participate in the rebellion, cowed and controlled by the
landowners. One scholar notes that Sheikh Said did not even invite
the peasants to join. The rebel tribes obviously thought that the
peasants would be worthless as fighters. Sheikh Said's rebellion
remained tribal. A large majority of the population of the town of
Diyarbakır was Kurdish in 1925. Yet none of the Kurdish notables of
the town supported the rebellion. One notable family even sided
with the Kemalists. One member of the Cemilpaşazade family,
Kasım, left the town in February before Sheikh Said's forces attacked
it on 29 February. While the strong Turkish army garrison and the
intelligence apparatus in Diyarbakır were deterrents to revolutionary activities, even with a reduced Turkish presence it seems unlikely that the Kurdish notables and middle class would jeopardize
their position with tribal forces led by sheikhs or the unproven
strengths of Kurdish nationalism. Striving to gain national pride,

civil rights, and better economic conditions was one thing, but to confront an armed Turkish response was another.

Neither did the lower-class and working-class Kurds in Diyarbakır or other larger towns in the rebel area rise. Some undoubtedly wanted the rebels to win, but they were not organized. The leaders of the rebellion obviously did not think they would be of much aid either. An effort to organize the lower classes or even to propagandize was obviously low on the agenda of the organizers of the revolt. The numbers and the potential effectiveness of such classes were small. The organization of the Azadi was secretive; events had moved very quickly since its establishment in 1921. In addition, Turkish intelligence was constantly on guard. All of these realities mitigated against extensive recruitment, especially the time-consuming task of inculcating nationalism in uneducated, poverty-stricken peasants or the lower classes. Not only were the peasants and working classes, small as they were, divided; the tribes were also divided, not only along Sunni-Alevi lines, but as a result of traditional tribal feuding. The only people who were in a position to overcome these differences, at least temporarily or partially, were the sheikhs. The first chapter discussed how the sheikhs had risen to such powerful positions in Kurdistan after the destruction of the emirates in 1847. The sheikhs, of both the Nakşbandi and Qadiri orders, had become seemingly necessary and hence powerful in fulfilling all of the political, religious, and psychic needs of the Kurds.

The Nakşbandi order and its sheikhs were the most important leaders of the rebellion. This was due to their traditional position and the high regard in which the Kurdish populace held them. It was also due to the fact that the Azadi leaders, most of whom were officers in the Turkish army, realized that the Kurdish populace would support and believe the sheikhs sooner than army officers. The sheikhs were to be "the overt leaders of the revolt."[16] After the arrest of hundreds of the leaders of the Azadi after the Beyt Şebab mutiny, the sheikhs were the only ones left to lead the rebellion. They had become indispensable. The supreme commander of the rebellion thus fell to the most respected, spiritually admired, and trusted nationalist: Sheikh Said of Palu and Hınıs. Sheikh Said's grandfather had settled in Septi, a village near Diyarbakır, sometime around the middle of the eighteenth century and then moved to Palu, where he continued his sheikhly duties and activities. Due to a dispute between the *ağa*s and *beg*s (notables and landowners) in which Sheikh Ali doubtless played a role, he was forced or thought it in his best interest to move. He chose to resettle in Hınıs, a district in the province of Erzurum. He married, gathered influence among the *ağa*s and *beg*s, and with their intervention was able to return to Palu. Sheikh Ali had five sons. The oldest, Mahmud, was the father of Sheikh Said. After Sheikh Ali's death, his tomb site (*türbe*) became an object of veneration and he was revered as a saint. During the following years, thousands of pilgrims visited his *türbe* and the gifts they brought enriched the family, which in turn increased its influence even more.

Sheikh Said was born in 1865 in Palu, which meant that he was around sixty years old at the time of the rebellion.[17] A few years after his birth, his father moved back to Hınıs, where Sheikh Ali had established a *tekke* (religious lodge). In Hınıs, Sheikh Said studied the Quran and the religious sciences, probably under the guidance of his father. When his father died, Sheikh Said became the head of the family and the head of the *tekke*s. As early as 1907, he had made a tour of the eastern *vilayet*s and became acquainted with the chiefs of the Hamidiye. It was apparently around this time that he was given the nickname Bedi uz-Zaman, because of the many poems and compositions of al-Hariri and Bedi uz-Zaman Hamadani that he had memorized. According to British intelligence reports, it was around this time that Sheikh Said urged the Kurdish deputies in the Grand National Assembly to form a radical party. Sheikh Said's five brothers settled in various places. Adil was killed in a place near Aleppo; Bahattin was killed while reading the Quran in Hınıs; Abdurrahim died in the same year as Bahattin. In 1925, two of his brothers, Mehdi and Tahir, both sheikhs, were still alive. Mehdi lived in Kelhasi village and suffered from some nervous disorder. Sheikh Tahir, who was one of the leaders of the rebellion, was still in the area, although after the rebellion he left Palu. In 1925, according to Metin Toker, more than twenty members of Sheikh Said's family still lived in Palu. One, Sadettin Gonur, became *müfti* (religious judge). Several other members of the family, including Sheikh Said's son Ali Riza, subsequently became leading members of political parties and members of the Grand National Assembly.[18]

The sheikh had pursued the usual practice of marrying his daughters and the daughters of his brothers to sheikhs and tribal chiefs who could contribute to the power and consolidate the influence of the family. Said himself had married a woman from the Kurmanci-speaking Cibran tribes in order to extend his influence beyond the Zaza-speaking area. His wife seems to have been an aunt of Halid Beg Cibran, making Sheikh Said and the first president of the Azadi cousins through marriage. In 1925, Sheikh Said was a very healthy, strong, and handsome man. His full white beard was dyed with henna and his eyes were sometimes tinged with antimony. Because of his position as sheikh as well as that of his two brothers, Said was probably one of the wealthiest men in Kurdistan. He owned large herds of sheep and employed around 120 shepherds to look after them. His sheep grazed mostly on lands between Palu and Hınıs. This meant that he was known in all of the villages between the two towns, in Diyarbakır and as far as Aleppo, where the sheep herds were taken for sale. Not only did Sheikh Said know everyone of any stature in the area of rebellion and beyond, but he and his lieutenants knew every inch of the terrain. His possession of large herds of sheep not only provided funds to purchase arms and ammunition; the herds were strategically located to provide food in the areas where the major fronts were to be established. One indication that the rebellion was to break out was that his son Ali Riza had driven twenty herds of sheep to Aleppo in December 1924 instead of the usual ten herds.[19] Turkish intelligence was probably aware of this as well.

Mela Hesen, who knew Sheikh Said, stressed in his interviews with van Bruinessen that he was an unswerving nationalist and was vehemently opposed to exploitation. The sheikh criticized "other shaikhs of his own Naqshbandi order who would have no dealings with the nationalists and seemed only concerned with their own interests." Sheikh Said had stated at one time that the Nakşbandi sheikhs in Kurdistan resembled more a "gangster ring" than a religious order. It can be inferred from this statement that one of Sheikh Said's objectives in promoting and leading the rebellion may have been to reform the Nakşbandi order in Kurdistan. Utilizing the nationalists and their objectives would have been one way of accomplishing this goal. The challenge of secularism would bring more order to the religious organizations of Kurdistan. The deterioration within the Nakşbandi order may suggest why the role of Sheikh Said as a holy man was more important in the rebellion than the organization of the Nakşbandi order. In spite of this organizational deficiency, the Sheikh Said rebellion was better organized than the Sanussi bedouins' rebellion against the Italians in Libya. Van Bruinessen attributes this to the fact that whereas the Sanussi sheikh sent his chief assistants (*khalifas*) directly to a tribe or subtribe, in Kurdistan the sheikhs had followers among more than one tribe.[20] For example, Sheikh Abdullah and Sheikh Said both had disciples (*murids*) among Kurmanci speakers, as well as Zaza. This was a deliberate policy cultivated through marriage.

As indicated in chapter 2, Sheikh Said was one of the most outspoken nationalists at the first Azadi congress held sometime in the late summer or early fall of 1924. When tribal chiefs and former Hamidiye commanders were cautious and reserved, Sheikh Said persuaded them of the need for rebellion. In all of the subsequent congresses and meetings of the Azadi, Sheikh Said was the dominant figure. The imprisonment of many of the Azadi leaders after the mutiny of Beyt Şebab made his leadership imperative.

Numbers of Kurdish and Turkish Forces Participating in the Rebellion

Most accounts of the rebellion state that the Kurds were able to mobilize about 15,000 fighters. Some estimates are as low as 10,000. I found few estimates lower than 10,000, and no sources stated that 20,000 or more fighters were mobilized. It would seem that a figure of 15,000 would be a good estimate. It is impossible to determine how many had horses, rifles, and sabers.[21] The number of troops mobilized by the Turkish government can be estimated much more exactly. British intelligence kept track of the Turkish army and the growing Turkish air force in the eastern provinces, especially as incidents increased along the Iraqi-Turkish frontier. After the Lausanne Treaty, regular reports were made and sent to concerned officials throughout the British government. The best report, and the one closest to the outbreak of the rebellion that I could find, on Turkish army estimates was that dated 20 May 1925, compiled by the headquarters of air intelligence in Baghdad. These reports were compiled by means of diverse sources. Air intelligence in Mosul was the most important. The estimates as of mid-April of Turkish forces employed in the area of the rebellion and within 170 miles of the Iraq frontier were 52,000.[22] The Air intelligence officer who wrote the report attached a note saying that the figures were conjecture. A minute from War Office intelligence states that the report's estimated figures of the rifle to ration strength of four to nine were similar to War Office estimates.

The 20 May 1925 report drew its information from another report issued simultaneously, which had slightly higher estimated figures of 53,000 total rations in the rebellion area. The difference of 1,000 between the estimates was derived from the fact that the draft report estimated 15,000 total rations for the Seventh Army Corps while the final report set the figure at 14,000. The draft report also put total rifles at 28,000; the final draft put the figure at 23,000. The draft report estimated 2,100 sabers and the final report, 1,920. The draft report also gave the location of the divisions: Fifth Army Corps Headquarters at Lice; Seventh Division at Hani; Forty-first Division

Table 2. Estimated Strength, Mid-April, of Turkish Forces Employed in Revolt Area and within 170 Miles of Iraq Frontier

Corps	Division	Rifles	Sabers	Guns	Airplanes	Total Rations	Remarks
HQ Vth Corps (mobilized)		350	150	20			
	7th Div.	5,100	50	16?			
	41st Div.	5,100	50	12	12	25,000	Only 4 serviceable 6/4
HQ VIIth Corps (partly mobilized)		650	150				
	2nd Div.	2,800	50				
	17th Div.	2,800	50	8		14,000	The mobilization of this corps was still in process on 14/4.
	1st Cav. Div.		660	8			
	14th Cav. Div.		660	8			
	5th Div. (VI Corps)	2,250	50	12?		5,000	
	12th Div. (IX Corps)	2,250	50	12?		5,000	
	11th Regt. of 3rd Div. (VIII Corps)	1,700				3,000	
Total		23,000	1,920	96	12	52,000	

Table 3. *Estimate of the Turkish Troops in the Eastern* Vilayets, *20 June 1925*

1. Force in the eastern *vilayets*, 15 February 1925

	Sabers	Rifles	Guns
VIIth Corps			
8th Cavalry Division	500	—	8
28th Infantry Regiment	—	500	—
1st Cavalry Division	500		8
14th Cavalry Division	500	—	8
2nd Infantry Division	50	3,000	24
17th Infantry Division	50	3,000	24
	1,600	6,500	72

2. Forces moved into that area by rail

	Sabers	Rifles	Guns
Vth Corps			
7th Infantry Division	50	6,750	24
41st Infantry Division	50	6,750	24
Corps troops	—	1,500	—
Reinforcements to VIIth Corps to make up their infantry regiments to war strength	—	9,250	—
For 1st Cavalry Division (nearly wiped out at commencement of rebellion)	500	—	—
	600	24,250	48

3. Other divisions that took part in the operations, presumably at war strength

	Sabers	Rifles	Guns
Vth Corps	100	18,500	48
5th Division	50	6,750	12
VIIth Corps	1,600	15,750	48
Corps troops	—	3,000	—
3 frontier battalions	—	3,000	—
Gendarmerie	—	7,000	—
	1,750	54,000	108

at Silvan. These divisions were completely mobilized. The Seventh Army Corps, thought to be only partially mobilized, was headquartered at Diyarbakır; Second Division at Bitlis; Seventeenth Division at Eghil (Eğil?); First Cavalry Division at Mardin; Fourteenth Cavalry Division at Mardin; the Sixth Army Corps, of which the Fifth Division was not mobilized, was north of Çabatca; the Ninth Corps,

Twelfth Division, also not mobilized, was between Gumgum and Muş. The Eighth Army Corps, Eleventh Regiment, of the Third Division was located at Çabatca.[23]

Major R. E. Harenc, British military attaché in Istanbul, submitted a report estimating Turkish troop strength in the rebellion area as of 20 June 1925 at 54,000. The figures he gives are 3,000 to 4,000 less than the mid-April estimates and may represent a slight decline in troop strength after the major defeats of the Kurds in March and April.[24]

As indicated by his figures, Harenc calculated that nearly half of the estimated 50,000 Turkish troops in the area of rebellion had been transported into the area by rail. This information makes it clear that substantially more than fifty percent of the troops deployed against Sheikh Said were moved into the area after the rebellion began. This also suggests that, in spite of good intelligence about the Azadi, the Turks seriously underestimated the scope of the rebellion that finally did take place.

As of 1 April 1925, the distribution, location, and officers of the Turkish forces deployed and mobilized against the Sheikh Said rebellion were as follows, according to British intelligence:

HQ 3rd Inspectorate
Ferik (General) Kazım Paşa
HQ VIIth Army Corps
Mirliva (Brigadier General) Mursalı
CSO (Chief Signal Officer) Kaymakam (Lieutenant Colonel) Yusuf
Ziya Corps artillery
   2 batteries, 8 field guns
   1 battery, 4 Schneider mountain guns
   1 battery, 2 antiaircraft guns (unserviceable; ammunition does not fit)
HQ 17th Division
Kaymakam (Lieutenant Colonel) Cemil Haci (acting), formerly on the staff of 3rd Inspectorate
   63rd Regiment
   Binbaşı (Major) Ismail Hakkı (acting)
   1/63rd Binbaşı (Major) Lutfi
   2/63rd Yüzbaşı (Captain) Nuri Veysi (acting)
   3/63rd Binbaşı (Major) Avni, formerly 2nd Section staff, VIIth Army Corps
   36th Regiment (attached to the 17th Division)
   Kaymakam (Lieutenant Colonel) Muhammad Şahin

1/36th Regiment Binbaşı (Major) Sukri
2/36th Regiment (two battalions only)
6th Regiment (attached to the 17th Division)
Kaymakam (Lieutenant Colonel) Ali Taymur
1/6th Regiment
2/6th Regiment
(2 battalions only), 2 batteries, 8 mountain guns
Under orders of OC (Officer Commanding) of 17th Division at
Harput
25th Regiment
Kaymakam (Lieutenant Colonel) Murad
1 battery field gun
HQ 2nd Division
Miralay (Colonel) Ali (acting)
18th Regiment (less 2 companies at Garzan [Karzan])
1st Regiment (Bitlis-Van)
62nd Regiment (attached to 2nd Division at Bitlis)
HQ 14th Cavalry Division
Miralay (Colonel) Subhi
3rd Regiment
5th Regiment
54th Regiment
14th Divisional Artillery (1 battery and 4 mountain guns)
1st Cavalry Division (reforming at Mardin)
HQ Vth Army corps
Mirliva (Brigadier General) Haci Paşa at Diyarbakır
Corps Artillery
1 battery, 4 howitzers
1 battery, 4 field guns
1 battery, 4 mountain guns
HQ 41st Division at Tel Alo, 3 miles northeast of Diyarbakır,
operating east of Diyarbakır toward Silvan.
Miralay (Brigadier General) Cemil Cahid
16th Regiment (3 battalions located at Kadi Köy north of
Diyarbakır as of 27 March 1925)
19th Regiment (3 battalions)
12th Regiment (3 battalions) at Sor
41st Divisional Artillery
1 battery of 4 field guns
2 batteries of 8 mountain guns
(See appendix VII for a selected list of Turkish officers serving in
the eastern provinces in April 1925.)

5. The Rebellion and Its Aftermath

WHEN THE Sheikh Said rebellion broke out prematurely on 8 February 1925, the rebel forces probably had around 15,000 fighting men. They were opposed initially by approximately 25,000 Turkish troops at ration strength, including the support troops not armed with rifles. If we accept the British intelligence calculation of a four to nine proportion between rifle and ration strength, the Turks were able to confront the rebels with less than 12,000 fighting men. By 1 April 1925, however, the Turks had some 52,000 ration strength in the area of rebellion, with close to 25,000 fighting men.

The rebellion broke out prematurely at a village called Piran. Sheikh Said was forced to declare general rebellion after there was an exchange of gunfire between his forces, which numbered over a hundred, and a gendarmerie force of ten men led by a lieutenant, Hasan Husni. The gendarmes were trying to arrest five outlaws who had taken refuge in Piran, seeking the protection of Sheikh Said. Said's brother Abdurrahim seems to have been the one responsible for issuing the order to fire on the gendarmes that resulted in killing one and wounding two others, including the lieutenant. This incident apparently made Sheikh Said apprehensive of the actions that the Turkish army might take, so he declared rebellion. One of Sheikh Said's supporters, Mudanlı Faki Hasanlı, was immediately appointed governor of the city.[1]

After the Piran incident, events quickly escalated. Sheikh Said's continuing calls for rebellion, denunciation of the Ankara government, and support for Kurdish nationalism and for religion and the restoration of the caliphate were fresh in people's minds. After the incident in Piran, the sheikh returned to the village of Serdi, where his brother Tahir lived. Plans were made to attack Lice, the district administrative center. On 10 February, Sheikh Tahir robbed the Lice post office; on 11 February, he robbed the Gence post office with a force of 200. After these two events, it was impossible to stop the progress toward full-scale rebellion.

Sheikh Said took control of the rebellion. He directed four of his commanders to capture Darahini on the south side of the Murat Su (Euphrates) River, which they did on 14 February, taking prisoner the *vali* and other civil servants. The same day, Sheikh Said issued a *fetva* that he was the *emir al-mujahidin* of the rebellion. In his *fetva* Sheikh Said emphasized that he was leader of the Nakşbandi *tarikat* and that he was the representative of the caliph and of Islam. He stated that he wanted everyone to join the holy crusade and become a holy fighter (*mujahidin*). Darahini was to be the temporary headquarters of a Nakşbandi caliphate. Captured Turkish soldiers were to be sent to Darahini; taxes were to be paid to his headquarters there; and fighters for the cause would be raised. Sheikh Said then assumed supreme leadership of the rebellion. There were to be four other main fronts, as described, at Melekan on 8 January. On 16 February, the sheikh left Darahini and moved south, galvanizing fighters along the way. On 20 February, Lice was taken and forces under the command of Hınlı Salih Beg were sent in the direction of Diyarbakır through the Hani (Hini) Pass. Firat claims that Salih Beg had around 10,000 men under his command.[2] It was here that the Kurds met the first resistance from the Turks on 22 February.

The Turks had sent the Twenty-first Cavalry Regiment, consisting of 120 to 130 sabers, to Piran and a squadron from the Seventh Army Corps with 70 to 80 sabers to Argana Maden. Before leaving to meet the Kurds, the Turkish commander, Lieutenant Huseyin Husni, commanding officer of the Twenty-first Regiment, protested against his regiment being sent on operations owing to its weakness. His apprehension proved to be justified; in the Hani (Hini) Pass area his troops were defeated by the Kurds. The regiment retired to the south and reformed into two squadrons. Huseyin Husni was relieved and imprisoned in Diyarbakır. The Seventh Army Corps Squadron also was forced to retreat in the face of the Kurds' attack. The squadron merged forces with the Twenty-first Regiment. As the result of these defeats, the First Cavalry Division, with the Eleventh and Fourteenth Regiments, was moved from Mardin in the direction of Piran, passing through Diyarbakır about 20 February and engaging in battles with the Kurds from 22 to 27 February; these forces were completely defeated and retreated to regroup at Mardin. Only one squadron with two officers succeeded in escaping intact to Harput. The Kurds captured four mountain guns, all ammunition, stores, and equipment, including automatic rifles. Most of the Turkish soldiers (a good portion of whom were probably Kurds) were made prisoners and disarmed, but they were later set free and told to return to their homes. Two officers were killed in the battles and twenty-six were taken prisoner. Lieutenant Colonel Kazım, commanding officer of the Fourteenth Regiment, was wounded and the commanding officer of the Eleventh Regiment did not return. Five other officers who managed to escape were imprisoned in Diyarbakır.[3]

It was also during the last part of February that Sheikh Said persuaded other tribes to join the rebellion through force. The Sasunah and Tatukan tribes in the Kiği area between Diyarbakır and Gence had refused to cooperate. Sheikh Said sent a force of 4,000, according to British estimates, to attack the two recalcitrant tribes. The chief of the two tribes, Haci Musa Beg, was killed along with 400 of his fighters. These actions persuaded the Sasunah and Tatukan to join Said's forces. After the battle of Hani Pass, Sheikh Said's main force marched toward Diyarbakır with forces now numbering around 7,000. The estimates of the Kurdish forces that attacked Diyarbakır vary widely. A reasonable estimate would be that more than 5,000 but certainly less than 10,000 attacked the city.[4] By 28 February, Sheikh Said had set up his headquarters north of Diyarbakır, from which he kept in contact with the other fronts. He asked for reinforcements and ordered Mahmud Beg, son of Ibrahim Beg, of the Milan tribe to attack Diyarbakır from the south. But after five days, there was still no answer from Mahmud.

Sheikh Said attacked Diyarbakır on 2 March. Ferocious battles took place for five days between the Kurds crying "Praises to God! Praises to God! Surrender! Surrender!" and the outnumbered but courageous Turkish army defenders. On the night of 7–8 March, seventy selected fighters managed to gain entrance by means of holes and tunnels in the walls with the assistance of some Zaza-speaking Kurds inside the walls. But Mürsel Paşa, the commanding Turkish general, galloped quickly from the fighting on the northern walls to the breached southern walls and defeated the rebel force. Failing to breach the walls or to tunnel under them and faced with the stout resistance of the Turkish force, Sheikh Said retreated.[5] Diyarbakır remained besieged until 27 March, when the Kurds were forced to leave their positions with the approach of large Turkish forces.

As Sheikh Said made preparations for the attack on Diyarbakır, actions were being taken on the other four fronts. As the rebels surrounded the walls of Diyarbakır, fighting was reaching its northern limits on the Kiği front by 27 February. It was, however, expanding in the southwest under the command of Sheikh Said's brother Abdurrahim. On 29 February, his forces took Maden and, a few days later, Çernik. At Çernik, Abdurrahim's force was joined by 500 men under the command of Sheikh Ayub from the district of Siverek. These combined forces then captured Erğani, after which they departed to join Sheikh Said's forces in Diyarbakır, according to van Bruinessen's account.

The western Harput-Elazığ front was commanded by Sheikh Şerif of Gökdere, who was aided by Saki Yado and the tribes west of the Çapakçur (Bingöl) area. These forces occupied Palu on 21 February and moved west toward Elazığ, which was entered on 5 March. Sheikh Şerif was able to enter Elazığ without fighting because the notables (*eşref*) had told the townspeople that "these sheikhs are going to reestablish the caliphate and the Şeriyet and it is your duty to aid them." The *müfti* (head religious judge) of Elazığ, Mehmet Efendi, was appointed as *vali* and the authorities in Dersim were notified of this by telegraph. It was apparently around this time, 6 March, that an explosion occurred in the ammunition depot at Huseynik, a village outside of Elazığ where Sheikh Şerif had made his headquarters. This explosion, which may have been caused by sabotage, created friction among the rebels and probably local townspeople (most of whom were Kurds) as well. Sheikh Şerif and Sheikh Yado were unable to contain the differences.[6] In spite of their peaceful admittance to the town, the rebels plundered, tortured, and raped. Government officials were imprisoned and prisons emptied. Some of the young men of the city became so outraged that they took to arms against the pillaging rebels and drove them from the city.

At about this same time, Turkish forces, taking advantage of the discord among the rebels and the Kurdish populace, under the command of Kazım Bey, arrived and drove the rebels north across the Murat Su River. Sheikh Şerif's forces took refuge in the foothills of the Dersim mountains, where they hoped to rally the Alevi tribes to their cause. But rather than join the rebels, the Alevis resisted, killing a number of them, and drove the rebels in the direction of Turkish forces in the plains around Palu. Here, on 3 April, in the Mendo Pass several thousand rebels hiding among the oak trees laid an ambush for Turkish forces led by Kazım Bey. In spite of the surprise attack, the Turkish forces were able to breach the pass and to scatter the rebels after twenty-four hours of continuous battle. Sheikh Şerif and a number of *hoca*s (religious leaders) and tribal leaders fled to Çapakçür in order to join Sheikh Said's forces. Kazım Bey pursued Sheikh Şerif to Çapakçür, which he entered on 6 April. Sheikh Said was there at the time and he was forced to flee with 300 cavalry to Solhan. After the departure of Sheikh Said, Kazım Bey set about restoring government control over the region. By 8 April, his forces

were reinforced by another Turkish force from Erzurum led by Lieutenant Colonel Sami Bey, to whom he turned over control. Kazım
Bey returned to Palu. The notables of Elazığ who had helped repel
the rebels from the town were not, however, treated kindly by the
Turkish government after the suppression of the rebellion. Many of
them faced trials and some were executed by the independence tribunal established by the government to prosecute the rebels and
their collaborators. Many of the leaders of the town were exiled to
western Turkey.[7]

The events surrounding the occupation of Elazığ were recorded by
a European resident of the city. This account is dated, however, to
cover events from 23 March to 15 April, hence some two and a half
weeks after the dates given by Firat and Dersimi. Since this report is
one of only two accounts of Sheikh Said's rebellion, except for the
accounts by British intelligence, it is worth examining extensively.[8]
(See appendix VIII for the European inhabitant's account of the attack by the rebels on Elazığ.) The report states that as the rebels surrounded Elazığ on 23 March, bank officials tried to secure the cash of
the Imperial Ottoman Bank. On 24 March, the *vali* fled in a car escorted by twenty-five mounted gendarmes. Soon afterward, 300
Kurds entered the town and proceeded to sack the Government
House, Department House, and Department of Justice. The prison
was then opened and the prisoners showed the rebels the houses of
the officers and rich men so that they could be looted. Many of the
porters and woodchoppers of the town, nearly all Kurds, joined in
the looting.

The following day (25 March according to the date on the report),
the pillaging continued. The depot of military material was half
emptied, then the Régie (state-owned but European-controlled) depot containing about 4,000 Turkish pounds of tobacco was pillaged.
Sheikh Şerif and Müfti Mehmet, the newly appointed *vali*, entered
the town and tried to regain order but were unable to do so. As a
result of the looting, the directors of the bank took all the valuables
in a car to Harput.

On 26 March, as looting continued, the notables of the town tried
to organize a militia, "but there was not much enthusiasm"; the
local population did not want to show arms for fear of being disarmed by the rebels. But one, Rassım Beg, an army officer, managed
to get some people organized and "they eventually attacked the
rebels; drove them out of the town, leaving 50 dead. There were an
equal number of casualties amongst the population." Four days after
the occupation of Elazığ, the rebels had been repelled and the directors of the bank returned. Telegraphic communication was restored.

Tension remained high in Elazığ in spite of Sheikh Şerif's withdrawal from the city because some of his forces remained in the vicinity and did not withdraw east or north of the Murat Su River. Nureddin Paşa, commander of the Turkish Army's Seventeenth Division, arrived with a sufficient number of troops to assure the recovery of the town, but not enough to attack the town itself. Elazığ remained in a state of panic as news reached it that Çemişkezek, north of Elazığ and north of the Murat Su River, had been plundered by the Dersim Kurds; a number of families fled to Malatya, south and west of the Murat Su River and outside the area of rebellion.

While the battle for Diyarbakır was being prepared and fought, actions continued in the north under the command of the sheikhs of Can: Ibrahim, Mustafa, and Hasan. On 17 February, Çapakçür was taken and Sheikh Hasan was made governor. The sheikhs of Can gathered forces totaling 2,000 and attacked Kiği on 20 February. The attack was not successful due to the strong resistance of the Turkish forces and the strong leadership of Binbaşı (Major) Tahsin, who, with a detachment of 200 gendarmes and militia forces, was able to fend off the rebels. The Turkish forces were joined by a contingent of some 300 Hormek (Shi'i) tribesmen in the Karir region led by chieftain Mehmet Hulasi Efendi. On 27 February, the rebels sustained fifteen casualties, ten dead and five wounded. The sheikhs of Can withdrew to Çapakçür without having conquered the territory or having secured the aid of the tribes necessary for the conquest of Erzincan or Erzurum. These same forces tried to take Varto but met tenacious resistance from Turkish forces of the Eighth Army. Even when forces of the Eighth Army sustained a defeat after being ambushed, they managed to drive the Kurds south, where they were joined by the Hormek and Lolan tribes, who fought enthusiastically against their Kurdish brothers, preventing the rebels from moving toward Erzurum and thereby stemming a wider rebellion and possibly revolution.[9]

The most important front, other than that of Diyarbakır, was the northeastern front, commanded by Sheikh Abdullah of the Melekan, Sheikh Said's son Ali Riza, Hasananlı Halid, and the chieftains of the Cibran tribes. The strategy on this front was coordinated by Ali Riza and was linked strategically with the northern front's efforts to capture Kiği. The Cibran chiefs were to occupy Solhan, Göynük, Varto, Malazgird, and Muş; Sheikh Abdullah would attack Erzurum and Hasananlı Halid and Ali Riza were to occupy Ağrı and Bitlis. Capturing Bitlis was a major objective of this front, with the goal of freeing Halid Beg Cibran and Yusuf Ziya Beg, the two main leaders of the Azadi, who were imprisoned in that town. After the rescue of the two men, it was thought that many other Kurdish tribes would join the cause and that this force would proceed southward to unite with the Kurdish forces in the Iraqi-Turkish border area. On 19 February, Sheikh Abdullah, Solhan tribal chief Mehmet Ali Çeto, and Girvaslu Haci Selim took command of the Ömerenan and Meneşkürt tribes, crossed the Şerafettin mountains, and occupied the Karlıova district, where the Cibran tribes predominated. At this point, Sheikh Abdullah gave the order to the Cibran chiefs—Kamil, Baba, Mehmet— to move on to Varto and to crush (*çiğneyip*) the Hormek tribal villages that stood in their path.[10] This decision proved to be disastrous.

On 17 February, the Hormek tribes learned of the advance of rebel forces and planned their resistance to the rebels in the village of Ürtükran. Veli Ağa, Ali Haydar, M. Şerif (the author of the book I use for this discussion), M. Halid, and Tatahlı Haydar were placed in command of a small force of 100 men, which then secured the adherence of the Lolan tribal villages of Kamer and Şelcuklu Huseyin: the Shi'i tribes moved to the defense of Varto. On 22 February, the Cibran and Hormek-Lolan forces clashed once again in the village of Kasman, south of Varto. This time the stakes were very high. It was not just tribal domination or Sunni-Shi'i differences to be determined, but the success or failure of a Kurdish nationalist and revolutionary movement. The battle lasted only half an hour, but it delayed Sheikh Abdullah's plans to conquer Varto and move toward Erzurum.

After the battle of Kasman Köy, Abdullah consulted with Halid Cibran's uncle Ismail, who resided in Varto, and retired major Kasım Cibran, who was one of the military strategists of Sheikh Said. The question was whether to attack Varto by passing around or through the Hormek villages. The attack, with a force of 2,000, was finally made on Varto on the morning of 11 March, three hours before dawn. Sheikh Abdullah was able to secure the support, probably with the influence of Ismail and Kasım, of 120 Kurdish gendarmes stationed in Varto. Most of the gendarmes were Zaza-speaking Kurds, as well as being *murid*s (adherents) of Sheikh Said from the area of Diyarbakır and Hazzo. These gendarmes prevented the acting governor of Varto from calling on the Hormek tribes for assistance. A small force of Turkish soldiers and a local militia put up a stiff defense before succumbing. Sheikh Abdullah's uncle Mahmud was among those killed. The resistance and challenge from the Hormek tribes forced Abdullah to abandon Varto after five days, on 16 March. This meant abandoning any hope of attacking Hınıs. On 17 March, Abdullah attacked the Arpa Pass (*devesi*) between Varto and Hınıs with 1,000 troops. The battle continued until nightfall, when Abdullah was forced to retreat to the village of Kirs. The last rebel forces numbering some 200, led by Ali Riza and Halid Beg Cibran's brothers Selim and Ahmet, evacuated Varto on 19 March and joined the forces of Hasananlı Halid in the Malazgird area. As yet unaware of the defeat at Arpa Pass, Abdullah was preparing with a contingent of 500 men to attack Muş. He was defeated. Met by a small force of gendarmes and local militia at the bridge crossing the Murat Su River north of Muş, the rebels were forced to retreat to Varto.[11]

Halid Beg Cibran and Yusuf Ziya Beg were hanged in Bitlis after the battle at Murat bridge around 19 or 20 March 1925. It is difficult to determine which had more influence on Abdullah's decision to retreat from the attack directed against Muş and Bitlis—the defeat at Murat bridge or the hanging of the Azadi leaders. The news of the latter obviously hurt the morale of the Kurdish forces, especially the more nationalistic leaders. The defeat at Murat bridge clearly influenced the local tribes not to join the rebellion. It also allowed the local government authorities to take stronger measures to secure law and order. By the end of March, the Kurdish rebels were meeting increasingly strong resistance from the Turkish army. On 20 March, in a battle with the Thirty-fourth Regiment that was advancing from Sarıkamış under the command of Talat Bey, the rebels lost forty men. As the Turkish forces continued to advance toward Hınıs, Abdullah decided to use some of his forces in an attempt to take the Arpa Pass. He did not succeed and lost ten more men in the battle. On the same day, the Twelfth Division with 3,000 men under the command of Osman Paşa reached Hınıs; on 24 March, Osman Paşa bivouacked on the north side of the Arpa Pass. One day later, on 25 March, Osman Paşa's fighters with the aid of the Hormek and Lolan tribes dealt a severe loss to Sheikh Abdullah. He and his forces fled into the Şerafettin mountains. While retreating to the mountains, they suffered more losses in the Gomo-gorgo Pass. It was here that Halid Beg Cibran's uncle Hasan and several others were killed by some of the fanatical Hormek tribesmen, eager to settle old scores.[12] Those among the remaining rebels that the Hormek were not able to kill were soon finished off by the cavalry of the Twelfth Division.

Osman Paşa established his headquarters in Varto and mapped out his subsequent strategy. The following several weeks were also filled with clashes and vendettas between the rebels and the Hormek tribesmen. The rebels viewed the collaboration of the Hormek and Lolan with the Turks as the worst kind of treachery. The battles raged with equivalent forces between 200 to 300 men. In each battle, several men were killed. The rebels did not give ground easily. On

27 March, Hasananlı Halid, Ali Riza, and Halid Beg Cibran's brothers Ahmet and Selim, among others, attacked Hınıs with 1,000 warriors after moving behind Osman Paşa's troops in Varto. At least twenty-seven men were killed by intense machine-gun fire. The rebels were forced to retreat in the direction of Malazgird. They were surrounded and attacked on 3 April by the Thirty-fourth Regiment commanded by Colonel (Miralay) Talat Bey. Hasananlı Halid, Ali Riza, and 150 others fled and finally reached the Iranian city of Maku. It is ironic that the rebellion suffered a further blow in Iran. Hasananlı Halid asked for refuge and surrendered his party's arms to the Iranian government, as did Ali Riza. But Kerim, the chief of the Zirgan tribe, refused to do so; a fight ensued with Iranian soldiers in which seventy-five of the rebels and a few Iranian soldiers were killed. Some of the main leaders of the rebellion were killed in this skirmish—Şemseddin, the son of Hasananlı Halid, Kerim, the Zirgan chief who initiated the battle, Suleyman, Ahmet, Abdulbaki, and one of Sheikh Said's sons, Giysuddin. Hasananlı Halid, Ali Riza, and one Fernande along with the remaining eighty men in their party immediately sought refuge with the Kurdish leader in Iran, Ismail Simko.[13]

By the end of March, most of the major battles of Sheikh Said's rebellion had been fought. The inability of the rebels to penetrate beyond Hınıs, ironically one of the two major areas in which Sheikh Said had considerable influence and was well known (he had a *tekke* there), excluded the possibility of extending the rebellion to Erzurum and beyond. Sheikh Said and the major leaders seemed to realize that their rebellion was in jeopardy. They gathered in the village of Kırvaz in the district of Solhan on 3 April to plan their strategy and their escape either to Iran or to Iraq from the enclosing Turkish forces of the Eighth Army and the Thirty-fifth Regiment of the Second Division under the command of Galip Bey, who by now had incorporated the Hormek and Lolan tribal forces under his command. A detachment from the Twelfth Division moved, destroying much of the area, toward the Boğlan Pass. By 6 April, the brigadier general (mirliva) who was commanding the Twelfth Division was confident that he had Sheikh Said surrounded.[14]

After 3 April, it was just a matter of time before Sheikh Said was captured. On 14 April, the sheikh and his retinue were prevented from crossing the Murat Su River bridge north of Muş by the Thirty-fourth Regiment commanded by Talat Bey. The sheikh was forced to retreat toward Varto, hoping to cross into Iran via Bulanık. On 15 April, Sheikh Said's retinue approached the Abdurrahman (some sources call it the Carpık bridge), where they were caught in an ambush by a battalion of soldiers and some Hormek of the Şelcuklu Huseyin tribe. It was here that Sheikh Said was captured. He, along with some fifty of his retinue, including Kasım, Ismail, Mehmet and Reşit Cibran, Sheikh Şemseddin, Ibrahim and Hasan, sheikhs of Can, and Haci Halid, surrendered to the Turkish battalion commander. Van Bruinessen states that his informants "generally claimed" that Sheikh Said was betrayed to the Turks by Kasım Beg Cibran, who was unhappy with the course of events.[15] The fact that Kasım Beg Cibran, his father, and his brothers escaped punishment and were not sentenced to death by the independence tribunals in Diyarbakır, as all the other leaders of the rebellion were, seems to give substance to the claim of treachery. The following day, 16 April, more members of Sheikh Said's immediate entourage were captured. A little over three weeks later, on 10 May, all of the leaders who had been captured or who had surrendered, almost all of them, were collected at Çapakçür and sent under the watchful eye of Lieutenant Colonel (Kaymakam) Sayim Bey to Diyarbakır. There, the independence tribunal (*istiklal makemesi*) sentenced all forty-seven of them to death.[16]

By the time that Sheikh Said was captured on or around 15 April, the peak of the rebellion had passed. The hardest-fought battles had taken place during the first two weeks of April on the northeastern front as the rebels tried to make a break through to Erzurum. But the effort to take Diyarbakır had failed by 9 March. The furthest limit of the southwestern front was reached at Siverek at the end of February. The westernmost extent of the rebellion was reached at Elazığ on 7–8 March. The maximum northern thrust of the rebellion at Kiği occurred at the end of February. On the hardest-fought front, the northeast, the tide of battle was definitely against the rebels by mid-March.

Many of the most important battles of the rebellion had taken place even before the Turkish forces had completely mobilized. As indicated in chapter 4, the 52,000 ration forces of the Turks were not reached until at least 1 April. If the proportion of ration forces to rifles was nine to four, this means that the Turkish forces fought the largest-scale battles of the rebellion in March with less than 25,000 rifles. The mobilization of forces up to 52,000 by early April allowed the Turkish forces quickly to contain and then crush the rebellion, although many small rebellions and skirmishes continued to take place right up to the major revolt of Ararat in early 1929. The forces organized by the Turks to fight against the Kurds were closely scrutinized by the British, who were concerned that the Turks were raising a large force in order to attack Iraq or at least to obtain a more favorable position for themselves concerning the Turkish-Iraqi border, then under discussion by a commission from the League of Nations.[17] The Brussels Line, eventually to become the border between Turkey and Iraq, established by the treaty of 5 June 1926, had been determined on 29 October 1924. This decision was confirmed by the Council of Nations on 16 December 1924.[18] Negotiations between Turkey and Great Britain continued apace during the Sheikh Said rebellion and its suppression. Except for the actual period of mobilization, as pointed out in the next chapter, the rebellion expedited the negotiations that resulted in the treaty of 5 June 1926.

British intelligence recorded the increase in the number of Turkish troops being sent east immediately after the Beyt Şebab mutiny. Their forces, it was specified, were to be used to put down the Kurds and to expel the Nestorians from the border area that would fall to Turkey if the Brussels Line was established as the eventual border, which, as things turned out, it was. On 4 November 1924, members of what British intelligence termed the Kurdish National Committee, which probably contained members of the Society for the Rise of Kurdistan as well as members of the Azadi, met with Turkish officers in Diyarbakır to discuss the question of Kurdish independence. These meetings were apparently related to the talks that took place during the first part of August, also in Diyarbakır. If the Turkish response was unfavorable, the British thought that the Kurds were prepared to rise in rebellion. The Turkish response was deemed unfavorable by the Kurds; on 20 November 1924, the governor (*vali*) of Diyarbakır was killed. Even before the talks between the Turks and Kurds on 4 November, the Turks had sent fifty to sixty train wagons of troops from Adana to Rasulayn (Ras al-Ayn). On 12 November, two field guns arrived in Mardin from Diyarbakır. On 20 and 26 November, a regiment of infantry and regiment of cavalry arrived in Mardin from Diyarbakır. Continual fighting ensued during November between Turkish forces and the Ziri Kurds. By 14 December, sixteen field guns had arrived in Diyarbakır from various sources. On 25 November 1924, 200 cavalry entered Diyarbakır. By the end of December 1924, the Turks had one cavalry regiment in Diyarbakır, one in the village of Kala (Kale) Mora, and one in Mansuriyah. In addition, they had four mountain guns in a church. As of 12 January 1924, Siirt was the headquarters of the Second Division under the command of Colonel (Miralay) Ali Bey. One regiment of infantry, less one battalion, was stationed in Bitlis with four mountain guns.[19] Thus, the Turks were prepared for resistance from the Kurds, but not for the scope of the rebellion raised by Sheikh Said.

British intelligence itself was not prepared to assess the extent of the rebellion. It was only two or three weeks after the outbreak of the rebellion that it was able to make assessments of its scale. It is possible that the Turks' lack of information limited the British, since British intelligence was in many ways dependent on Turkish intelligence. Both Behçet Cemal and Metin Toker cite the lost opportunities of Turkish government authorities properly to weigh information they received about the rebellion. By 1 March, however, extensive information on the rebellion began to appear in the weekly intelligence report, as well as in many other sources. On 1 March 1925, the commander of Turkish forces at Jezira (Jazirat Ibn Umar or Cezire) arrested, and subsequently hanged, four chiefs of the Milli Kurds (including Nawaf Ibn Mustafa and Ali Barhan) for inciting their tribes to attack Jezira. By 3 March, the British speculated that the Turks intended to establish a force of 12,000 at Darbaziyah. By 14 March, reports recorded the battle on the outskirts of Bitlis in which 150 Turks were killed, with heavy casualties suffered by the rebels as well. By 14 March, after the failure of Sheikh Said to take Diyarbakır on 7–8 March, executions of supposed collaborators of the rebels were taking place daily.[20]

By early March, there were reports of up to 25,000 troops mobilized under the command of Deli Nuri in Adana that were due to pass to Diyarbakır and the area of rebellion along the railroad through Syria. In addition to troops being sent from Izmit, Ankara, and Adana southward, there were also forces being sent from Sivas, Sarıkamış, and Kars in the north. By 2 April, British intelligence was making estimates of the Turkish forces that resulted in a mid-April figure of 52,000. The mobilization of troops was accompanied by Turkish efforts to secure more and newer artillery from Krupp and from Skoda. This effort was facilitated by the return of Kemaleddin Sami Paşa, a hero of the Turkish war of independence and then ambassador to Germany, who was to be in overall command of operations against the Kurds. British intelligence thought Kemaleddin Sami was the second-best general the Turks had—the best general was Asin Paşa, commander of the Eighth Army Corps at Erzurum.[21]

Before leaving Berlin for Turkey, Kemaleddin Sami, according to some sources, had asked a German businessman knowledgeable about weapons, Friedrich Wilhelm Hayer, to get in touch with poison gas specialists. When Kemaleddin Sami arrived in Turkey, he had two German poison gas specialists in tow. Hayer's business associate told British intelligence that he understood that the gas was to be used in airplane bombs. I found no evidence of its use in subsequent files, however, and British intelligence never stated that the Turks used poison gas against the Kurdish rebels. Hayer, however,

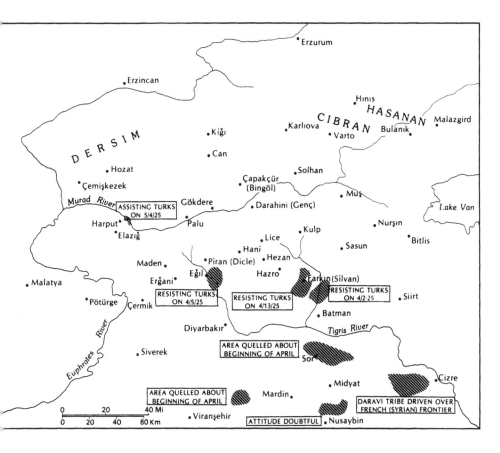

Map 2. The Deployment of Turkish Forces against Sheikh Said

apparently wanted to use the gas in bombs, since that was the primary reason for his January visit to Istanbul. The German firm of Hayer, Schroeder, and Froehlich sold the Turkish government 50,000 water bottles, 50,000 pairs of boots, and material for uniforms. The contracting was done by Huseyin Husni Bey, an important Turkish army contractor in Istanbul.[22]

By 1 April, British intelligence began to record the names of leaders and chiefs of the rebellion who were either killed in the fighting or subsequently hanged. Tribal leaders and sometimes entire tribes began to flee into or toward Iraq. Accounts of the major battles on the northeastern front were recorded in some detail. After the capture of Sheikh Said in the middle of April, the Turks brutally pacified the areas they occupied. Efforts were made to disarm all Kurds, houses and entire villages were burned, and the process of expelling some Kurdish leaders and tribes to western Anatolia began. These harsh measures were partially responsible for the continuing Kurdish resistance and rebellion throughout 1925 and early 1926. By June, the British had information that the Zaza-speaking Kurds living in Diyarbakır and its vicinity had been rounded up and "after being confined were practically annihilated by bombs, two companies of infantry being employed for this purpose, bombs being hurled amongst the prisoners for a period of over one hour."[23]

The Turks also employed their fledgling air force against Sheikh Said. In early 1925, the Turks had a very small air force. While I have no exact figures on the number of airplanes that the Turks possessed as of 1 January 1925, they did have eighty-seven by the end of that year, some of which had arrived in order to be used against the Kurds:[24] ten war stock, twenty Bregeut, ten Junker, thirty Caudron, and seventeen Sovoia. The planes were purchased from France, Germany, and Italy. Fourteen Bregeut were delivered during 1925 as well as ten Junkers for reconnaissance and bombing. The Sovoia were hydroplanes, all but one of which had been purchased from Italy and delivered in 1923. Due to wrecks, lack of spare parts, and so forth, many of the planes that the Turks had in early 1925 were unusable.

At the outset of operations against Sheikh Said, the Turks had one squadron (*filo*) consisting of seven airplanes, only two of which were serviceable, stationed at Mardin. Shortly thereafter, four more arrived. Out of the eleven planes, however, only six were serviceable, one of which was a single seater. These six airplanes carried out two bombing raids a day from the airfield at Diyarbakır. They returned to Mardin at night, apparently to lessen the possibility that they would be destroyed by the Kurds. Three airplanes at the Diyarbakır airport had been destroyed by the Kurds two days before the 2 March attack by Sheikh Said. Also, fuel and bombs could be received by rail from Istanbul at Mardin. Only two or three of the pilots were regular Turkish army officers who had been trained by the Germans. Each squadron was commanded by a captain. The other pilots were civilians wearing uniforms and badges according to the rank of pay they received.[25] The information concerning the impact of the Turkish air force in the suppression of the rebellion is sparse, but its role seems to have been minimal. The rugged terrain in much of the area in rebellion limited air operations. Unreliable planes and poorly trained pilots seem to have contributed to the limited impact of the fledgling air force.

Nevertheless, the Sheikh Said rebellion was the first major combat situation in which the Turkish air force participated and provided invaluable combat experience for the pilots, as well as mechanical and logistical training. The suppression of the Sheikh Said rebellion was one of the major factors in the subsequent growth of the Turkish air force. The Turks had witnessed the efficacy of the RAF in Iraq, especially after the Air Ministry took command from the War Office in August 1922. The forward policy of the British air commander in Iraq, Sir John Salmond, was initiated largely with the intention of testing the effectiveness of the RAF and its bombing policies in efforts to subdue the Kurds and Arabs in northern Iraq as cheaply and with as little force as possible. One of the results of this RAF forward policy was to drive the Turks and the Turkish officer, Özdemir Paşa, out of Rawanduz. By the end of 1926, the Turkish air force had a total of 106 airplanes, of which 80 were serviceable. They also had a command structure headed by Colonel Muzzafer Bey as the inspector general. All of the air force officers were well paid, especially compared to army officers of equal rank. Mobilization was expedited rapidly in March. Recruits were called for the years 1904–1905 in Adıyaman and for 1903–1904 in Aksaray; orders were issued finally that all Muslims born in the years 1889–1900 were to be called up. Christian recruits for the years 1901–1904 were called up and sent to labor battalions near Mersin.[26]

After the capture of Sheikh Said, extensive operations were continued in order to break the back of any possible future Kurdish nationalist movement. The Turks did not want to reduce their troop strength until they were assured that there would be absolutely no possibility of another rebellion on the scale of Sheikh Said's. At the same time, their large forces were to be used in an attempt to gain as much leverage as possible against the British in the dispute over the Turkish-Iraqi boundary. By 1 June 1925, the Turks had even moved to allow some of the Nestorians to return to their villages, from which they had been driven during the past six months. Malik Kosaban, leader of the Lizan Assyrians, was given permission for his people to return to their villages. The Turks also reacted favorably to a request from Tawris Khanum (a leading Assyrian and spokeswoman) to the French to grant passports to the Assyrians so that they might return to the Tiari country in Turkey. British intelligence speculated that the Turks wanted the Assyrians to return to their homes and farms for reasons of productivity, to use them as a balance against the Kurds, and to prevent them from being recruited as levies in the Iraqi army. The Assyrians were already the mainstay of the Iraqi army's infantry, along with Indian troops. Also by June 1925, 1,000 to 2,000 Turkish soldiers had occupied the Goyan territory and remained in the area fighting throughout June. In the middle of June, Kurds were still resisting in the area of Maden. Another 1,000 to 2,000 Turkish troops were employed for operations in the Jebel Tur region, and a 1,000–1,200-man contingent arrived in Midyat around 20 June. Throughout June and July, there were reports that Turkish troops and soldiers were rounding up large flocks of sheep, sometimes up to 3,000 head, and selling them at auction. In the Lice and Diyarbakır areas alone, 30,000 sheep were auctioned. Activities of this kind were reported to have taken place elsewhere.[27]

As the Turkish forces occupied the towns and pacified the villages throughout June and July, some of the remaining Kurdish leaders decided to engage in guerrilla warfare, such as the Sigo and Hayter tribes in the area of Muş; after the Turks quashed the resistance, some of the same leaders escaped and attempted guerrilla warfare in the areas of Hizan, Garzan, Bişiri, and Sosan, which continued throughout the rest of 1925. Only in November 1925 did Nuh Beg, the leader of the guerrilla activity, seek refuge in Iraq with the Iraqi Kurdish leader, Sheikh Mahmud.[28] British air intelligence reports dealing specifically with the Sheikh Said rebellion carry accounts until 1 March 1927. These reports contain detailed accounts of the continuing resistance of the Kurds to the Turkish forces. Some reports from part II of the Air Ministry files that deal specially with the events of 18 June to 12 September 1925 show the extent of the rebellion.[29]

One of the most serious areas of rebellion for the Turks was the revolt of Sayyid Abdullah, son of Abdul Qadir. The latter was hanged in Diyarbakır on 27 May along with one of his sons, Sayyid Mehmet, and Haci Ahta, Palulu Kör Sadi, Bitlisli Kemal Fevzi, and Hoca Askeri. Sayyid Abdullah renewed strong resistance and guerrilla activity in the area of Van, Bitlis, and Hakkari, a harbinger of the future. His revolt was to continue for many months despite the fact that none of the Kurdish tribes in Iraq joined his rebellion even when Abdullah exhorted them to do so. Even Turkish soldiers seeking refuge from Abdullah's guerrillas among the Kurdish tribes in Iraq were turned over to the Turkish army by Iraqi authorities. Abdullah's resistance, especially in the Şemdinan region, was stiff. Two hundred Turkish soldiers were killed. Only the aid of the settled Kurdish tribes of Geravi and Sarafan lessened Kurdish losses. Naturally, the nomads from these tribes did not aid the Turks as did their settled brothers. The strength of small rebellions and continuing resistance persuaded French intelligence that the rebellions of August and September were more serious than that of Sheikh Said. The French were convinced that this time the British were working with the Kurds.[30] By late August 1925, British intelligence estimated that

357 Kurdish notables had been sentenced to death by the independence tribunals.

On 16 September, Sayyid Abdullah, who had escaped from the Turkish forces at Şemdinan, held talks with Sir Henry Dobbs, the British high commissioner in Iraq. Abdullah asked for asylum for himself and the 700 people who had accompanied him to Iraq. Dobbs gave him permission on the condition that he not attack Turkey. Dobbs added, "Unless the Turks refused to abide by the decision of the League of Nations in regard to the Frontier of Iraq and resorted to hostilities to achieve their ends then a conflict might result which might make it possible for Great Britain to assist *the Kurdish nationalists*. In the meantime, however, Sayyid Abdullah must have no expectations" (emphasis added).[31] Dobbs's statement to Sayyid Abdullah provides a fitting political end to Sheikh Said's rebellion. By 16 September 1925, Dobbs was of the opinion that Turkey would abide by the 29 October and 16 December 1924 League of Nations decision regarding the boundary between Iraq and Turkey.

The Sheikh Said rebellion occurred at a crucial time in the developing domestic politics of Turkey, as noted at the end of chapter 3. As a result of the struggle for power between the ardent Kemalists and those who opposed some of the policies of Mustafa Kemal (the Second Group and Kazım Karabekir, Ali Fuad Cebesoy, Rauf Orbay, Refet Bele, Adnan Adivar, Halide Edip, etc.), Atatürk thought it imperative to call Ismet Inönü back to the government, which he did on 21 February. On 24 February, Mustafa Kemal, Ismet Inönü, Fethi Okyar, and their advisers had a seven and a half hour meeting at which the main topic of discussion was the rebellion. It was apparent from the meeting that Ismet Inönü wanted to adopt a much harder line and to mobilize more military force against the rebellion than the prime minister, Fethi Okyar. Mustafa Kemal sided with Inönü and his hard-line approach. Inönü criticized the press that was opposed to Mustafa Kemal, saying that it indirectly encouraged the rebellion because of its opposition to the government's secularization policies. He was especially critical of Huseyin Cahit Yalçın, editor of the newspaper *Tanin*; Velit Ebuziya, editor of the newspaper *Tevhidi Efkâr*; Ahmet Emin Yalman, editor of the newspaper *Vatan*; and Eşref Edip, editor of *Sebilürresat*, a newspaper supporting religious elements. Behçet Cemal characterized Huseyin Cahit Yalçın as belonging to the CUP faction, Ahmet Emin Yalman as belonging to the Rauf Orbay group, and Velit Ebuziya as being partial to groups supporting the caliphate.[32]

On 25 February, the government proclaimed martial law in all of the eastern provinces and stated that all persons supporting the rebellion were liable to the law of treason. Supporting religion as a political weapon against the government was to be considered treason. Many in the government were quick to characterize the rebellion as a reactionary (*irtica*) revolution. Ismet Inönü's group characterized it as a large counterrevolutionary movement aimed at toppling the government, while Fethi Okyar thought the rebellion was limited and could be contained in the eastern provinces.[33]

After losing a vote of confidence within the People's party on 2 March, Fethi Okyar resigned on 3 March 1925 and Ismet Inönü again became prime minister with a mandate from the government and from Mustafa Kemal to pursue strong measures against Sheikh Said. The very next day, 4 March, Inönü got the Grand National Assembly to pass the Takriri Sükun Kanunu (Restoration of Order Law). This law allowed for the reactivation of the independence tribunals for a period of two years. Granted dictatorial power to convict, imprison, and execute rebels or traitors against the government, the independence tribunals were to be operative in Diyarbakır and Ankara. The Ankara tribunals were to be utilized to prosecute individuals opposed to the Kemalists. The tribunal in Diyarbakır was to be used primarily to prosecute and sentence the rebels and their collaborators. The great significance of the Restoration of Order Law was not lost on the opposition to Mustafa Kemal, which realized that it could and would be used to limit or stop all newspapers and publications that stated views differing from those of the government. It was hotly debated in the Grand National Assembly and passed by a vote of 122 to 22. With the legal mechanism in force to quell the rebellion as well as the opposition, Mustafa Kemal gave an exhortatory speech on 8 March stating the great danger of the rebellion to the peace, economy, and productivity of Turkey and insisting that every Turk should oppose it with staunch patriotism.[34]

By the middle of March, the independence tribunals were ready to go to work. The Diyarbakır tribunal consisted of a president, prosecutor, two members, and an assistant. The president was Mazhar Müfit (Kansu) of Denizli. Eight months later, because of illness, he was replaced by Hacım Muhiddin (Çarıklı) of Giresun, who served for ten months. On 6 December 1916, Ali Saip (Ursavaş) of Urfa became president. The prosecutor was Süreyya Özgevren of Karesi. The members were Ali Saip, who upon becoming president was replaced by Ibrahim Kocaeli, and Lutfi Müfit of Kırşehir. The assistant was Avni Doğan (Bozak). It was this court that sentenced Sayyid Abdul Qadir, his son, and four others to hanging on 27 May 1925 and Sheikh Said and 46 others on 29 June. Many others were sentenced to death by the Diyarbakır tribunal; but, as mentioned above, by late

August 1925, British intelligence estimated that 327 Kurdish notables had been sentenced to death and more were sentenced later. The Turkish government itself announced that in the two and a half months after 15 February it had arrested over 1,000 people, tried 900, and executed 57; 800 others had been arrested for brigandage. Before their abrogation, the independence tribunals arrested a total of 7,440 people and executed 660.[35]

As early as 5 July 1926, there were reports that Turkey was planning to settle Muslim Albanians from the Kossovo region in the Kurdish areas of rebellion. There were also reports that the Turks hoped to settle 40,000 to 50,000 Circassians in the Kurdish areas. Throughout 1927, the British ambassador, Sir George Clerk, reiterated information from the Air Ministry intelligence that deportations of Kurds continued throughout 1926 "on a scale which to some extent recalls the mass deportations of Armenians in 1915." Clerk stated further that "it would hardly be an exaggeration to say that not less than 20,000 men, women and children will have been forcibly driven from their homes before the deportations are completed." By December 1927, British reports stated that "the country was now terrorised, but would never remain quiet if the large military force was removed, the Kurds had hidden 90 per cent of their arms."[36] The Grand National Assembly voted 1,500,000 lira for increasing the gendarmerie in the eastern *vilayets* for 1928 and Ibrahim Tali Bey was appointed inspector general of all of the eastern *vilayets* with authority over all *valis* in November 1927. He left Ankara to assume his new office in Diyarbakır on 8 January 1928. Ibrahim Tali Bey's appointment was indicative of the Turkish government's concern about its inability to pacify the Kurds in spite of a Law of Amnesty promulgated on 9 May 1928. Some Kurdish leaders who had taken part in Sheikh Said's rebellion did, however, take advantage of the amnesty law. On 12 August 1928, Sheikh Mehdi and Sheikh Abdurrahim, brothers of Sheikh Said, turned themselves in to government officers in Mardin.[37]

It is difficult to determine how many casualties the Turkish forces or the Kurdish rebels sustained from the outbreak of the rebellion on 8 February to the death of Sheikh Said on 29 June. Based on the figures of 52,000 for the number of mobilized Turkish forces with a four to nine ratio of rifles to ration forces, which would mean 25,000 rifles as a high estimate, it is difficult to believe that the Turkish forces suffered more than 5,000 killed. It seems likely that the ratio was less. The reports in some sources that the Turks suffered 50,000 casualties seem gross exaggerations. Even figures of 15,000 to 20,000 killed would seem to be highly exaggerated. It is impossible to determine how much the suppression of the Sheikh Said rebellion cost in monetary terms. The only figures that I came across were those quoted by Mete Tuncay's book, in which the figure of 20,000 British pounds was given. Abdul Rahman Ghassemlou, a nationalist Kurdish leader and writer, states that the rebellion cost 60,000,000 Turkish lira.[38] The massive mobilization of the Turks and the materiel needed for the effort were obviously very expensive for the Turkish government. The need to sustain large forces in the area of the rebellion and throughout the eastern provinces was to be a continuing drain on the budget in subsequent years.

The Kurds also suffered. It seems unlikely that the Kurds mobilized a force much over 15,000 mounted and fighting men. This would mean that at the peak of mobilization of both forces their ratio of fighting men was probably about 25,000 to 15,000 or five to three. The Kurds incurred heavy losses in the battles during late March and early April, but it is unlikely, in my view, that the numbers killed constituted twenty percent of their fighting forces. It must be remembered that the Kurds lost few men until the battles of late March and early April. It seems to me improbable that they sustained 3,000 to 4,000 killed. If the number was less than 3,000, it would put the number killed at twenty percent of their fighting forces. Also, it must be remembered that the Kurds quickly reverted to guerrilla warfare, which further reduced their potential number of casualties. The largest numbers of casualties seem to have been sustained when forces were ambushed. While it is possible that the number of dead from both sides could have reached 7,000 to 8,000, it seems to me that these figures are extremely high. The figure of 5,000 killed, from both sides, in the rebellion from 8 February to 29 June would be more reasonable. Figures of 15,000 to 20,000 killed seem farfetched.

The greatest suffering of the Kurds was not from the numbers killed or the casualties they sustained, but rather from the lands destroyed, villages burned, people deported, and persecution and harassment by Turkish officers, soldiers, and gendarmes. While these brutalities were greatest during the period of the rebellion and its aftermath throughout 1925, the harsh tactics of the Turks continued unabated throughout 1926 and 1927. After a brief respite, similar tactics and measures were again employed during the rebellion of 1929–1930 (Şimşir cites many British documents to this effect).

Nothing can better describe the great amount of energy, men, money, materials, and time that the Turkish government spent on trying to suppress and contain Kurdish rebellion and Kurdish nationalism than the admission of the Turkish armed forces that of the eighteen armed engagements between 1924 and 1938 that the armed forces were involved in suppressing, seventeen occurred in Kurdistan. One of these was the Assyrian (Nestorian) rebellion of 3–4 September 1924 of Beyt Şebab, which, as indicated above, was itself very much related to the Sheikh Said rebellion.[39] In other words, of the major nineteen military engagements in which the Turkish armed forces participated from 1924 and 1938, all but two were against or connected with efforts to suppress Kurdish rebellions and nationalism. Only two engagements, that of Menemen in December 1930 and the action in Alexandretta (Hatay), were not connected with the Kurds. In the post–World War II period, with the exception of Korea (1951–1953) and Cyprus (1974–present), Turkish armed forces' actions have been solely against the Kurds. For historians of Turkey not to record or to recognize this fact is akin to studying the history of the United States without studying the history and impact of its black population or studying the history of the Soviet Union without mentioning the influence or impact of the Muslims.

The hanging of Sheikh Said and most of the leaders of the rebellion on 29 June occurred at a time when Turkish forces were in control of most of the rebellion area. Sheikh Said had led the largest armed and most sustained Kurdish nationalist rebellion of the twentieth century. He himself had been in command of the rebellion for over two months (8 February to around 15 April) and became a symbol of the continuing resistance until his death. Indeed, stories continued to circulate after his death that he was still alive. Said's leadership had indeed aroused messianic as well as nationalistic expectations among some of his followers. Sheikh Said's death also meant that Turkey and Great Britain, as well as other countries, would have to consider the broader international implications and consequences of his rebellion.

6. The International Aspects of the Sheikh Said Rebellion

THE OBJECTIONS raised by the Middle East Department and the director of intelligence at the War Office in late autumn 1921 regarding possible British support of a Kurdish rebellion in Turkey still obtained during the period of the Sheikh Said rebellion. They were: (1) the great expense and support it would entail on the part of the British, perhaps more than for the Arab revolt, which had cost some £21,000,000; (2) the terrain in which the rebellion would be mounted was extremely rugged; (3) armed action against Turkey would be interpreted in some quarters as antagonistic to Islam; (4) a rebellion could not be discontinued at will; and (5) a rebellion raised the possibility that the Kurds would be abandoned by the British and then left to be massacred by the Turks.[1] In my research in the Public Record Office I found no documents to indicate that the British changed their policy regarding support for Kurdish rebellion(s) and revolt(s) in Turkey. The policy as established in November 1921 remained in effect up to the outbreak of Sheikh Said's rebellion on 8 February 1925, in spite of the differences between Great Britain and Turkey resulting over the failure to resolve the Mosul question.

Recent works by the Turkish scholars Ömer Kürkçüoğlu and Bilal Şimşir rely totally on British documents and come to the conclusion that the British did not have a role in the Sheikh Said rebellion as the Turkish press was stating at the time, at least during the first days of the rebellion.[2] As far as I know, there are no Turkish archival sources to support the charges of British involvement, although some British officials took obvious delight in the difficulties the rebellion created for the Turks, especially the damage to the Turkish claim to Mosul on the basis that "the Turks and Kurds are indivisibly united by racial affinity."[3] A British Foreign Office official remarked in a minute on Ismet İnönü's statement before the Grand National Assembly of Turkey on 7 April 1925 that the prime minister "is careful to lend no colour to the accusations of the Turkish press that foreign &

especially British influence is behind the rebels." On 22 April, Sir Ronald Lindsay, British ambassador to Turkey, in a dispatch to Austen Chamberlain, the foreign minister, stated that there were documents being published charging British involvement from Iraq but that "the documents seem to refer to period of 1919 & 1920 when ideas of Kurdish autonomy were very much to the fore."[4]

In fact, there are documents in the Public Record Office that indicate some British intelligence analysts in Istanbul and James Morgan in particular thought the Sheikh Said rebellion might have been planted by Turkey. Kürkçüoğlu cites Morgan's concerns and speculations as further proof that the British did not support the rebellion. Morgan gave various reasons as to why Turkey would support the revolt:

(1) If the present rising has been engineered by Angora and exists, attracting to itself, numerous "deserters" from the Turkish regular forces. We may hear that the successful rebels have determined to free their brothers in the Mosul Vilayet, and for that purpose have crossed the present frontier, aided by the deserting Turkish troops, in order to take possession of the Mosul Vilayet, probably surrender to Turkey, leaving Turkey in possession of the conquered territory.[5]

(2) Another possibility is that a successful rising in Turkey (countenanced by Angora) might be taken as a pretext for a rising of Kurds in Irak (also engineered by Angora) to throw off the Irak yoke and proclaim union with the Turkish Kurds, all ultimately submitting to Angora.

(3) A further possibility is that the rising may afford a pretext for a concentration of Turkish troops on the Irak frontier, who might ultimately find it their duty to pursue flying Turkish rebels across the Irak border.

(4) "The Turkish govt. pretended to take the view that the movement is reactionary and due to certain influences playing on the religious instincts of the rebels. The attempt to use religion as a cloak for treason is strongly condemned. At the same time reactionary and rel. movement affords the govt. opportunity of seeking out under cover of martial law its opponents of whatever colour and of dealing with them. Perhaps 'independence tribunals' will again be set there.

Turkey will certainly do all in her power to crush any movement tending to create an independent Kurdistan. The Turanian ideas of the CUP [Committee of Union and Progress] are still prevalent in Turkish Govt. circles. Turkey wishes to extend her influence toward & be in close relations w/ the Central Asian Moslems and the rise of any buffer state in E. Asia Minor would be an obstacle to her plan & will certainly be crushed."

D. A. Osborne at the Foreign Office suggested that the British should "remain alive" to the possibilities mentioned by Morgan, but that he did not believe the rebellion was fictitious or exaggerated, as some French military and intelligence officers had indicated, because: "(1) the Turks will not be affected by a show of military force; (2) the rebellion involved a rejection of the Turkish claim to Mosul; (3) it caused considerable discredit in the eyes of the world to the present Turkish regime, however; (4) once the revolt broke out its seriousness may have been exaggerated to enable Kemal to reinstate Ismet [Inönü] as Prime Minister and to institute a variety of repressive measures against the rising tide of criticism and oppression."[6] Additional evidence that the British might have to fear a Turkish attack was provided in a report by the British military attaché, Colonel Harenc, who wrote in April 1925 that Recep Peker, the Turkish minister of defense, had asked Colonel Neyroni, the Italian navy attaché, to imagine a situation in which a 60,000-man army, but a small air force, would confront an army of only 4,000 or 5,000 men, but one with a strong air force. "Would you," asked the Turkish defense minister, "be able to prevent the invasion of your country by the larger force with little or no air force to speak of?" It did not take British officers long to decide that Recep was referring to the relevant Turkish and British forces in Iraq. The British ambassador was quick to inform the Foreign Office that progress on the Mosul question could not be made in face of such reports.[7]

More evidence that the British were not eager to be associated with the Sheikh Said rebellion occurred on 24 March when the British Chancery in Paris reported "a gentleman called Messoud Famy Bey, describing himself as 'Governor of Djebeli-bereket' or alternatively as 'Ex-Governor of Cilica' called to-day and asked to see a member of the Chancery. On being asked what he wanted, he stated that he wished to discuss the present political situation in Kurdistan with special reference to the revolt in those parts. He was told that this was a matter concerning Turkey alone and that we could not discuss the question at all. He thereupon departed, shaking the dust of his feet upon us." Although Osborne wrote in a minute, "It might have been interesting to hear what he had to say," he was overruled by a more senior official, Lawrence Oliphant, who wrote, "Far better to keep out of it." It appears the British, even in Paris, wanted to keep their distance from the Sheikh Said rebellion. By June, there were still few official Turkish charges of British complicity. On 2 June, Lindsay reported to Chamberlain, "Curiously little has transpired *or been allowed to transpire* as to any British instigation of or part in the Kurdish movement. Mention has been made of one, Templi (?Tamplin) who, three or four years ago, was supposed to be a British agent, but turned out really to be a Turkish agent provocateur. I have no ideas who this man can have been. It is also said Sheikh Said hoped, after taking Diyarbekır, to get in touch with the British authorities via Gezireh. This is about all the mention made of British activity reported so far in the newspaper accounts" (emphasis added). Tampling, it seems, had previously been in the Allied police and "had entered into a highly compromising correspondence with Seyyid Abdulqadir via Keur Sadi, one of his agents." Lindsay stated that Tampling and his associate, a certain Hulse, "were looked at rather askance by British authorities, as they were understood to be willing to work for foreigners but on the other hand they had been employed by (a Britisher) Sir A. Block on a forged bank note case." In June 1925, Lindsay believed Tampling was no longer in Turkey but that his associate Hulse was still in Istanbul, "in pay of and working for the Russian Bolshevik authorities."[8]

It is not surprising that there were few official Turkish charges against British complicity in the Sheikh Said rebellion. On 18 April 1926, when it was clear there would soon be a peace treaty concluded between Turkey and Great Britain, Lindsay reported to Chamberlain that on that very day he had met with Ismet Inönü and stated bluntly to him:

> If we wanted to cause trouble in Turkey we could have lighted up rebellion from one end of the country to the other, but we had not done so, and he must know it. Did he not remember an observation I made to him last year [1925] in March when Sheikh Said's rebellion was at its height? I had then said to him that doubtless Turkey would soon crush the rebellion; that prisoners would be taken and cross-examined and close enquiries pursued; but that I could tell him, in advance, that no trace of British instigation of the revolt would be found. And now I said what trace of British instigation did you find?

"This," stated Lindsay, "seemed to strike Ismet forcibly, and he did not attempt any accusation that we had had any part in the Kurdish rising of 1925."[9]

If we have established with some degree of certitude that neither

Great Britain nor Turkey was involved in inciting the Sheikh Said rebellion, then we must ask what was Britain's policy? Why didn't it attempt to stir up the Kurds against Turkey, especially since the Mosul question in early 1925 did not seem readily soluble? Ömer Kürkçüoğlu summarizes Britain's position as follows: because of its interest in the Kurdish question, Britain closely followed the Sheikh Said rebellion but tried to avoid the position of supporting it. One of the reasons that Britain did not support the rebellion was that it was having enough trouble controlling the Kurds in Mandated Iraq, Sheikh Mahmud being the best example. Britain was in the process of changing its policy toward the new republic and did not want to fragment Turkey and probably again push Turkey toward the Soviet Union. A Kurdistan tied to Britain would increase its security in the Middle East, but if Turkish-Soviet relations once again became close, the strong advantages Britain had gained in the Straits at Lausanne would be endangered. By demonstrating friendship toward Turkey, Great Britain would be able to ensure its security in the Straits and in the Arab Middle East.[10]

As Kürkçüoğlu states, these were British objectives, but as long as the Mosul question and the Turkish-Iraqi boundary dispute were not settled, the British thought rebellion in Turkey was in their interest since it would pressure Turkey to negotiate over the Mosul question to British advantage. But the British did not support a Kurdish movement that would lead to independence. Furthermore, British opinion was that the Sheikh Said rebellion demonstrated that the Turks could not live in peace with the Kurds in Turkey and consequently weakened their claim to Mosul with its Kurdish majority. Great Britain also realized that, in spite of Turkey's mobilization of some 50,000 troops on the Iraq-Turkey border, Turkey still wanted to avoid military intervention. Turkey's struggle with the Kurdish rebellion would only increase Turkey's resistance to negotiations over Mosul.[11] In short, Kürkçüoğlu speculates that the Sheikh Said rebellion, like the first years of the Turkish war of independence, allowed Great Britain the opportunity to "give the Kurds hope"; but after the rebellion broke out, the British did not aid the Kurds. It seems likely that Great Britain's policies and Turkey's accurate perception of these policies greatly expedited the negotiations that led to the Turkish-British treaty of 5 June 1926.

There were, however, several factors other than the Sheikh Said rebellion that compelled Turkey to seek agreement with Great Britain over the question of Mosul. In 1924 and 1925, Turkey found itself increasingly isolated in world affairs. Turkey had rejected the League of Nations Tripartite (Uçlu) Commission report of 16 July

1925 that dealt with the Turkey-Iraq border as being unfavorable. But it is important to note that, when the commission's report was being discussed by the League of Nations from 3 to 19 September 1925, Tevfik Rüstü Bey, the Turkish foreign minister, stated that Turkey had no disagreements with Great Britain other than the Mosul question. He added, however, that the Mosul question could not be resolved if the British, and the League of Nations, citing protection of Kurdish rights, attempted to use the Kurds of Iraq against Turkey, the country in which the majority of Kurds lived. Tevfik Rüstü was reiterating a policy that had become clear during the negotiations at Lausanne in 1923—namely, that the Turks viewed the Kurds as affecting both their internal and external security. The memories of British support for Kurdish autonomy at Sèvres and for inciting the Kurds against the nationalist forces in 1920–1921 were fresh in the minds of the Turks in 1923 and still so in 1925. The problem was perceived in the same light: if the Kurds were left to Great Britain and, in the future, if the British gave the Kurds autonomy, the Kurds in Turkey would put forward the same demands.[12]

After Turkey's rejection of the League of Nations Commission's report, the dispute was taken to the Permanent International World Court of Justice, which on 21 October 1925 basically accepted the World Court's opinion and that of the Tripartite Commission of 16 December 1925 with regard to the boundary line between Turkey and Iraq. On the basis of these favorable opinions, Great Britain made a new treaty with Iraq on 18 January 1926 that was passed unanimously by the Iraqi Parliament. There were 58 votes in favor and 19 abstentions. An Iraqi police intelligence operative noted on 9 January 1926 that "those in favor of the treaty, on whatever grounds, use the argument that the treaty is not only essential for the retention of the Mosul Wilayat but is also essential for the actual existence of the independence of Irak and its monarchy. . . ." In this fashion, it seems that the Sheikh Said rebellion not only facilitated Iraq's acceptance of the new relationship with Great Britain—less than five months later, it resulted in a treaty between Great Britain and Iraq and Turkey. By December 1925, most European nations, either directly or indirectly through the League of Nations and with British encouragement, were opposed to Turkey's policies. The forced expulsion of the Nestorians during the course of suppressing the Sheikh Said rebellion had added to the strong disapproval of Turkey in Europe and in the League of Nations and increased Turkey's isolation at this crucial juncture.[13]

By the end of 1925, Great Britain was using the League of Nations not only with regard to the Mosul question but as an effective instrument of its foreign policies. Austen Chamberlain utilized the league as a tool for fostering the unity of the Locarno Powers in order, he hoped, to void "the divisions in the ranks of the Allied Powers which had hampered British policy during the Lausanne Conference." If members of the league expected Britain to underwrite sanctions on a worldwide basis (e.g., through the Geneva Protocol of 1924), they should not drag their feet on the Mosul question. "Are the sanctions available," queried Chamberlain, "only if Britain applies them for someone else's protection?" In spite of his annoyance over the hesitancy of some league members with respect to Mosul, Chamberlain remained a staunch advocate of the "New Diplomacy" of employing multilateral and third parties to arbitrate disputes previously settled only on a bilateral basis. "Is Mosul," he asked, "to be allowed to destroy what has been accomplished?" In fact, Peter J. Beck asserts that Chamberlain's interest in the utilization of the League of Nations as an instrument of British policy was such that his "contacts with the great powers were supplemented by the attention he paid to the three members of the council's subcommittee," Guani (Uruguay); León (Spain); and Branting (Sweden); and subsequently Undén (Sweden). Chamberlain concentrated his attention first on León of Spain, who sought British support for Spain's policy in Morocco and also support for a permanent seat on the council.[14] The close personal attention paid by the British foreign minister to members of a subcommittee of a council of the League of Nations is an indication of Chamberlain's policy to pressure Turkey through the league.

Turkey was also apprehensive of Italy, under the dynamic new leadership of Benito Mussolini, who, much to Turkey's consternation, seemed to be courted by Great Britain and by Austen Chamberlain in particular. The menace of Italy's designs on Turkey during and after World War I was fresh. It seems that Turkey was aware of the rumors that Italy was stockpiling war materiel and sending troops to Sicily in May 1924 for possible use against Turkey, although an Italian representative denied this was the case. There were further reports in June that Italy and the Soviet Union had signed an agreement to invade Turkey within six weeks. There were still other reports, or perhaps one should say rumors, that Italy, Yugoslavia, and Greece were waiting to attack Turkey at an opportune moment; Italy would be free to do as it pleased in Anatolia, Yugoslavia would annex Albania, and Greece would take eastern Thrace. When the Sheikh Said rebellion broke out, fears surfaced that Italy would act as it had in 1908. Turkish fears of Italy were not unfounded. Britain sought Italian help, especially from the Italian air force and navy, against Turkey, if such need arose. Turkey was aware of the rapprochement between Great Britain and Italy as indicated by the Chamberlain-Mussolini meeting and the Rome Accords of December 1924.[15]

In April 1925, at the height of the Sheikh Said rebellion, the British government recognized Italian economic rights in Iraq. In December 1925, Great Britain and Italy exchanged notes providing for the mutual recognition of their respective concession claims in Ethiopia. Peter J. Beck has written, "in fact, the exchange of notes has resulted in claims, which are unsupported by the evidence, that the Ethiopian agreement was a quid pro quo for Italian help over Mosul." It is very probable indeed that the Turks thought this to be the case. Chamberlain's visit to Rapallo at the end of December 1925 "provided *not* just a further opportunity, to meet Mussolini but also served, for Turkey's benefit, as another outward manifestation of Anglo-Italian harmony" (emphasis added). One scholar states, "British efforts to create a kind of 'Triple Entente' between Britain, France and Italy were clearly helped by the relative coincidence of interests existing between them in respect of Turkey, although recent events, such as the Locarno Conference, the Greco-Bulgarian dispute and the Ethiopian question also promoted harmony." Even if frightening the Turks was an unexpected bonus and not a planned policy, the Rapallo talks did succeed in making the Turks apprehensive. Indeed, Turkey was nervous about Italy's policies right up to the signing of its treaty with Great Britain on 5 June 1926. In addition to the British-Italian rapprochement, the Locarno negotiations and agreements in winter 1925 sought to make Germany once again a member of the European and international political communities. It was reported that Gustav Stresemann, the German foreign minister, had reprimanded Herr Nadolny, German ambassador to Turkey, for encouraging Turkey to look for German support on Mosul.[16] It became clear by late 1925 that Turkey could not look to Germany for aid, at least with regard to the Mosul question and/or conflicts with Great Britain.

The French also felt that the Locarno treaties had stopped any potential German support for Turkey. On 28 October 1925, the secretary general of the French Foreign Ministry, Philippe Berthelot, informed Miles W. Lampson of the British Foreign Office that the Locarno treaties had been signed and

had affected Turkish circles. The Turkish Government had been anticipating that in the future, as in the past, they would have been able to draw upon German resources for help in such matters as the training of the Turkish army, etc., etc. It has now been borne in upon them that any such hope after Locarno was vain. There thus remained to Turkey only the possibility of Russian support, which was another factor upon which they had been counting. He (Monsieur Berthelot) had little doubt that the French Govt. could get something of the kind from the Russians (Monsieur Chicheron) to pay the Russian debt to France. This he thought would lead to the opening of some formal negot. with Russia which might even, ultimately, lead to the entry of Russia into the League & her re-admission to the comity of nations. Now, if all of that came to pass, the result would be that Russian support would also be w/d [withdrawn] from Turkey, and Turkey, left to her own resources, would speedily see that it was to her interests to come to friendly arrangement with Great Britain.[17]

Berthelot finished his memorandum by saying that, in light of the above, the movement of Turkish troops eastward along the Pozanti-Nusaybin railroad was not as important as the British thought. The reduction of the number of Turkish troops using the portion of the railroad that passed through French-controlled Syrian territory had been requested by the British as early as May 1925, when the peak of Sheikh Said's rebellion had passed. But it was not until the first part of November that Aristide Briand, the French foreign minister, announced that no more troops would be allowed to pass eastward than passed westward—that is, the troops going eastward must be reliefs and not reinforcements.[18] Thus, by November 25, the French had not only decided to impede Turkish troop movements along the railroad to prevent or reduce the possibility of a Turkish attack on Iraq but also attempted to prevent the Soviet Union from supporting the Turks by providing avenues allowing it to repay debts to France and to reenter the "comity of nations."

Briand was eager to maintain Anglo-French solidarity not just on the Mosul question but for the wider interests of France in the Middle East, especially in Syria, and also in Europe, especially with respect to Germany. As a result, he did not want French commercial and oil interests to profit from Turkey's acquisition of Mosul to damage the broader interests of France. He thought, too, that perhaps the oil interests could be satisfied by French requests that Great Britain allow French interests to participate in the oil development of the Basra *vilayet* and in the transferred territories. Briand was also doubtless aware that Mosul might establish a precedent for Turkish claims to Alexandretta (Hatay) and Aleppo. He furthermore wanted Britain's cooperation in quelling the Druze rebellion, which had broken out in Syria in July 1925, just after the Sheikh Said rebellion. Briand even responded to Chamberlain's request to pressure the Swedish rapporteur, Osten Undén, of the league's sub-council committee on Mosul. He even offered to allow the British to use Syria as an air base to attack Turkey if necessary. By December 1925, in spite of a few disagreements over the activities of the French delegate, Paul Boncour, during the council session and Turkish troop movements along the Pozanti-Nusaybin railroad, French-British relations were excellent.[19] They improved further: on 1 December 1925, the French ambassador, Monsieur de Fleurian, in conversation with British officials, suggested that British-French relations could be even better in the Middle East. In particular, he said, with regard to the Mosul question, France might become more cooperative after the commencement of the Druze revolt and nationalist rebellion in Syria during the summer and autumn of 1925.

On 20 October 1925, C. W. Rendel, a Foreign Office official, stated in a memorandum to the Colonial Office and Air Ministry that the "question of the attitude of the French in Syria towards the possible Turkish threat to Irak has been quite separate from that of our attitude in Transjordan towards the Druze rebellion." Rendel admitted that British attempts to prevent Transjordan from giving the Druze assistance had been "of a purely local ad. [administration] nature. . . . We have hardly succeeded in doing more than clear ourselves of the suspicion of disloyalty to our neighbors [the French]." But Rendel now thought that "the juxtaposition of these two questions [i.e., the possible Turkish threat to Mosul and the Druze rebellion in Syria] suggests the idea that possibly a useful connection might be best. If we should be able to make some effective gesture of cooperation with the French in their difficulties in Southern Syria, the impression of the Franco-British solidarity which would be created might have a very salutary effect on Angora, while any real assistance we could give the French, besides enabling them to pay more attention to their northern frontier, & to the north-eastern corner of Syria, where they have lately been obliged, from lack of men, to tolerate illegal Turkish outposts."[20] It was in such fashion that two incipient nationalist rebellions—that of Sheikh Said, which led to the "possible Turkish threat to Mosul," and of the Druze in Syria—led to closer, albeit tenuous, cooperation between the two major imperialist powers in the Middle East. The Sheikh Said rebellion in Turkey and the Druze nationalist rebellion in Syria are excellent examples of how incipient but uninstitutionalized nationalisms led to and created the need for greater cooperation between the imperialist and nationalist empires of Great Britain and France in the Middle East. The British-French cooperation of 1925 did not eliminate all of the undercurrents of mistrust and suspicion between the two countries, especially Britain's dislike of French support for Turkish policy in Alexandretta. The closer cooperation dictated by the two rebellions, as suggested by British and French officials in the Middle East, juxtaposed nicely with the policies of Aristide Briand and Austen Chamberlain calling for closer relations between France and Great Britain in Europe and elsewhere in the world.

By December 1925, then, the Turks were quite isolated in foreign affairs. The only country they could turn to was the Soviet Union. On 17 December 1925, Turkey and the Soviet Union signed a treaty of friendship encompassing nonaggression and neutrality clauses. Moscow in 1925 felt as isolated as Turkey, suspicious that the Locarno treaties were directed against it and furthermore that Germany's reinduction into European politics was anti-Soviet. The Turks, by signing the treaty with the Soviets, hoped to obtain leverage against Great Britain. However, the British were not overly concerned about the treaty. By December 1925, they knew Turkey was nearly ready to negotiate about Mosul and that the Soviet Union wanted an independent Turkey as well as an independent Iran, rather than reactionary or imperialist governments in Ankara or Teheran. This meant that, as far as the British were concerned, the Soviet Union would not support the Kurds or Kurdish independence in Turkey. If the Kurds were not to be used as an instrument of Soviet policy, the Soviets could exercise little influence over Turkish policy or a Western-oriented Turkish policy. As C. W. Rendel summed it up just prior to the signing of the treaty: "All of our information goes to show that the Turks are making use of the Russians, but the Russians have not yet succeeded in making use of the Turks." Herr Nadolny, the German ambassador, was certain as late as 4 October 1925 that the Turks would not sign a treaty with the Russians, and, if they did, it would be "a purely temporary affair." Nadolny added that his information was that "the Turks were obstructing all progress on neg. [negotiation] of a commercial treaty."[21]

As noted above, the Turkish-Soviet treaty was seriously limited by the fact that both countries wanted to reduce their isolation in world and particularly European affairs. France and Great Britain continually held out the incentive of supporting Soviet membership in the League of Nations, something the Soviets wanted badly. The fact that this was achieved in 1932 by both Turkey and the Soviet Union is sufficient testimony that neither followed policies too disruptive to Western policy from 1925 to 1932 and that their 1925 treaty was only of limited bilateral usefulness. Indeed, according to the treaty, if Turkey went to war with Great Britain over Mosul, the Soviet Union was not obliged to come to its aid. In fact, a Turkish historian has suggested that the Soviet Union thought the treaty would increase tensions between Turkey and Britain and thereby improve relations between the Soviets and the British, which would in turn enable the Soviets to eliminate those aspects of the Locarno treaties detrimental to Soviet policies. Kürkçüoğlu also states that the treaty allowed Turkey some "comfort" (*rahatlığı*) to pursue a pro-Western foreign policy without excessively irritating the Soviet Union. He thinks that the fact that the treaty lasted for twenty years supports this contention. The British ambassador seemed to think that the policy of Turkey toward the Soviets, as exemplified in the treaty, was a wise one and that it would facilitate and expedite the negotiation of a treaty between Britain and the Turks by cushioning the adverse impact of the League of Nations decision on Mosul in Turkey. Furthermore, Lindsay was of the opinion that the Soviet Union would not impede a British-Turkey treaty over Mosul while it was in need of economic aid from Western Europe. The diplomatic and economic needs of the Soviets, coupled with the Soviet "fear of a reactionary or an imperialist regime before Turkey has recuperated her strength," made it imperative that the Soviets keep the "strength of the British empire available as a reserve both for the immediate and for the distant future."[22]

The rapid movement toward conclusion of a treaty with Britain in the spring of 1926 also impelled Turkey to sign a treaty of friendship with Iran on 22 April 1926. Sir Percy Loraine, British ambassador to Iran, concluded that "this treaty can be explained on simple premises"—namely, Turkey had been for some time "inordinately anxious regarding the policy of Reza Khan in Kurdistan, suspecting doubtless that his lenient treatment of Simko *indicates some sympathy with the project of an autonomous Kurdish state* embracing, under Persian suzerainty, the Kurds of Turkey, Persia and Iraq" (emphasis added). Loraine was of the opinion that "it seems probable that it was with a view to force an issue in their relations with Persia that the Angora Government increased the tariff coefficient to eight and threatened to impose a consumption tax on the goods in transit"; but, as Loraine stated with authority, the Persian government, "always acutely conscious of the danger of Turkish irredentism in Azerbaijan, and fearing a Russo-Turkish combine against them, were all too willing to yield to such pressure." But in spite of Iran yielding to Turkish pressures, the results were still advantageous to Iran and to Great Britain because the instability threatened by dis-

orders in Azerbayjan would be diminished and the economic development of the northwestern provinces could be pursued. In addition the
"menace" of too close cooperation between Turkey and the Soviet
Union was "for the moment" averted. The Turkish-Iran treaty, continued the ambassador, would allow Reza Khan to turn his energies
to internal reorganization. Most importantly, stated Loraine, "the
conclusion of this treaty should render it easier for the Persian Government to proceed with the recognition of Irak." Most of Loraine's
assessments, it should be noted, turned out to be accurate, except
that a treaty between Iraq and Iran proved more difficult to achieve
than he had anticipated.[23] In addition, Reza Khan's admiration for
Kemal Atatürk's reforms apparently facilitated the agreement.

But Rouhallah Ramazani, a student of Iranian foreign policy, writing in 1966, agrees with Loraine's view expressed in 1926 that "the
Shah was determined to emancipate the economy of northern Iran
from dependence on Soviet Russia by finding access to new markets
through Turkish ports." In addition, article 5 of the treaty stipulated
that both countries agreed "not to allow in their territory the formation or presence of organizations or groups of persons whose object
is to disturb the peace and security of the other country or to change
its government, or the presence of persons or groups of persons to
attack the other country by propaganda or by any other means."[24]
From the Turkish point of view, article 5, which was directed against
any Iranian support for Kurdish movements for autonomy and/or independence, was the most important feature of the treaty.

There was sufficient cooperation from Iran, in spite of continuing
Kurdish rebellions in eastern Turkey, that the Turks and Iranians
were able to sign a definitive frontier treaty by 23 January 1932 that
is still in force. Feeling more secure on its eastern boundary with
Iran, less than a month and a half later, Turkey signed a treaty with
Great Britain and Iraq. The diplomatic activities leading up to the
Turkish-Iranian treaty of friendship led Sir Ronald Lindsay in Istanbul to conclude eight days before the treaty was signed: "On the
whole Turkey is weak, and her Government is now conscious of her
weakness. There is unquestionably a strong desire to come to terms
with His Majesty's Government over the frontier and *a settlement
can be had cheaply*" (emphasis added). The British were also of the
opinion that the treaty would allow Reza Khan to cooperate more
effectively with the British to control Sheikh Mahmud "rep. [repre-
senting] as he does independent Kurdistan." Sheikh Mahmud was
thought to be the most powerful and influential Kurdish leader in
Iraq and Iran, where many other sheikhs were loyal to him. If Sheikh
Mahmud ever "attempted to increase his sphere at the expense of

Persian territory he would have a sure ally in Ismail Agha Simko, an enemy of Persia."[25] In other words, a treaty between Turkey and Iran that called for suppressing a Kurdish nationalist movement and its leaders would give some confidence to Turkey that Great Britain would not support then or in the future an independent Kurdistan or Kurdish autonomy.

It should be mentioned that Reza Khan was satisfied that Turkey had not taken advantage or interfered in any way during the Turcoman rebellion in eastern Iran, which began in November 1924 and continued throughout 1925. The rebellion, led by the Serdar of Bujnird, chief of the Şadilli Kurds, was intense and widespread and required a force of 10,000 to 15,000 to suppress. The Soviet Union's attitude toward the Turcoman rebellion that occurred on its frontier with Iran and was at its peak during 1925 (the same time as the rebellion of Sheikh Said) also made the British confident that the Soviets would not impede a Turkish-British settlement of the Mosul question. While the Soviets would attempt to embarrass the Iranians and to leave the Turcomans and Kurds in Khurasan in a semi-autonomous position, the British were quite sure that the Soviets would not openly support the rebellion against the Iranian government because it "was too inconsistent with the Eastern policy of the Soviets."[26]

The Soviet attitude toward the Turcoman and Kurdish rebellion in eastern Iran in 1925 and its actions toward Sheikh Said's rebellion in Turkey during the same year bear certain similarities, the major one being that the Soviets favored the regimes of Kemal Atatürk and Reza Khan to alternative regimes that could possibly be more hostile to the Soviet Union. The corollary of this policy was one that sought rapprochement with Great Britain or, at least, with Western Europe. Turkey and Iran, as well as Great Britain, interpreted the policies of the Soviet Union in this way as they combated the Sheikh Said and Turcoman-Kurdish rebellions during 1925 and, indeed, subsequently.

The Turkey-Iran Treaty of 22 April 1926 also put a final end to the suggestion by Lindsay on 20 November 1925 that some Kurdish-populated territories in Iraq between Amadiya and Rawanduz be transferred to Iran in order to ease the way for a final settlement with Turkey over Mosul. The Foreign Office thought Lindsay's proposal was prompted by Ismet Inönü's remarks to the British ambassador that "so long as any large number of Kurds are included in Irak the Turkish Government would have perpetual trouble on their eastern provinces and *trouble would arise automatically, however loyally the British authorities might act as neighbors*" (emphasis added). This was an admission, it seems, on the part of Inönü that a strong Kurdish nationalist movement existed and a presumption by Lindsay that, without an adjustment on the frontier substantially different from the Brussels Line, a peace treaty between Great Britain and Turkey would not materialize. Sir Henry Dobbs, British high commissioner in Iraq, however, quickly threw water on Lindsay's suggestions. Dobbs stressed that the Kurds were essential to the security, financial, and political stability in Iraq and that Turkish policy was to eliminate the "Kurdish wall which is interposed between herself and the Turkish population of the Persian province of Azerbaijan." Dobbs was of the opinion that the Turks themselves, including Inönü, notwithstanding his remarks to Lindsay, would be opposed to the transfer of the Kurds between Amadiya and Rawanduz because "it would give Persia a wedge on the flank of the Turkish route to Azerbaijan" and "would defeat the object of the Turks in their Kurdish policy." Dobbs believed that the Turks "would prefer to see the Kurds remain under Irak." In addition, Chamberlain noted, the transfer of Kurds to Iran would not meet the League of Nations stipulation regarding use of Kurdish language and officers, especially if League of Nations control expired in 1928.[27] The realization that Great Britain, Iraq, and Turkey did not desire the transfer of Kurdish populated territory also probably hastened the signing of the friendship treaty of 22 April 1926.

The last remaining hurdle to the conclusion of a treaty between Great Britain and Iraq and Turkey was in the final analysis Great Britain itself. In addition to many favorable international developments through 1924–1925 that had strengthened Great Britain's position vis-à-vis Turkey, there were also internal changes in Turkey favorable to Britain's rapprochement. The most favorable of these changes was the abolition of the caliphate on 3 March 1924, a clear indication that Turkey intended to pursue a Western-oriented foreign policy and a laic or secular policy domestically. As one Turkish scholar has put it, "The Turks, to be Western, fought the West."[28] By March 1924, it was also clear that a corollary of Turkey's turn to the West would be a reduction in the appeal of Bolshevism and a cooling of relations with the Soviet Union. It was becoming clear in early 1924 that Turkish-Soviet relations would remain in the context established later by the Turkey-Soviet Treaty of 17 December 1925, discussed above. The abolition of the caliphate also reduced the possibility of the opposition utilizing the caliphate against Mustafa Kemal and his government.

Indeed, in spite of the abolition of the caliphate in March 1924, Sheikh Said raised the banner of Islam in his nationalist uprising less than one year later. Kürkçüoğlu has suggested that as long as the Mosul question was not resolved, Turkey could have used the caliphate and Islam as a weapon against Great Britain, which, as the British were fond of saying, was the largest Muslim country in the world—but Turkey didn't. Kürkçüoğlu suggests that Turkey did not use Islam because it would have contradicted the new republic's secular policies, and would have thrust Turkey back into the politics of the Arab world. The acquisition of the Mosul *vilayet* would necessarily and perhaps inextricably have tied Turkey to the politics of the Arab world and the politics of Islam would have figured more strongly in its domestic policy, to say nothing of the geopolitical threat to Great Britain's Sharifian policy in the Middle East. In the opinion of Kürkçüoğlu, this is why it was probably as early as March 1924 that Turkey wished to signal Great Britain that it would not use Islam—as it had earlier—against British interests in the Middle East or India.[29]

The Turks gave a clear signal in March 1924 that they would not support other Muslim countries in their struggle to gain independence from Western imperialism and from Great Britain. Lindsay wrote in February 1926 that a secular Turkey reduced the danger of Muslims to the British Empire. When the Sheikh Said rebellion was at its height in March 1925, he said that he continually stressed to Ismet Inönü that "it was not in our interest that Turkey should be diverted by internal disorder from the task of peaceful reconstruction." Furthermore, Lindsay told Inönü that the secularization of Turkey's domestic policy would be paralleled internationally by Turkey's joining the League of Nations, whatever the league's verdict on Mosul. These developments would be facilitated, thought D. A. Osborne in the Foreign Office, by the fact that "Ismet realized capital can only be got from London." The Turks, like the Soviets, would have to look west for capital if they wanted to develop their country. In November 1925, Ronald Lindsay reported that he emphasized to Inönü that Turkey's policy of modernization was threatened by its demand "for restitution of Mosul which was purely Arab." Lindsay reported that "Ismet took up the point at once. He admitted that Mosul was Arab or mainly Arab, but added that there were other 'elements' of population in those regions. 'These two policies,' he said 'are, as you remark, contradictory and mutually destructive of each other, the one must be sincere, and the other not sincere; and I leave your excellency to decide for yourself which is which.'" Lindsay commented he was inclined to attribute the form of Ismet's answer to his imperfect command of French, but he wanted to point out to Chamberlain the "sound common sense that underlies it."[30]

The British interpreted modernization and the orientation this implied, rather than Mosul (i.e., oil), to be the sincere Turkish policy with regard to Ismet Inönü's studied ambiguity about the contradictions of Turkey's policy on modernization or Mosul.

The one factor that had always been and still remained the main issue between Great Britain and the Turks was Britain's policies and intentions toward the Kurdish question, with respect to both Britain's imperial policies in the Middle East and its pursuit of the Sharifian policy after World War I. To the Turks, Britain's policies toward the Kurds from 1920 to 1925 must have seemed very similar to its policies toward the Zionist movement in Palestine and the larger implications of that policy for the Ottoman Empire from 1880 to 1918. The Turkish government in 1925 still contained many diplomats and bureaucrats thoroughly familiar with Britain's support for the Zionist movement and for Jewish settlement in Palestine.[31] While the Turkish archives are not open for the years under study here, the Turkish arguments made by Ismet Inönü at the Lausanne conference and subsequently, as well as those by Tevfik Rüstü, demonstrate clearly that the Turks thought the British were trying to create a national home for the Kurds. The British, it seems, were clearly thinking along these lines. As the probability of a settlement with Turkey increased in the fall of 1925, British authorities addressed this question more directly.

On 16 October 1925, Sir Ronald Lindsay wrote that international and domestic developments were pointing to "a return of good relations" between Great Britain and Turkey. But, he said, "the Kurdistan rebellion of last year was a terrible shock to this policy. There is nationalism in Kurdistan, but it is Kurdish and not Turkish, and the Turkish nationalism, inculcated by the Govt. is too narrow and sectarian in character. Small wonder that the tribes broke into revolt.—(Turkish) Govt. feels that at any cost it must suppress Kurdish nationalism; yet it finds that just across the border H.M. Govt. *proposes to find a sort of Kurdish national home"* (emphasis added). "And so we return to the point from which we started—that the Mosul Question is the only stumbling block in the path towards Anglo-Turkish friendship. After the agitations [Sheikh Said] of the past month or two it looks as if the game is fairly in the hands of H.M.G. and that they can play it out as they like. *Perhaps H.M.G. are already irretrievably committed to fostering nationalism in Southern Kurdistan,* if not, there are strong reasons for wishing the League will not impose on the mandatory power any obligation in that direction" (emphasis added). Four days later, Lindsay reiterated his belief that *"Kurdistan constitutes the most serious menace in sight to the present regime"* (emphasis added). He was of the opinion that "even before the end of Abdulhamid's reign the young Turks were at loggerheads with Kurdish nationalism, and with the disappearance of the Armenians the last reasons for tolerating it have gone. Between it and the secular-minded young republic, there can be nothing but irreconcilable hostility." He added, "The only question is whether, so long as the republic lasts, shall we see a series of revolts followed by repression; or whether the task will be too great for the government and Kurdistan will be left severely alone with its own local ad. of sheikh-Beys. . . ."[32]

As Lindsay penned his predictions regarding the serious menace of Kurdish nationalism to the Turkish government, the Eastern Department of the Foreign Office submitted a long memorandum regarding the factors that "would influence or decide Turkish policy in the question of Mosul."[33] Lindsay's sanguine prognostications of a return to good relations with Turkey were substantiated by the policy memorandum. There were two internal political issues that the Turks had to consider. One was the need for prestige and the second was the question of Kurdistan. The memorandum stated that Mustafa Kemal's policy was to assimilate the Kurdish population. But the policy of Great Britain "was to plant the seeds of autonomy among the Iraki Kurds." This in turn would strengthen the resolve of the Kurds in Turkey not to assimilate with the Turks. If the Kurds of Turkey "sooner or later" claimed their right to unite with their "semi-independent brothers in Irak, it would mean the loss of valuable population and territory to Turkey—a threat which must be averted at all costs." The British thought that it was this concern that explained the Turkish suggestion of a guarantee of the Turkish and Iraqi frontiers. In addition, it speculated, three external factors were influencing Turkish policy: Mustafa Kemal wanted Turkey to join the League of Nations; Turkey wanted to join the League of Nations to take advantage of the protection it offered against potential invaders; and Turkey's desire to join the League of Nations was a top priority because the Locarno treaties had demonstrated strongly the isolation of the Soviet Union: Turkey did not want the same thing to happen to it!

The memorandum also spelled out the financial needs of Turkey and stated that "to flaunt the League" would lessen Turkey's chances of obtaining financial aid from its members. Military operations against Iraq would prove costly to Turkey, but the authors of the memorandum thought there was a slim possibility that Turkey might think the wealth of the oil deposits worth the risk. When it came to military considerations, the drafters of the memorandum advanced several cogent arguments against the possibility of a Turkish invasion of Iraq. For example, Turkey might take Mosul, but could it hold the city, especially in light of the Sheikh Said rebellion? Britain could get reinforcements from India. Turkey's lines of communications were very tenuous. The Turks would have to remember that the Kurds were in back of them and would be vulnerable to British attacks from the sea, and the interior of the country would be vulnerable to attacks from the RAF. Finally, such an attack would be an indirect violation of League of Nations decisions and the political and economic costs of these violations would be high.

The authors of the memorandum concluded that a military adventure on the part of the Turks would be a policy of desperation and would have doubtful success. But Mustafa Kemal's position did not seem desperate. The policy memorandum stated that a Turkish attack on Mosul was unlikely, although it was speculated that there might be an intensification of "military bluff" on the part of Ankara. The Turks might continue what the British termed a policy of obstruction and of legal objection "as long as the game plays." It also broached the possibility that Great Britain might obtain a compromise settlement with Turkey *without the aid* of the League of Nations. In order to obtain compromise, two conditions had to be met: some kind of guarantee against the loss of Turkish Kurdistan; and some face-saving device by which Mustafa Kemal could justify himself to Turkey. Three possibilities were offered with regard to the latter: that Turkey and Great Britain could bring off "a spectacular burying of the hatchet"; the former might involve a treaty of friendship and arbitration, although such a treaty could not guarantee Turkish borders against the Soviet Union; and it was "unfortunately too late to offer her a share in the Mosul oil development scheme." This is a reminder that however much current negotiations concerned security affairs (i.e., Kurds and boundaries), the importance of oil always loomed large to British officials.

The drafters of the policy memorandum thought that there were several other factors that restrained the Turks. For one thing, winter was coming on. The Turks would be able to attack only on the western end of the Brussels Line, exactly where the British forces were concentrated; also, a Turkish attack would be slowed considerably by British air power. It was made clear in subsequent memoranda that the RAF would be responsible for stopping, deterring, or defeating any indirect attack. The conclusion of the memorandum was that there were simply too many internal, external, military, and financial restraints on Turkey to make possible an attack on Mosul or combat with Great Britain. The conclusions and recommendations of the memorandum were in harmony with the objectives and direction of Britain's foreign policy and diplomacy as they were then developing and would continue to develop with respect to Turkey and the Kurds.[34]

In early November, Britain continued to press Turkey for a diplomatic settlement. On 5 November, Chamberlain answered Lindsay's concerns that the League of Nations would not impose any obligations on Great Britain "in the direction of fostering nationalism in southern Kurdistan." Chamberlain told Lindsay, "I fully appreciate the force of your contention that Anglo-Turkish relations could be placed on a satisfactory footing if only means were found to eliminate the direct menace to the very heart of Turkey policy which is implied in the proposal *to found a sort of Kurdish National Home* in northern Irak, just across the southeastern frontier of Turkey" (emphasis added). Chamberlain continued, "His Majesty's government are, however, in an unfortunate dilemma in this matter for the commission of the council of the League of Nations had stipulated as essential conditions for union with Iraq of the territory south of the Brussels line that due consideration must be paid to the desire of the Kurds to use Kurdish, to build schools, and to have autonomy in local administration in the hands of Kurdish officers and police." As early as 3 September 1925, Chamberlain informed Lindsay that L. S. Amery, secretary of the colonies, had informed the council that the British were already carrying out its wishes, which would be "made more effective." On 4 September, Amery stated to the council that "the Kurdish population enjoys wide measure of racial autonomy at this moment, *and we are prepared to extend it . . . but we shall not create an autonomous Kurdish State*" (emphasis added). This means, said Sir John Shuckburgh, head of the Middle East Department, that "we are in our usual unhappy position of facing both ways. Our obligations to the League *require us to foster Kurdish Autonomy* (within limits); our relations with the Turks to make it appear that we are doing nothing of the kind" (emphasis added). This could be especially embarrassing to "the Turks in dealing with their own Kurdish problem."[35]

As negotiations over resolution of the Mosul question accelerated in spring 1926, the Turks had cause for concern. As of March 1925, Kurds, who represented seventeen percent of the total population of Iraq, formed twenty-four percent of the entire police force of Iraq, fourteen percent of the army, and twenty-three percent of the railway employees. The police, army, and railways of Iraq had a total personnel of 20,000, of whom twenty percent or 4,000 were Kurds. Furthermore, sixteen out of twenty-five schools in Kurdish districts used Kurdish as the language of instruction. In four other schools Kurdish and Arabic were both used freely. Fifty-two Kurdish teachers taught in the schools; there were only eight non-Kurdish teachers. Moreover, twenty-two Kurds taught in areas outside the Kurdish districts. In addition to these measures, Great Britain and the Iraq government were doing "everything possible . . . not only to permit, but actually to encourage, the free use of the Kurdish language." Despite Great Britain's policy, sanctioned and promulgated through the League of Nations, to create "a National Home for the Kurds" and the threat this implied to Turkey's sovereignty and territorial integrity as expressed in the National Pact of 1920, Turkey was compelled to sign a treaty with Great Britain and Iraq on 5 June 1926. Sixteen of the eighteen articles of the treaty dealt with the frontier and with the Kurds. Articles 6 through 13 and articles 15 and 16 dealt specifically with "Good Neighborly Relations"—the control of the Kurdish populations.[36]

The only article of the treaty, number 14, that did not deal with the frontier or the Kurds stipulated that the Iraqi government would pay the Turkish government ten percent of the royalties it received from the Turkish Petroleum Company under article 10 of its concession of 14 March 1925. The exchange of the ten percent for 500,000 pounds sterling and other matters pertaining to the oil concession were dealt with in an annex to the treaty and did not even merit an article in the treaty itself. This was done to shield the transaction from as much public scrutiny as possible, as the British conceded that it "is somewhat in the nature of a bribe." It also demonstrated that oil was not the only significant factor in the settlement of the Mosul question. In fact it is rarely mentioned in the Foreign Office, Colonial Office, or Air Ministry records in the Public Record Office in direct relation to the frontier dispute with Turkey or with regard to wider policy implications of the British and, as far as can be determined on the available evidence, the Turkish policies toward the Kurds. Indeed, Turkish receipt of part of the oil revenues in lieu of receipt of a cash payment only cropped up in the negotiations between Ronald Lindsay and Tevfik Rüstü in April and May 1926.[37] On 21 April, Tevfik Rüstü told Lindsay that Turkey was not primarily interested in territory and raised the demand that Turkey be allowed to participate in the oil exploitation of Iraq. Although Great Britain was prepared to purchase Turkish acquiescence with oil, Sir Ronald Lindsay's instruction did not specifically mention it as an inducement for Turkey to sign the treaty. The alacrity (there was not much haggling) with which the Turks accepted whatever the British offered with regard to oil revenues suggests strongly that the Turks were much more interested in security, and in controlling the Kurds in Iraq, than they were in oil. In fact, it seems to me quite possible that the Turks raised the issue of participating in Iraqi oil exploitation and/or revenues as a guise to conceal their profound and real interest in the security measures of the treaty, which they very much wanted to obtain in the wake of the Sheikh Said rebellion.[38]

Recent studies by Helmut Mejcher, Peter Sluglett, and Marian Kent and older studies by Karl Hoffman and Elizabeth Monroe stress that oil was the center of the Mosul question. In the light of my research and arguments offered here, these assertions seem somewhat forced. Even if oil was the most important issue for Britain, which it was not, it certainly was not for Turkey, whose foremost concern was the Kurds and the accompanying problems of security. It seems to me that oil was probably not the most important factor for Great Britain with regard to the Mosul question: imperial, strategic, ethnic, and political considerations were probably commensurate with the concern for oil. As William Stivers has demonstrated, the control of oil in Iraq was crucial to British imperial policies in the Middle East and elsewhere in the world. The British even sought at different times to utilize the oil of Mosul to induce the United States oil companies to support British imperialism. The American oil companies were happy to oblige when they thought it would provide them an entrée to Middle East oil. Subsequently, however, Great Britain, the United States, and the oil companies had serious differences over access to Middle East oil, especially during negotiations that led to the Red Line agreement in 1929. In this sense, the British government, as Mejcher suggests, was more concerned with British interests in Mosul than with Iraq's, but not especially or only with respect to oil.[39]

The assertions of the British government and its representatives— Bonar Law, Lord Curzon, Ramsey MacDonald, and Austen Chamberlain—that oil was not at the heart of the Mosul question are correct, at least for the period to 5 June 1926. The arguments of the British that ethnic and/or racial and strategic interests were at the center of the Mosul question are accurate in my judgment. The reason for the imbalance in the more recent studies and the others mentioned above is that they are concerned with oil policy or with the wider implications of British imperialism in the Middle East and the rest of the world; very few address problems posed by the Kurds except in the most cursory manner. The rebellion of Sheikh Said, for example, and its international consequences have been virtually overlooked. Furthermore, the profound implications of the Sheikh Said rebellion for the internal politics of Turkey—the major concern of Turkey—are never mentioned at all. Yet in the Colonial Office, Foreign Office, and especially Air Ministry records, there are literally thousands of pages devoted to the Sheikh Said rebellion itself. Rather than oil being the crucial factor of British policy in the Mosul question, and in the Middle East, it was generally the British policy of fostering Kurdish nationalism and establishing "a National Home for the Kurds" that was among paramount issues in 1925–1926. It was this policy that the Turks thought so threatening to their external and internal security. If the only concern between Turkey and Great Britain had been oil, it is unlikely that the Mosul question would have been resolved in June 1926, as a result of the ramifications of the Sheikh Said rebellion in 1925. Without the Sheikh Said rebellion, Great Britain and Turkey very likely would have resolved their differences anyway, but at a later date and probably on terms advantageous to Turkey.[40]

The treaty between Great Britain and Turkey was also probably facilitated by the perception of both the Turks and the British that the Kurds were a group of diverse tribes incapable of ruling themselves and of achieving real independence.[41] Whether this was the true assessment of Ronald Lindsay or Kemal Atatürk is difficult to determine, but its mutual announcement helped to consolidate the agreement of 5 June 1926. It is possible that the British perception that the Kurds would not achieve the degree of nationalism sufficient to jeopardize their Sharifian and Middle Eastern policies encouraged them to continue their policy of support for a national home for the Kurds, an autonomous entity to keep the central government in check that would allow sufficient British control to ensure that an independent Kurdistan would not emerge. The policy was to be sufficiently ambiguous to allow Kurdish nationalists to hope that an independent Kurdistan could be achieved in future propitious circumstances. It may be that British views were influenced by what they considered as the great success already obtained by their support of a national home for the Jews in Palestine.

Consequences

The major international consequences of the Sheikh Said rebellion, then, may be summed up as follows:

(1) It facilitated the negotiations that led to the resolution of the Mosul question, with all of its consequences, in the treaty between Great Britain and Turkey and Iraq on 5 June 1926.

(2) It allowed Great Britain to utilize even more effectively the League of Nations as an instrument of British and European policy

against Turkey and subsequently as an instrument to implement British imperial policy.

(3) As a result, Turkey thought itself challenged by Greece, Yugo-slavia, and Italy and deprived of any support diplomatically or other-wise from Germany or the Soviet Union, both of which wanted to reestablish themselves in European politics through the League of Nations and through bilateral relations. In addition, Great Britain, through the League of Nations and bilateral arrangements, had es-tablished good relations with Italy and France that increased Tur-key's isolation in 1925. As soon as Great Britain and Turkey signed their treaty, in fact even prior to signing it, relations between France and Italy improved. On 30 May 1926, France and Turkey signed a treaty of friendship and relations with Italy improved.[42]

(4) It became clear during the Sheikh Said rebellion that the Soviet Union would not interfere in Turkey's internal affairs and support Kurdish nationalism, just as in 1924–1925 it had not challenged Reza Khan during the Turcoman-Kurdish rebellion in Khurasan. It became clear in 1925 that the Soviet Union, therefore, would not challenge a resolution of the Mosul question between Turkey and Great Britain. A stronger Turkey was more in the interest of the So-viet Union in 1925 as a buffer against Great Britain than as a weak and fragmented state. In addition, many Turkish and Soviet Com-munists viewed the Sheikh Said rebellion as feudal and counter-revolutionary.[43] In short, for various and different reasons, both Great Britain and the Soviet Union supported Mustafa Kemal's na-tionalist Turkey.

(5) The Sheikh Said rebellion, aiding as it did the expeditious reso-lution of the Mosul question, contributed to the success of Great Britain's Sharifian policies in Iraq and therefore to the suppression of Arab nationalism—hence the need for closer relations between Iraq and Syria and their mandatory powers.

(6) The Sheikh Said rebellion was instrumental in bringing about the treaty of friendship between Turkey and Iran on 22 April 1926 and the signing of a definitive border treaty in 1932. It also led to the demise of Turkish hope, as realized by the British, and of breaking down the Kurdish wall between Turkey and Azerbayjan.

(7) The rebellion had the consequence of Turkey's eschewing in-terference in the internal affairs of other countries and contributed to the Turkish motto: peace at home and peace abroad.

(8) The Sheikh Said rebellion forced Turkey to abandon any hopes it may have nursed for an assertive foreign policy and to form a non-interventionist foreign policy.

(9) The rebellion helped force Turkey to accept the British policy

of creating "a National Home for the Kurds" in Iraq with the potential consequences of its development if not constrained by the security measures of the 5 June 1926 treaty. The treaty meant that Great Britain and Turkey would have mutual interests in preventing a Kurdish national state of Kurdish autonomy other than in Iraq while at the same time pursuing drastically different policies toward the Kurds and Kurdish nationalism.

(10) The Sheikh Said rebellion and its aftermath helped to promote a wider rapprochement between Great Britain and Turkey. Among its key elements was the fact that Great Britain wanted to prevent close relations between Turkey and the Soviet Union.

(11) The rebellion excluded or reduced Turkish access to the oil of Mosul *vilayet* and it allowed Great Britain to use it to consolidate support for the British Empire by allowing foreign oil companies, especially American, to participate in the exploitation of the oil.

(12) The rebellion forced Turkey to concentrate on internal construction, to expedite secularization, and energetically to encourage Turkish nationalism.

(13) The rebellion led to the suppression of Kurdish nationalism in Turkey.

(14) The Sheikh Said rebellion reduced the utility of Islam as a vehicle of challenge and/or opposition to the other governments in the Middle East and in other Arab and Muslim countries. It also reduced the ability of those who wished to use Islam as a vehicle of cooperation with other Muslim states or to include it in international objectives.

Conclusion

THE SHEIKH Said rebellion was the first large-scale nationalist rebellion by the Kurds. The role of the Azadi was fundamental in its unfolding. Kurdish intellectuals and military officers lay at the heart of the nationalist movement, in terms of organization and recruitment. The paramount influence of the more secular or noncleric Kurdish nationalist organizations must be separated from the rebellion itself and its sheikhly leadership. The Sheikh Said rebellion was led largely by sheikhs, a deliberate determination by the leadership of the Azadi from 1921 onward. These decisions were defined and given force in the Azadi congresses of 1924.[1] The fact that the rebellion had a religious character was the result of Azadi's assessment of the strategy and tactics necessary for carrying out a successful revolution. While the Sheikh Said rebellion was a nationalist rebellion, its mobilization, propaganda, and symbols were those of a religious rebellion. It must be remembered that it was and continued to be characterized by most Turkish scholars (such as Behçet Cemal and Metin Toker) as a religious rebellion, instigated by reactionaries, who happened to be Kurds, against the secularizing reforms of the Kemalist government from 1922 onward (especially the abolition of the caliphate on 3 March 1924 and the National Law Court Organization Regulation among others).

It should be noted, however, that recently some Turkish scholars have also characterized the rebellion as "a nationalist rebellion in religious garb." The basis of this is the fact that Sheikh Said was an ardent nationalist, as demonstrated by his earlier career. The consensus of scholarship in the 1960s and 1970s (much of it emanating from Western social scientists and orientalists) that nationalism and genuine religious commitment and spirituality, especially Islamic, are incompatible is not valid in the case of Sheikh Said's rebellion. The Iranian revolution of the 1970s and 1980s has demonstrated forcefully the fallacy of this sort of reasoning. Martin van Bruinessen, the only scholar who has studied the rebellion in any detail, has stated emphatically that "the primary aim of both [Sheikh Said and the Azadi leaders] was the establishment of an independent Kurdistan."[2] Sheikh Said is an example of a man who was simultaneously an ardent nationalist and a committed believer. Many of the leaders of the Azadi and of the rebellion may have been genuinely upset by the abolition of the caliphate. For the average Kurd who participated in the rebellion, the religious and nationalist motivations were doubtless mixed. Most of the Kurds thought that the sheikhs who led the rebellion were religious and, more importantly, Kurds.

Many other crucial events, factors, and developments played a role in the rebellion. Many of the leaders wanted to protect their land, their domination of the markets for their livestock, and their control of the legal system, all or some of which seemed to be threatened by the secularizing and centralizing reforms of the central government in Ankara. The Sheikh Said rebellion was a turning point in the history of the Kurds in that nationalism was the prime factor in its organization and development. This is indicated by the fact that the subsequent large rebellions by the Kurds were nationalist and religious, employing nationalist symbols and propaganda. The Sheikh Said rebellion clearly demonstrated the direction that Kurdish nationalism was to take. In the Zeylan (1930) and Ağrı (1926–1932) rebellions, nationalist Kurdish slogans were used extensively.

This does not mean that traditional motivations of banditry and tribal feuds, as well as personal vendettas, were not prominent causal factors in the rebellion. In this and in other senses, the rebellion could be described as "primitive," as Amal Vinogradov describes the Iraqi revolt of 1920. But the Sheikh Said rebellion, like the Iraqi rebellion, was a genuine national response to fundamental dislocations in the political and socioeconomic spheres.[3] Like their Kurdish counterparts who had gained so much experience by their participation in the Hamidiye Regiments and in World War I, the Iraqi tribesmen (some of whom were Kurdish) who fought in the Ottoman army benefited from the military experience they gained in World War I. One of the interesting developments concerning the Sheikh Said rebellion of 1925 and the Jangali rebellion of Kuchak Khan in northern Iran from 1914 to 1921 is the supposed efficacy of arms and technology in supporting revolution and rebellion by dissident and nationalist minority groups. The participation of Kurdish, Arab, and Iranian tribesmen in the Ottoman, Qajar, and British armies and their familiarity with the substantial technological and military changes that had been occurring since the 1880s may have contributed to their conviction that these weapons and organizational methods could be used effectively in their own national movements. Their assessments may have been sound. It was the misfortune of all three rebellions, however, that they were challenged and defeated by more powerful forces and stronger nationalisms. In the case of the Kurds, it was the stronger state and more developed nationalism of the Turks. For Kuchak Khan in Gilan, the same was true. But, in addition, the Jangalis were deprived at crucial junctures of aid from the Soviet Union and the Communist movement. The Jangalis' opponent, the Iranian government, backed and supported by the British, was able to defeat the rebels. Unlike the Sheikh Said rebellion, British forces played a major role in the suppression and defeat of both the Jangali movement and the Iraqi revolt. It is possible that exposure to modern weapons, but not to modern diplomacy, may have caused the leaders of all three rebellions and/or revolts to act prematurely.

The Sheikh Said rebellion was tribal. The proportionate number of nomadic tribesmen who took part in the rebellion was much higher than in the Iraqi and Jangali rebellions.[4] Few tribal or peasant cultivators participated in the rebellion as combatants. Indeed, as indicated above, the leaders of the rebellion did not even try to recruit the tribal and peasant cultivators, either because they thought little of them as fighters or because they thought that the peasants were simply too much under the thumb of the landlords through fear, coercion, or indifference. The role of the tribal and peasant cultivators was much greater in the Iraqi and Jangali rebellions. It is difficult to know how much land was owned by *derebeys* and/or *ağas* within the area of rebellion, although there were a number of large landowners in the extended area (e.g., Diyarbakır) of the rebellion (see map 2). If tribal chiefs are classified as *derebeys* or *ağas*, then it seems that most of them were engaged in animal husbandry. But the landlords of the Diyarbakır plains opposed the rebellion. They played a principal role in assuring that Diyarbakır remained loyal to the Turkish government when it was attacked and besieged by Sheikh Said. The cooperation of these *ağas* with the government is another indication of the strong ties that the Kemalists had already established with many Kurdish *ağas* and chiefs. It was a premonition of a future when they were to become one of the mainstays of the Atatürk coalition.[5]

The rebellion did not demonstrate much tribal coordination with urban dwellers. Diyarbakır, heavily Kurdish, did not rise in support of the rebels. The populace of Elazığ initially surrendered without fighting, only to turn against the rebels because of their excessive looting and pillage. Again urban participation in the Iraqi and Jangali rebellions was greater than in the Sheikh Said rebellion. The coordination with urban groups was inhibited by the territorial isolation of the core area of the rebellion. Communication, except on horse or donkey, was impossible, especially after the telegraph lines were cut. Also, telegraph lines had not yet been extended to many towns. The establishment of Azadi in Erzurum after 1921, in addition to the split in the Kurdish nationalist movement, resulted in less contact with the Kurdish nationalists in Istanbul, although, as we have seen above, contacts between Azadi and İstanbul were maintained." The ulama and sheikhs played a large and influential role in the Jangali and Iraqi rebellions, as they did in the rebellion of Sheikh Said. Their input in the rebellion of Sheikh Said was significantly greater than in the other two. This could also suggest, as I argue above, that the nationalist tenor of the Sheikh Said rebellion was even stronger than that of the other two rebellions.

The Sheikh Said rebellion, then, was a prototype of a post–World War I nationalist rebellion. Its weaknesses were the usual ones: intertribal rivalry and Sunni-Shiʿi differences, especially as represented by the Hormek-Cibran tribal conflict, contributed to the lack of success of the rising. These cleavages were exacerbated by the Nakşbandi/non-Nakşbandi differences as well. These, rather than the differences between Zaza and non-Zaza speakers, played an important role in the evolution of the rebellion and in the growth of Kurdish nationalism. Urban-rural cleavages, tribal-peasant and landowner-tribal hostilities, and antithetical secular-religious orientations among its leaders all contributed to its lack of success. The Sheikh Said rebellion represented an incipient nationalism that was also challenged by a strong Turkish nationalism that had been mobilized in the course of the past thirty years, gathered strength during World War I, and was further energized by the war of liberation with the power of an organized state behind it. Turkish nationalists claimed the territory on which the Kurdish nationalists wanted to create an independent Kurdistan. The Turks also proclaimed a nationalism that was inclusive of the Kurds, however prejudicial, while Kurdish nationalism, imperatively so, was exclusive of the Turks and their nationalism. This made Turkish nationalism initially stronger ideologically than Kurdish nationalism.

The Sheikh Said rebellion demonstrated, territorially and politically, the increased vulnerability of the Kurds as a result of the displacement, deportation, and massacre of Armenians during World War I. The removal of the Armenians also removed the buffers of protection that their presence and nationalism offered the Kurds. The situation of the Kurds and the suppression of their nationalism was even more ironic in light of their eager participation in the deportation and massacres of the Armenians in 1915 and subsequently. The truly tragic meaning that the elimination of the Armenians held for the Kurds and Kurdish nationalism was recognized, as mentioned earlier, by some of the Kurdish nationalist leaders such as Halid Beg Cibran.

In assessing the effect of the rebellion on Turkey's history and politics, my position differs from that of Erik Jan Zürcher and that of Metin Toker. Zürcher in his recent study assigns the Sheikh Said rebellion and its aftermath only two paragraphs, while he devotes an entire chapter to the purges of 1926.[7] Metin Toker, on the other hand, wrote an entire book on the subject of the Sheikh Said rebellion, in an attempt to demonstrate that it represented a turning point in the history of the modern Turkish republic. To be sure, Toker states that one has to make a distinction between the event of the rebellion itself and its consequences. As an event, says Toker, the rebellion was not much. As soon as the Turkish armed forces were able to mobilize, it was crushed. The tenor of my argument here is that the Sheikh Said rebellion, even as an event, was much more important than Toker suggests and profoundly more so than Zürcher indicates.

Metin Toker is correct, however, in asserting that the consequences of the rebellion for Turkey, especially the Kemalists, were far more important than the rebellion itself. The main reason for this is that Toker is convinced, rightly in my judgment, that military action by the Kurds—even if they had displayed much more unity, cooperation, and coordination than they did—would never have withstood a focused attack by the experienced Turkish forces. However, the rebellion as an event was more important than Toker asserts because he refuses to acknowledge that it represented a challenging nationalism in competition with Turkish nationalism and, hence, threatening to the Turkish state.

In terms of domestic Turkish politics, the rebellion was, in my opinion, nearly as important as Toker suggests. According to Toker, the rebellion gave the Kemalists, or "radicals" as he calls them, an opportunity to silence the criticism of the Istanbul press, which was aligned with oppositional groups and, shortly thereafter, regional newspapers as well. It also established the legal means via the Restoration of Order Law and the creation of independence tribunals to arrest the leading members of the opposition forces when the time was ripe, in June 1926 after the discovery of a plot in Izmir to assassinate Mustafa Kemal. Soon after the discovery of the alleged plot, twenty-one members of the Progressive Republican party and eleven of the most important members of the Committee of Union and Progress were arrested. Some escaped arrest only because they were abroad or went into hiding. Less than one month after the discovery of the plot, fifteen members of groups opposed to the Kemalists were condemned to death. Even the heroes of the revolution and of the war of liberation, such as Refet Bele, Rauf Orbay, and Kazım Karabekir, who managed to escape death, were never again to play significant roles in the politics of Turkey. The only exception was Fuad Cebesoy.[8]

The suppression of the opposition to the Kemalists in wake of the discovery of the assassination plot in Izmir in June 1926 has been dealt with adequately elsewhere.[9] The point that I wish to make here is that the machinery to facilitate the crushing of the opposition both politically and legally was put into place in the effort to suppress the Sheikh Said rebellion. Ironically, many of those sentenced to death in the Izmir assassination plot had voted for the very independence tribunals to which they fell victim. While the Kemalists had to wait until the purges of June–July 1926, nearly a year after the suppression of the Sheikh Said rebellion, to rid themselves of remaining opposition, the formal and organized opposition as represented by the Progressive Republican party was eliminated when the party was banned on 3 June 1925.

Metin Toker writes that it was only after the Sheikh Said rebellion that three "revolutions" were able to occur: the Code of Civil Law (Medeni Kanunu Devrimi) of 4 October 1926; the Dress and Headgear Law (Kiyafet Kanunu Devrimi) of 25 November 1925; and the Alphabet Law (Harf Kanunu) of 1 November 1928. These kinds of reform would only have been possible in a Turkey under the Restoration of Order Law. Indeed, Toker sees similarities between the period of 1925 and that of 1957–1960. In both instances, Ismet Inönü was able to assert his authority to restore order to the Kemalist program. Unfortunately, argues Toker, Celal Bayar and Adnan Menderes did not have in 1957–1960 the same power and legitimacy that Ismet Inönü and Mustafa Kemal possessed in 1925.[10]

In short, for Toker, the Sheikh Said rebellion remains a symbol of the impediments—conservativism, religious fanaticism, Muslim brotherhoods, and formal democratic opposition—that the "radical" Kemalists had to suppress or contain in order to proceed with their Western-oriented, capitalist-directed, heavy industry–biased modernization program. The Sheikh Said rebellion emphasized to the Kemalists that this program might be delayed through continuing political infighting or might not be carried out at all. The decisions to pursue the Kemalist road to modernization were probably determined a few years earlier, but certainly there was a solid core that wished to pursue this course expeditiously by 1924. It was the Sheikh Said rebellion that created the atmosphere and the mechanisms to carry out the purges of 1926. In this sense, Toker's analysis is correct. Zürcher does not sufficiently emphasize the atmosphere and context of the purges of 1926. The reason why the Sheikh Said rebellion is so important for Turkish history is that the laws and institutions created for its suppression were agreed to by those who opposed Kemalism. They agreed, no matter how reluctantly, because no patriotic Turkish official could tolerate a contending nationalism. Here we have a good example of laws and institutions created to suppress an "external" enemy that are later used by the group in power to quash "internal" opposition. The Kemalist opponents and Fethi Bey realized this and therefore tried to depict the rebellion as a regional uprising, certainly one that was not counterrevolutionary. But the fact that the rebellion was Kurdish and nationalist severely limited any objections that they could make. More strenuous opposition would have produced the charge that they were traitors. As it was, the members of the Progressive Republican party were charged with complicity in the rebellion, although such complicity was never proven.[11]

The Sheikh Said rebellion gave the Kemalist government a certain justification for categorizing serious opposition as being in league with the Kurds, having sympathy for Kurdish nationalism, or favoring ideologies that would strengthen Kurdish nationalism or Kurdish ethnic power. If the red flag of the leftists was hoisted beside the green flag of Sheikh Said (representing Kurdish nationalism as well as Islam), the menace of the rebellion's legacy would be even more of a threat to Kemalism and, possibly, in the future, to the Turkish state itself. The rebellion proved an opportunity to reduce the opposition to Kemalist modernization through the closing on 30 November 1925 of all *tarikats* (orders), *tekkes* (lodges), *zaviyes* (cells), and *türbes* (religious tombs). Religious titles were abolished and wearing of clerical garb was prohibited. The Dress Law was passed on 25 November 1926, aimed against religious centers of opposition as well as political groups that opposed implementation of the law for the purpose of enhancing its legitimacy against the Kemalists. What is important to note here is that these laws were passed in an atmosphere of political consciousness on the part of Turkish public that their implementation and acceptance would reduce the threat of Kurdish nationalism.

The Sheikh Said rebellion created and provided a means whereby most serious subsequent opposition to government policies or comprehensive disagreement with its progress laid open the possibility that the disaffected groups would be labeled as traitors. In the aftermath of the rebellion, it was relatively easy to color opposition forces with a hostile ethnic tinge. The vehicles created and the laws passed for the suppression of the rebellion and the symbols of opposition to the Kemalist program that it generated meant that the consolidation of the Turkish state and of Turkish nationalism were greatly expedited by the suppression and perceived threat of Kurdish nationalism. The nationalist aspirations of ten percent of the population had to be denied if the nationalist goals of the other ninety percent were to be achieved. It is in this sense that the Sheikh Said rebellion, its suppression, and its aftermath were more important than the purges of 1926, which simply eliminated the remaining opposition to the Kemalists' programs. Most of those who were purged or sentenced to death agreed or would have agreed with the position subsequently adopted by the Turkish government vis-à-vis the Kurds and their nationalism. After all, when opportunities arose after 1950 for different policies to be followed or implemented, they were not.

The suppression of the Sheikh Said rebellion contributed to the consolidation of the new Turkish republic, the evolution and domination of the Republican People's party (Cumhuriyet Halk Firkası) and the one-party state it represented up to 1950, and the greater articulation of the Turkish nationalism on which the party and the state were based.[12] The creation of a one-party state conditioned the lack of serious discussion of policy alternatives, which in turn meant that there was a monodimensionality to the possible ideological solutions to the problems and challenges that the young republic would confront. It is this unidimensional approach that led to the great surprise of the Republican People's party at the strength and appeal of the Democrat party in 1946. The inability of the Republican People's party to learn from the lesson of 1946 led inexorably to its defeat in 1950. In this sense, one of the reasons for the defeat of the People's party in 1950 was the legacy of the monodimensionality that the Sheikh Said rebellion and its consequences introduced into the Turkish polity. In fact, the entire post–World War II period, when the military was in power in 1960–1961, 1973, and from 1980 onward, follows a pattern shaped by the political and ideological consequences of the rebellion. Many factors contributed to the emergence of the modern Turkish polity—the Kurds and Kurdish nationalism may not be the single most important factor. But their influence on the development of modern Turkey has been most underestimated by scholars and students of Turkey.

It was stated in chapter 5 that seventeen of the eighteen military engagements in which the Turkish military fought from 1924 to 1938 occurred in Kurdistan. Information about post-1938 Turkish military engagements is not available, but, if it were, a similar situation would probably be noted. Turkey's armed forces intervened in Hatay in 1938, in Korea in 1950–1953, and in Cyprus in 1974. The military engagements against the Kurds far exceed the number of external interventions and engagements. By the 1980s, Turkey's military actions against the Kurds had assumed external as well as internal proportions. In 1983, 1985, 1986, 1987, and 1988, Turkish forces entered Iraq in order to suppress and contain Kurdish nationalist and guerrilla groups. The struggle against Kurdish nationalism, in which certain patterns of policies were implemented and against which certain nationalist, ideological, and psychological premises and attitudes were initially adopted in 1925, continued to play an important role in Turkey's policy decisions more than fifty years after the Sheikh Said rebellion. These factors will quite likely continue to influence Turkish policy well into the twenty-first century. Kurdish nationalism, articulated and symbolized by the Sheikh Said rebellion, will also continue far into the next century.

The objectives and policies of the third major party involved in the Sheikh Said rebellion, Great Britain, have been discussed in chapter 5. There is, however, another aspect to the international consequences of the rebellion that should be mentioned. Great Britain had consolidated its power in northern Iraq through its forward policy, adopted after the Air Ministry assumed control of military operations from the War Office in August 1922. From 1922 to 1925, the RAF, under the command of Sir John Salmond, who replaced Sir Hugh Trenchard as chief of the Air Staff in 1929, pursued a vigorous bombing policy against the Kurds and Arabs in northern Iraq. The bombing forced the Turkish forces led by Colonel Özdemir to retreat from Rawanduz in June 1923. In many ways, the formal treaty between Turkey and Iraq on 5 June 1926 was shaped by the success of the British bombing policies. As we have seen above, the new Turkish republic was quick to learn from the British. By the end of 1926, Turkey had acquired 106 aircraft. In the following years, air power was used extensively in military operations against the Kurds. Air power was an effective means by which the new Turkish republic consolidated its state power, especially against the Kurds, just as British air power was instrumental in consolidating Britain's imperial power in the post–World War I Middle East. The lessons learned regarding the use of air power in northern Iraq, especially during the period 1922–1925, were used to good advantage by the British in Sudan, the Northwest Frontier, Palestine, and other places. These examples are illustrative of the relationship between established empires and new states when the two are not in direct military conflict but both wish to subdue third parties following policies antagonistic to the empire or to the new state. It became easier for Britain and Turkey to bomb Kurds "than to make political concessions to Kurdish nationalism."[13]

In the period prior to the Sheikh Said rebellion, the Kurds (and Turks, too) had to face the new technology of massive bombing, including incendiary bombing at night. In the post–Sheikh Said period, the Kurds had to face the might of an experienced British air force, as well as the burgeoning and increasingly effective Turkish air force. It would be more than thirty-five years before the Kurds had adequate antiaircraft guns. In the intervening years, the Turks and the British (Iraqi) forces were able to extend their control over areas of Turkey and Iraq that were predominantly Kurdish. By 1926, the same bombing policies against the Kurds were followed by Reza Khan in Iran. The effective use of air power and its implied threat played an important role in the origins and consequences of the Sheikh Said rebellion. The psychological terror it induced in the peasant and nomadic peoples of Iraq and Turkey and Iran, especially through incendiary night bombing, proved to be especially effective. Iraq was, according to L. S. Amery, the British colonial secretary in 1925, "a splendid training ground for the Air Force."[14]

One of the results of this effective British use of air power between World War I and World War II largely against the peoples of British colonies was that it contributed to the unpreparedness of British air defenses against the Germans at the outbreak of World War II, what A. J. P. Taylor has called the RAF's "doctrine that overwhelming superiority was the only defence." "Right up to the outbreak of the second World War and even during it," the policy Lord Hugh Trenchard, who was chief air marshal from 1919 to 1929, had established was followed: "Bombing," he held, "could win a war all by itself; it was also the only means of not being bombed by others. Trenchard and his successors persistently neglected air defense." Trenchard had first witnessed the great effectiveness of strategic air bombing, sometimes in coordination with infantry, in northern Iraq during the early 1920s. Taylor was of the opinion that the successful use of British air power in northern Iraq contributed to the deterioration of the British army, the lack of mechanized vehicles, and the failure to create a sufficient air defense system in the 1920s and 1930s.[15] British success against Turkey and then against the Kurds and Arabs in northern Iraq in the early 1920s may have contributed subsequently to the RAF's lack of preparedness against the Germans on the eve of and during the early years of World War II. Recent studies have confirmed Taylor's judgments.

Uri Bialer in his study of British air and defense policy in the 1930s concludes: "There can be no doubt that one of the main arguments against going to war in 1938 was the fact that Britain was defenceless against German bombers." Jafna Cox in his study of the role of the RAF in Iraq from 1919 to 1932 concludes that the British emphasis on bombers in Iraq led to the development of an unbalanced air force. He suggests that the extent to which this policy "may have influenced strategic doctrine during the Second World War is perhaps worthy of further attention."[16] Insofar as the successful suppression of Kurdish nationalism by use of air power contributed to the lack of British air defense preparedness to meet the German challenges and threats in the 1930s, one may say that Sheikh Said, so to speak, had his revenge: it proved very costly to Great Britain, Europe, and the Western world.

Appendix I: British and Turkish Army Officer Equivalents and Abbreviations

British

General Officer Commanding	GOC
Officer Commanding	OC
Other Ranks	ORS
Aide de Camp	ADC
Chief Signal Officer	CSO
Regiment	Regt.
Squadron	Squdr.
Battalion	Bttn.
Infantry	Infy.
Cavalry Detachment	Deth.
Company	Coy.
Small Arms (ammunition)	SA
Sycees (animal handlers)	

Turkish

Ferik (Fariq)	General of a Division
Mirliva (Mir Liwa)	Brigadier General
Miralay (Mir Alai)	Colonel
Kaymakam (Qaimaqam)	Lieutenant Colonel
Binbaşı (Binbashi)	Major
Yuzbaşı (Yuzbashi) Yuzb.	Captain
Mülazım (Mulazim) Mul.	Lieutenant
Mülazım-i-evvel (Awal)	First Lieutenant
Mülazım-i-sani (Thani)	Second Lieutenant

Appendix II: Draft Law for a Proposed Autonomy of Kurdistan as Debated in the Grand National Assembly on 10 February 1922

(FO 371/7781 Eastern [Turkey], E 3553/96/65, no. 308; telegram from Sir H. Rumbold to the Marquess Curzon of Kedleston, [received April 3])

8. The following is a summary of the draft law referred to above:

(1) The Great National Assembly of Turkey, with the object of ensuring the progress of the Turkish nation in accordance with the requirements of civilisation, undertakes to establish an autonomous administration for the Kurdish national in harmony with their national customs.

(2) For the area, the inhabitants of which are in the majority Kurds, a Governor-General may be chosen by the dignitaries of that nation, together with an Assistant Governor-General and an inspector, who may be Turks or Kurds as the Great National Assembly may decide.

(3) The Great National Assembly shall also choose a Governor-General who must be an experienced administrator, with an honourable reputation, and respected by all the Kurdish nation.

(4) The Governor-General shall be nominated for three years; at the expiration of that period the nomination of the new Governor-General shall be made by (Kurdish) National Assembly, unless the majority of the Kurdish nation should desire the maintenance of the former Governor-General.

(5) Although the Great National Assembly may decide whether the Assistant Governor-General shall be a Turk or a Kurd, he shall, nevertheless, be elected directly by the Kurdish National Assembly. The nomination of the Governor-General, the Assistant Governor-General and the inspector must, however, be submitted for the approval of the Angora Government.

(6) The Kurdish National Assembly shall be formed in the eastern provinces by elections based upon universal suffrage, and the mandate of each Assembly shall be for three years. The Assembly shall meet on the 1st March each year, and will sit for four months. If, during this period, the Assembly is unable to complete its labours, the period may be prolonged at the request of a clear majority of members and with the approval of the Governor-General.

(7) The General Assembly shall have the right to examine the budget

of revenue and expenses of the administration of the eastern provinces and to enquire into injustices to which subordinate civil and administrative officials may be exposed. The Assembly may take definite decisions concerning the advancement and the prosperity of the country, and all these decisions shall be communicated to the Angora Government for the information of the Great National Assembly.

(8) The Great National Assembly shall decide in all disputes between the Governor-General and the Kurdish Assembly, and both parties must submit to its decision.

(9) Pending the settlement of boundaries by a mixed commission, the administrative area of Kurdistan shall consist of the provinces of Van, Bitlis, Diyarbekir and the sanjak of Dersim, together with certain casas [*kazas*] and nahies [*nahiyes*].

(10) With regard to the administration of Kurdistan judicial organisation shall be created in harmony with local usages for special areas. For the time being this organisation shall consist of competent officials, half of whom shall be Turkish and other half Kurdish. Upon retirement of the Turkish officials they may be replaced by Kurds.

(11) From the date of the application of this law no taxes shall be imposed either under the form of war contribution or any other form. All fiscal contribution hitherto in vigour shall be abandoned at the discretion of the local administration, and payments of taxes shall be made once a year only. The proportion of net revenue to be paid to the Angora Government shall be settled by a mixed commission consisting of Deputies of the Great National Assembly of Angora and the Kurdish National Assembly.

(12) A corps of gendarmerie shall be formed to maintain order in the eastern provinces. The Kurdish Assembly shall elaborate the law governing this body, but the chief administration of the gendarmerie shall be in the hands of high Turkish officials until the conclusion of peace, when those who desire may return to their own country.

(13) Kurdish officers and soldiers in the Turkish army shall remain in their present service until the conclusion of peace, when those who desire may return to their own country.

(14) After the conclusion of peace the value of all animals and materials requisitioned both during and after the general war shall be a first charge, and shall be paid within twelve months at the latest.

(15) The Turkish language only shall be employed in the Kurdish National Assembly, the service of the Governorate and in the administration of the Government. The Kurdish language, however, may

be taught in the schools and the Governor may encourage its use provided that this shall not be made the basis of any future demand for the recognition of the Kurdish language as the official language of the government.

(16) The primary duty of the Kurdish National Assembly shall be to found a university with a law and medical faculty.

(17) No tax whatever may be imposed by the Kurdish National Assembly without the approval of the Governor-General and before the Great National Assembly of Angora shall be informed.

(18) No concessions of any kind shall be granted without first consulting the Great National Assembly of Angora and securing its consent.

It will be understood from this summary why the draft law was opposed with such energy by the Kurdish Deputies as described above.

I have, &c.
Horace Rumbold
High Commissioner

Appendix III: Azadi Membership as of September 1924

(Air 5/566; Kurdish names appear as written in the British documents.)

ERZERUM.

Miralai Khalid Beg.
(Head of the Society; previously Commander of Erzerum Garrison, now a merchant in Kars.)

Qaimmaqam Salim Beg.
Qaimmaqam Kuckuk Kazim Beg.
Miralai Kuchuk Raghib Beg.
Haji Maulud Effendi.
Notable of Erzerum.
or
Haji Dorsum Effendi.
Qaimmaqam Arif Beg.
Now Civil Qaimmaqam of Khinis.

Abdul Huda Jafar Beg.⎫
Arslan Beg. ⎬ Brothers.

CONSTANTINOPLE.
Saiyid Abdul Kadir Effendi.
(Head of Branch.)
Abdul Rahim, Lawyer.

KARS.
Yuzbashi Tawfiq Effendi.
(Head of Branch.)

BAYAZID.
Shaikh Ibrahim.

MELASHGIRD.
MENASGIRD.
Kur Hussain Pasha of Haidaranli tribe.
(Head of Branch.)

VARTAVA
(NEAR MELASHGIRD)
Khalid Beg.
(Head of Branch; distinct from President of Society.) Chief of the Hasserahli Kurds and Colonel of a Tribal Regiment.

KHINIS.
Rushti Effendi.
(Head of Branch.)
Yuzbashi Rashid Effendi.

MUSH.
BITLIS.

Yusuf Zia Beg, Ex-Deputy.
Binbashi Haji Hassan Beg.
Abdul Rahman Agha.⎫
⎬
Haji Darsum Aghi. ⎭
VAN.
Mullah Abdul Majid Effendi.

Sa'adun Beg, Kara Hisar.
Binbashi Arif Beg, Shamsaki.
Ali Beg.

(Head of Branch.)
Bitlis.
Shernakh (now in prison
   in Sairt).
Of Mush.

Brother of Mullah Sa'id
   Kurdi.
(Head of Branch.)
Chief of Hassaran Tribes.
Chief of Shamsaki Tribes.
Brother of Arif.

(**Note.** In early September informant heard that the well known Mullah
Sa'id Kurdi had left Constantinople for Van via Bitlis.)
SAIRT.

Yuzbashi Ihsan Beg.
Haji Abdullah Effendi, Merchant.
Darwish Beg, Inspector of Customs.
Qaimmaqam Razzak Beg.

Miralai Wais Beg.
SHERNAKH.
Sulaiman Agha.

JAZIREH.
Haji Dursun Effendi.
Abdul Wahab Effendi.
Abdul Muttalib Effendi.
DIARBEKIR.
Jamil Pasha Zadah Akram Beg.
Doctor Fu'ad Beg.
Abdul Ghani Beg.
Doctor Nasim Beg.
Binbashi Mustpha Beg.
Qaimmaqam Adhan Beg.

(Head of Branch.)
Sairt.
Sairt.
Now Qaimmaqam of
   Belajik.
(Sent by Governor of
   Anatolia.)
Retired.

(Head of Branch.)
Haji Bairam Tribes.

Mudir of Sloopi Nahiyah.

(Head of Branch.)

1st Cavalry Division.
Native of Diarbekir
where he is known as
an enthusiastic
nationalist.

MARDIN.
Haji Khidr Effendi.
Qaimmaqam Khidr Beg of Dersim.   (Sent there from Dersim.)
                                                   Was OC 6th Regiment.
ERZING[J]AN.
KHARPUT.
DERSIM.
Kangor Zadah Ali Haidar.   (Head of Branch.)
                                                   (Tribes whom Azadi
                                                       counted on to give
                                                       them support.)

BITLIS AREA.
Haji Musa Beg and his sons.
Jamil Chatto.   Pachinar tribe.
Shaikh Salahuddin.
Mustapha Agha.   Gharzan tribes.
Ali Agha s/o Mustapha Agha.
VAN AREA.
Karawilli Dezgin Agha.   Artushi tribes.
Abu Bakr (brother of Lezgin).
Ismail Agha.   Gevdan tribe.
Umar Agha.   Mamkhuran tribe.
Ismail Agha Simko.   Shikak tribe.
Shaikh Abdul Rahman Effendi.   Berwardi tribe.
Shahin Agha.
Yahya Agha.   Jirikan tribe.
Yaqub Agha.   Aruh tribes.
SHERNAKH AREA.
Ali Khan Agha.
Mustapha ibn Abdul Rahman Agha.   Haji Bairam tribes.
Shahin ibn Sulaiman Agha.
'Agid Agha.
Umar Timur Agha.   Chief of Batwan tribes.
Shaikh Tahir.   Batman tribes.
MARDIN AREA.
Rammo Agha of Zangard.
Aiyub Beg.   Milan tribes.
Isa Agha.
Ibrahim Agha.   Dakouri tribes.
Faris Agha.
Mahmud Beg ibn Ibrahim Pasha.   Milli tribes.

Appendix IV: List of Kurdish Officers Who Deserted after the Mutiny of Beyt Şebab

(Air 23/279; Kurdish names are given as rendered in document.)

Name/Rank	Arrived-Departed
Abdul Majid/Yuzbashi	20/3/24 −25/8/24
Abbas Eff./Mulazim awal	26/8/24 −31/8/24
Khorshid Eff./Mulazim awal	20/9/24 −21/9/24
Ahmad Adib Eff./Yuzbashi	20/9/24 −10/10/24
Ihsan Nuri/Yuzbashi	27/9/24 −24/10/24
Towfiq Eff./Mulazim awal	27/9/24 −24/10/24
Rassim Eff./Mulazim awal	27/9/24 −24/10/24
Said Fahmi/Yuzbashi	24/10/24−28/10/24
Ahmad Bey/Civil Qaimaqam	25/10/24
Sayid Mohammad/Imam	27/11/24−22/1/25
Mohammad ibn Shaikh Abdullah/Imam	12/12/24−12/12/24
Abbas Eff./Yuzbashi	15/12/24−21/12/24
Shakir/Teacher	7/3/25 −10/3/25
Khalil ibn Musafa/Private	8/8/24
Ahmad/Private	8/8/24
Abdur Rahman/Private	21/9/24
Mustafa/Private	21/9/24
Ali ibn Shaikho Ibrahim/Private	18/10/24−24/2/25
Saleh/Private	1/11/24
Mohammad/Chaush	1/1/25 −13/1/25
Cholo/Private	17/1/25 −3/2/25
Abdur Rahman/Private	17/1/25 −3/2/25
Wali/Private	17/1/25 −3/2/25
Mohammad ibn Abdur Rahman/Chaush	18/1/25 −18/1/25
Jama'a ibn Mustafa/Private	30/1/25 −3/2/25
Wali ibn Ayub/Private	30/1/25 −3/2/25
Aziz ibn Khalil/Private	30/1/25 −3/2/25
Shukri/Private	30/1/25 −3/2/25
Ahmad Hamdi/Mulazim awal	7/4/25
Abdul Karim/Mulazim awal	22/4/25

Appendix V: Intercepted Letter from Turkish Intelligence Meant to Implicate Ihsan Nuri as a Spy

(Air 23/436)
VERY SECRET

SPECIAL INTERCEPT
TRANSLATION OF TURKISH CIPHER LETTER

Addressed to: Q. 40. (Q = Turkish letter Qaf).

Comrades!
We will soon see the sun of salvation which will rise as the day when our beloved MOSUL will once more be united to our Fatherland with the help of God.

The Turkish Government has secured the inclusion of a Turkish mission, composed of young, active and honourable men, in the neutral Commission appointed by the League of Nations which is going to MOSUL. The Commission of the League of Nations accompanied by our delegates will go to MOSUL by land in the second week of January by car via ALEPPO and DAMASCUS. In our mission are the KIRKUK deputy NAZIM Bey and the SULEIMANIYEH Deputy FETTAH Bey and some Foreign Office officials. We announce this good news to you. We deem it necessary that your Committee should secure from now the following means to show the Commission, which will arrive there to examine the question, by deeds that the Nation desires union with the Fatherland.

1. It is necessary that the MOSUL Committee, which will control the public opinion in MOSUL in accordance with the wishes of the Turkish Government and Nation, should be prosperous. Therefore you must inform us what moral or material assistance is required to achieve this end.

2. The Committee should have influence not only in MOSUL but also in every caza, Nahiyeh and village and it should lead and instruct how to act. In view of the fact that some of the members may occasionally be arrested and disappear, in order not to prejudice the organisation and activities of the Committee, Committees should be set up with all possible speed all over the Vilayet. Committees thus established should be reported.

3. Men approved by your Committee, especially those individuals, chiefs of tribes and sheikhs of the localities to be visited by the Commission, will receive suitable gifts through you. On this point send your proposals with all speed.

4. Your decision, as regards to the holding of demonstrations by the people against the British and the Government of IRAQ in the places where

the Commission of Enquiry of the League of Nations will go, has been approved. If the people make demonstrations in favour of TURKEY in districts visited by the commission, our cause will derive much profit. In order that advantage may not be taken by the British of the League of Nations commissioners' ignorance of the language and that the demonstrations may not be diverted to the profit of the English, it would be well to carry a Turkish flag during the demonstrations. As far as the situation allows it would be well for one or more big and small flags to be carried or that everyone should produce a small flag from his pocket.

5. As the English have prepared several memoranda against us and sent them to the League of Nations, it would be very effective if your Committee could produce several memoranda with lots of signatures from different places in the Vilayet showing their desire for union with TURKEY and give it or have it given to the Commission. This is very important.

6. In short, the people of MOSUL must strain every nerve either by demonstrations or preparing memoranda or by any other means to show their love for and the ties that bind them to TURKEY. They must not fear of the threats or propaganda which the English might make at this time. In fact, as the English Government has officially accepted this Commission of Enquiry, they will not dare to bring any pressure to bear on the people under the eyes of the Commission. Apart from this, every action or pressure brought to bear will be met by protests and interpellation by the Turkish Government. If the populace of MOSUL wish to be saved in a ?peaceful? way, they should take advantage of the arrival of the Commission of Enquiry, and this is possible for them.

7. There are few officers, who during the activities of the NESTORIANS in and near MOSUL, turned traitor and betrayed their country and deserted. Strong measures must be taken to stop the activities of these men. These men were afraid of fighting and ran away. They are regarded as traitors by the Government and therefore are not reliable persons.

8. In the near future posters will be sent printed in Turkish and Kurdish by the Government addressed to the honourable population of MOSUL. These must be distributed to the populace and those interested before the arrival of the Commission. In addition to this 60 copies of the memoranda which were submitted by our government to the League of Nations claiming that MOSUL belonged to TURKEY, must also be distributed to all concerned, such as chiefs and sheikhs, etc.

9. In short, it must be thoroughly understood that our Government insists in its claims and views about the MOSUL Vilayet, and with the help of God, will achieve our object. Only that, as the English have stated that they would accept the verdict of the League of Nations, we must make sure that the League of Nations gives a verdict in our favour. For this reason it is necessary for the inhabitants of the MOSUL Vilayet to make manifestly clear to the commission or, directly to the League of Nations by words and deeds, that they do not desire the British and Iraqi administration.

10. In addition to this our Government informs you and declares that, in order to secure the union of the MOSUL Vilayet with the Fatherland, no

stone has been or will be left unturned. The Government is working hard and will not lose this opportunity. If the population of MOSUL also work in a self-sacrificing and energetic manner the end will be easily obtained. Courage and perseverance are the keys that open the doors of success! God gives victory!

11. We have secured that these 10 paragraphs be communicated, through suitable means, to His Excellency SHAIKH MAHMOUD. You should communicate this to KIRKUK and ARBIL and they will distribute it to Cazas and Nahiyehs.

12. You must, in the way of propaganda, publish the facts that it has been decided to proclaim a general amnesty to those who served the British and worked with them, some to secure a livelihood, others to get position in order to turn their opinion in our favour.

13. You must make sure that the enclosed letter for IHSAN Effendi falls into the hands of the British Intelligence.

14. Please send a reply to this with all speed and let us know all your requirements by the hand of your most reliable agent. Dated: January 7th, 1925. Signature: D. 92. (D = Turkish Letter Dal)

VERY SECRET

TURKISH SPECIAL INTERCEPT

From: J. M. DIARBEKIR. To: Captain IHSAN Bey. Deserter 2nd Division. Date: 5.1.25.

Dear Brother,

I have received your long letter for which I have been waiting for a long time. The news you have supplied has been highly appreciated, and it has been decided to reap the benefits of this in future. You know that the Commission of League of Nations is shortly coming there. According to our previous decision you are requested to send (one or two words) immediately by a sure hand to . . . (about two words) . . .

Authority has been obtained for the increase of your allowance. It will be sent with the first of our men who come. Please instruct your colleagues about their duties in the places where they are domiciled . . . (about three words) . . . as the time has arrived for the solution of this question, you are requested to . . . (about three words) . . . in favour of TURKEY among the people in accordance with your promises and undertakings.

I end my letter and wish you success in your patriotic efforts. Compliments and greetings to other friends.

Your brother,
J. M.

Appendix VI: Colonel (Miralay) Özdemir's Proclamations to the Kurdish Tribes

(CO 730/32)

COMMAND OF THE NATIONAL OTTOMAN
MOVEMENTS IN SYRIA AND PALESTINE.
No. 41 of the 5th Shawat 340.
[5 June 1922]

In the name of God.

To the honourable and zealous nationalist AHMAD SHAKIR Agha,

Chief of DERAHIN.

After compliments, let it be known to you that we have come to this country for Jihad for the sake of God and his word and for defending our mother country, getting back Ottoman territories now in the hand of Foreign Governments.

God has said: "The real faith in God is Islam; God has grace and also his prophet and his faithful" and "Oh Prophet, ask the faithful to fight" and also "God's promises are good, he prefers the fighters (Mujahids) to those who sit down."

I have shown all my options in the way of how to raise the Millice (national) formations, and about the national movements, to Omar Agha Chief of the Jelian tribe; kindly meet him and he will let you understand whatever is necessary. God will help you in vanquishing.

(Sd.) EUZDAMIR,
Chief of the General National
Formations and Movements

Headquarters of the Syria and Palestine Committee of Organisation and National Liberty.

To: RASUL AGHA, Chief of the DIZAI tribe.

Dear Chieftain,
There is not a single Mohammedan who has not so far realised how great and serious was the calamity which befell our country in the Great War and also during the period which has elapsed since the Armistice. There is not a

single Mohammedan who does not understand the real and true purpose of the British, which has caused the occupation of Holy STAMBUL the seat of the Caliphate, by elements hostile to Islam, and the reduction of the Caliph, the "Pride of Mankind" (Glory and Praise be unto him), also to slavery; it has forced him by low means to comply with their orders; and finally, to sow hostility and dissent among the Mussalman population, and to break them finally, created the present objectionable situation in SOUTH KURDISTAN.

There is not a single soul who does not understand the spirit of the Government of FAISAL, a despicable instrument in the hands of the British. But this deplorable situation has affected the Honour of God, and therefore He, in order to prove the Miracles of the Prophet, who said in the holy words of the Koran that Islam would live until the Day of Resurrection, has thrown into the battlefield one MUSTAFA KEMAL to remove the enemy occupation from Ottoman territories and save them from desecration and turning out the foreigners who were in occupation of an important part of our country and, thank God, the country is regaining its independence.

For this reason the government was unable to render any important assistance in SOUTH KURDISTAN and in the MOSUL VILAYET. Now, thank God, we have come into this region in order to break the legs of the foreign forces ruling here and to save our Holy Country. With the mercy of God, we shall begin shortly to organise the people for a general movement.

I now advise you to attack the enemy with your tribe from the interior, as soon as we have started our operations in the north, provided that you remain at the head of your tribe. On this point there is no reason for hesitation or delay. We shall do our utmost in order to save our MOSUL VILAYET. I expect your co-operation with our action in due course. As assistance not rendered when it is due is of no use whatever to us, I do not want any promises from you in this matter.

I propose a meeting between yourself and our delegate who has been detailed to see you at any place you like and to explain our aims and plans in a more explicit language. If you wish, you may ask for an interview with us at any convenient place.

I send my greetings and respects to you and to the Chiefs of your tribe.

Dated 26th June 1922.

> EUZ DEMIR Commander of the al Jazirah and Iraq Organisation and General Movement

Appendix VII: Selected List of Turkish Officers in the Eastern Provinces in April 1925

(Air a3/?81; Turkish names are rendered as written in the British documents.)

IIIRD INSPECTORATE, ADV. HQ DIARBEKIR.

Inspector General	Fariq Izz ud Din Pasha.
CSO	Mir Alai Kazim of Kamakh (formerly OC 2nd Division).
Operations	Qaimaqam Fakhri.
Cavalry Adviser	Qaimaqam Hussain Nuri (formerly OC 9th Cav. Brigade).
Pioneer Adviser	Mir Alai Nafith of Erzinjan.
Infantry Adviser	??? Qaim. Jamil Hadi (reported Act. OC XVIIth Division).
Transport Adviser	Qaimaqam Abdullah of Kharput.
Medical Adviser	?
Veterinary Adviser	Mir Alai Ali Riza (formerly Veterinary Officer Al Jazirah Front).
Communications	
Records	

VIITH ARMY CORPS HQ DIARBEKIR.

GOC	Mir Liwa Mursal Pasha.
ADC	Yuzb. Ramis.
Military Secretary	Yuzb. Fadhil.
Chief Staff Officer	Qaimaqam Yusif Zia.

1st Section	Qaimaqam Mohammad Nuri.
(a) Operations	Yuzb. Jalal.
(b) Intelligence	
2nd Section (Personnel)	Binbashi Baha Bey.
3rd Section (Judicial)	Ibrahim Bey (Civilian).
Court Martial Officers	Qaimaqam Mihri.
	Binbashi Alias.
4th Section (S. and T.)	Mir Alai Khalis.
(a) Pay Office	Binbashi Ismail Haqqi.
(b) Supplies	Binbashi Osman (Act.).
(c) Ordnance	Binbashi Khalis.
5th Section (Medical)	Qaimaqam Ismail Haqqi.
6th Section (Veterinary)	
7th Section (Records)	Yuzb. Towif.
Inspector of Artillery	Binbashi Mustapha Rasim.
Markaz Qumandani (Camp Comdt.)	
Military Police	Yuzb. Salah ud Din.
HQ Cavalry Squadron	Yuzb. Tahsin.
	Mul Awal Bahjat (Sulamani).
HQ Guard Coy. (Infantry)	
Central Hospital	
Skilled Works Battalion	Binbashi Suliman.
Building Coy.	Yuzb. Suliman.
	Yuzb. Jamil.
Ordnance Workshops	Yuzb. Abdul Qadir.
Engineer Coy.	Yuzb. Nazim.
	Yuzb. Kazim.
Signal Coy.	Yuzb. Badri.
OC Wireless Telegraph	Yuzb. Zia (African).
OC Field Set	Yuzb. Siddiq.
OC Mountain Set	Mul. Thani Amin (Qonia).
OC Transport Coy.	Yuzb. Ahmad Hamdi.
OC Section	Mul. Tahir.
Animal Transport Coy.	Yuzb. Ali Ratib.
OC Section	Mul. Thani Zia (Stamboul).

HQ Artillery Battn. (Regiment?)
CO AA Battery
Liaison Officers:
  Jerablus   Yuzb. Nishat.
  Nisibin   Yuzb. Akram.
  Jazirah   Yuzb. Nazim Nafatchi
                                     (Kirkuk).
                                     Suliman Fff. (Kirkukli).

IIND DIVISION: HQ BITLIS.

GOC	Mir Liwa Kazim Pasha.
ADC	Yuzb. Ismail Haqqi.
Chief Staff Officer	Binbashi Yunni.
1st Section	Yuzb. Lutfi.
(a) Operation Mul. Awal	Mul. Awal Nuri.
(b) Intelligence	Mul. Thani Jawdat.
2nd Section (Personnel)	Yuzb. Mohammad Salim (Kharput).
3rd Section (Judicial)	Yusuf Bey (Civilian).
4th Section (S. and T.)	Binbashi Shawkat (Damascus).
(a) Pay Office	Regtl. Clerk Towfiq (Damascus).
(b) Supplies	Asst. Bn. Clerk Sayid Amin (Kirkuk).
(c) Ordnance	" " " Ismail Haqqi.
5th Section (Medical)	Qaimaqam Shukri.
6th Section (Veterinary)	Qaimaqam Nur ed Din (Anatolian).
7th Section (Records)	Mul. Awal Jamal.
HQ Cavalry Batt.	
HQ Infy. Coy.	
OC 2nd Infantry Brigade	Mir Alai Ali Bey.
Staff Officers, Infy. Brigade	Yuzb. Fakhri (Damascus)

2ND DIVISIONAL ARTILLERY REGT.

OC Regt.	Qaimaqam Munir.
OC 1st Battalion	Binbashi Towfiq (Smyrna).
OC 1st Battery	Yuzb. Sadiq.
OC 2nd Battery	Yuzb. Nur ed Din.
OC 2nd Battery	Binbashi Fawzi (Baghdad).
OC 3rd Battery	
OC 4th Battery	

1ST INFANTRY REGIMENT.
OC Regiment
OC 1st Battalion — Binbashi Anvar.
OC 2nd Battalion — Binbashi Mazhar.
6TH INFANTRY REGIMENT.
OC Regiment — Qaimaqam Ali Taimur.
OC 1st Battalion — Binbashi Omar.
OC 4th Coy. — Yuzb. Hilmi.
OC 2nd Battalion — Binbashi Faiq.
18TH INFANTRY REGIMENT.
OC Regiment
OC 1st Battalion, Acting — Yuzb. Ismail Haqqi (Oghuz).
OC Coy. — Yuzb. Ahmad Faiq.
OC 2nd Battn. — Binbashi Fuad.
OC Coy — Yuzb. Mustafa Hami (or Kamil).
Reported attached 18th Regt. — Binbashi Hussain.
but required confirmation. — Binbashi Suliman Fakhri.
XVIITH DIVISION:
GOC — Qaimaqam Jamil Hadi, formerly Infy. Adviser, IIIrd Inspectorate. Vice GOC Nur ed Din Pasha, Mir Liwa, OC Kharput area.
CSO — Binbashi Jawdat.
ADC
1st Section
2nd Section
3rd Section
4th Section — Binbashi Ghalis.
5th Section
6th Section
7th Section
OC 17th Infy. Brigade — Mir Alai Osman Bey.
ADC, OC
17th Infy. Brigade — Mul. Awal Lutfi.
17TH DIVISIONAL ARTILLERY REGIMENT.
25TH INFANTRY REGIMENT.
OC 1/25th Infy. Regt. — Qaimaqam Murad (Trebizond).
OC 1/25th Regt. — Binbashi Zaki (Arbil).

62ND INFANTRY REGIMENT.

OC 62nd Infy. Regt.	Qaim. Hassan Faiq.
OC Depot	?Towfiq.
Regtl. Clerk	Yuzb. Rasim.
OC 1st Battn. 62 Regt.	Binbashi Hassan Tahsin.
2nd in command, 1st Battn.	Mul. Awal Hamdi.
Doctor, 1st Battn.	Binbashi Ismail Haqqi.
Supply Officer 1st Battn.	?Suliman Eff.
OC 1st Coy. 1st Battn.	Yuzb. Talaat,
Coy. Officer	
OC 2nd Coy. 1st Battn.	Yuzb. Ibrahim ?Haqqi.
Reported OC 2nd Coy.	Yuzb. Hassan Fahmi.
Reported Coy. Officer	Mul. Thani Ihsan.
OC 3rd Coy. 1st Battn.	Yuzb. ?Ibrahim Haqqi.
Coy. Officer	Mul. Thani Bushar.
OC 4th, Machine Gun Coy.	Yuzb. Osman Other
	Officers reported attached
	to 1st Bttn.
	Mul. Awal Khalil.
	Mul. Thani Zia.

2ND BATTN. 62ND REGT.

OC 2/62nd Regt.	Binbashi Hussain Nazif.
2nd in command, 2nd Battn.	Binbashi Akram.
Supply Officer, 2nd Battn.	?Suliman Eff.
Coy. Officer	Yuzb. Hussain.
3rd Battn. 62nd. Regt.	
OC 3rd Battn.	Binbashi Bekr Sidqi.
	Officers reported
	belonging
	same battalion.
OC Coy.	Yuzbashi Qadir.
OC Coy.	Mul. Awal Nashat.
OC Coy.	Mul. Awal Shukri.
	Mul. Thani Saim.
	Mul. Thani Sanri.

63RD INFY. REGIMENT.

OC 63rd Infy. Regt.	Qaim. Mohammad Shahin.

1ST CAVALRY DIVISION, HQ MARDIN.

OC Acting	Mir Alai Adham (OC Brigade).
	Vice OC Mir Alai 'Arif reported unposted since

defeat of Division in
operating against Kurds
April 1925.

ADC — Yuzb. Saif ud din.
CSO
OC 1st Cavalry Brigade — Mir Alai Adham, Act. OC
Division.

ADC to OC Brigade
11TH CAV. REGIMENT.
OC 11th Cav. Regt. — Qaimaqam Nuri.
2nd in command, 14th Regt. — Qaimaqam Jamil.
21ST CAV. REGIMENT.
OC 21st Cav. Regt. — Qaim. Hussain Husni.
Doctor, 21st Regt. — Qaim. Hassan Basri.
Other officers reported
attached this Division
but Unit thereof not
known:
Binbashi Akram Qadhi
Zada.
Yuzb. Hussain Hilmi.
Yuzb. Shawkat.
Mulazim Rijab Munir.
Mulazim Abdullah.

XIVTH CAVALRY DIVISION. HQ URFA.
OC — Mir Alai Subhi.
CSO — Binbashi Hamid.
ADC — Binbashi Farid.
1st Section
2nd Section
3rd Section
4th Section — Binbashi Khairi.
5th Section — Qaimaqam Jalal.
6th Section — Qaimaqam Zia ud din.
DIVISIONAL ARTILLERY REGIMENT HQ

??Husni Bey.
3RD CAV. REGIMENT. — **QAIMAQAM FARHAT.**
5TH CAV. REGIMENT.
OC — Qaimaqam Jamil.
ADC — Yuzb. Faiq.
54TH CAV. REGIMENT.
OC

OTHER OFFICERS ATTACHED SAME DIVISION.

Reported Sec OC Artillery Battn.	Yuzb. Mustafa.
" " "	Yuzb. Khamis.
" " "	Yuzb. Hafiz Hilmi.
Reported OC 1st Squdn. 3rd Cav. Regt.	Yuzb. Hilmi.
" OC 2nd Squdn. " " "	Yuzb. Khamis.
" OC 3rd Squdn. " " "	Yuzb. Lutfi (Urfa).
" OC 4th Squdn. " " "	Yuab. Hussain (?Husni).
" Doctor to 3rd Cav. Regt.	Qaim. Kazim.

Appendix VIII: Diary of Events at Mezreh [Mamouret-el-Aziz], 23 March to 15 April

(From a letter written by a European inhabitant of the town.)

(FO 371/10837)

23rd March

News of the approach of the rebels was received, and in the evening a state of siege was proclaimed. The Vali when questioned endeavoured to re-assure the informant. He offered to transfer the cash at the Imperial Ottoman Bank to his house for safe-keeping. This was refused as there were no safes in the Government building.

24th March

Towards sunset sound of guns and firing of rifles and machine guns. The Vali in a car escorted by 25 mounted gendarmes fled.

Soon afterwards 300 Kurds entered the town and proceeded to sack; first the Government House, and then the Department House, and then the Department of Justice. They then opened the prison, and the prisoners showed the Kurds the houses of the officers and rich men so that the first could be made prisoners and the houses of the latter looted. In this looting the porters and woodchoppers of the town, mostly Kurds, also joined.

25th March

The rebels continued pillaging. Firstly the depot of military material, which was half emptied; then the Regie depot which lost about LT [Turkish Lira] 4000 tobacco and also the richer men of the town.

It was learnt that Sheikh Sheriff was in command and he entered the town about midday, went to the Konak (Government house) and promised to en-quirers that he would maintain order, but was unable to do so.

Later in the day, the population of the town, elected by a petition of 500 signatures, Mehmed Nouri Effendi, son of Ali Bey, an ex deputy and ex mufti of the town, who with Sheikh Sheriff went round the town and reas-sured the population that order would be maintained; and incidentally, the Director of the Imperial Ottoman Bank, on the request of the Vali and in-terim assured the Sheikh that they had not suffered any loss.

However, since the looting continued, towards the evening the directors of the Bank took away all the valuables in a car to Kharput.

26th March

During the day, the notables of the town tried to organise a militia amongst the population but there was not much enthusiasm, for although most of the population was armed as it always is, they did not like to show their arms for fear of being disarmed by the rebels.

However, one Rassim Bey an officer of the army managed to get some courage into the people and they eventually attacked the rebels; drove them out of the town leaving 50 dead; there were an equal number of casualties amongst the population.

27th March

Soldiers and officers came out of their hiding places and some of them put on their uniforms. Some rebels still held a house outside the town which the militia attacked without success.

28th March

The Vali and interim announced the opening of all government services and the directors of the bank returned to the town.

The Government at Angora sent its congratulations to the people and announced the early arrival of troops. Telegraphic communication which had been censored and letters had to be posted open.

Between the 28th of March and 16th April, Noureddin Pasha commanding the 17th Division arrived with some troops not enough to ensure the safety of the town as the rebels had not retreated east of the Murad river; the town was still in a state of panic for the pillaging of Chemishghezek north of Mezreh by the Dersim Kurds caused a great number of families to emigrate to Matlatia.

Notes

1. The Emergence of Kurdish Nationalism

1. The best discussion of the reign of Sheikh Ubaydallah is Wadie Jwaideh, "The Kurdish Nationalist Movement: Its Origins and Development," pp. 212–289, the first work to describe it as a movement with nationalist characteristics. See also John Joseph, *The Nestorians and Their Neighbors: A Study of Western Influence on Their Relations*, pp. 107–113. Joseph does not seem to have utilized Jwaideh's dissertation; it is not cited in his notes, although he does include it in his bibliography (p. 264). Maarten (Martin) van Bruinessen, *Agha, Shaikh and State: On the Social and Political Organization of Kurdistan*, is the best source, along with Jwaideh, on the social-political and national history of the Kurds in the nineteenth and twentieth centuries, although it allots only a few pages (328–329, 444 n. 84) to Sheikh Ubaydallah's movement. Basil Nikitine, *Les Kurdes: Etude sociologique et historique*, also has a brief discussion of Ubaydallah's rebellions and wars. My account of Sheikh Ubaydallah's movement relies on Jwaideh. For the rule of Bedir Khan Beg, see Jwaideh, "The Kurdish Nationalist Movement," pp. 176–212.

2. For the great influence of Muslim orders (*tarikats*) in Kurdistan, see van Bruinessen, *Agha, Shaikh and State*, pp. 249–339; Butrus Abu Manneh, "The Naqshbandiyya in the Ottoman Lands in the Early 19th Century," *Die Welt des Islams* 22/1–4 (1984): 1–35; Hamid Algar, "The Naqshbandi Order: A Preliminary Survey of Its History and Significance," *Studia Islamica* 44 (1977): 124–152; Albert Hourani, "Shaikh Khalid and the Naqshbandi Order," in *Islamic Philosophy and the Classical Tradition*, ed. Albert Hourani, S. M. Stern, and Vivian Brown, pp. 89–104. For a fuller treatment of the Nakşbandi movement in the Islamic world, see *Les confréries soufies dans le monde arabo-islamique: Les Naqshbandis*, ed. Alexander Popoviç and Marc Gaborieau, to be published in 1989.

3. Van Bruinessen, *Agha, Shaikh and State*, p. 225.

4. Jwaideh, "The Kurdish Nationalist Movement," p. 202. Bedir Khan Beg left another legacy. He was reportedly the father of some ninety children, several of whom, no doubt inspired by his legacy, became Kurdish nationalists. See Chris Kutschera, *Le movement national kurde*, p. 20.

5. Arshak Safrastian, *Kurds and Kurdistan*, pp. 62–63, who quotes from Vice-Consul Clayton's report dated 11 July 1880, p. 7 (Turkey, no. 5, 1881). Joseph, *The Nestorians and Their Neighbors*, pp. 109–110, includes a similar letter that states Ubaydallah's reasons for attacking Iran, which he did in October 1880. In this letter, Ubaydallah puts the Kurdish population

at 500,000 families. Calculating 5 persons per family, this would mean a population of 2.5 million people. Joseph cites *Parliamentary Papers* 100 (1881), cmd. 2851, no. 47 as his source.

6. Jwaideh, "The Kurdish Nationalist Movement," pp. 225, 215.

7. Ibid., p. 133. For highly interesting observations of some Kurdish sheikhs in the 1970s, see van Bruinessen, *Agha, Shaikh and State*, pp. 296–332. See also the same author's "Vom Osmanismus zum Separatismus: Religiöse und ethnische Hintergründe der Rebellion des Scheich Said," in *Jahrbuch zur Geschichte und Gesellschaft des Vorderen und Mittleren Orients 1984*, ed. Jochen Blaschke and Martin van Bruinessen, pp. 148–151.

8. Ibid., pp. 229–333. The sheikhs were only one of the groups that benefited from the Ottoman Land Code of 1858: *aġas*, rich merchants, and local government officials also profited. For more on this subject, see Albertine Jwaideh, "Midhat Pasha and the Land System of Lower Iraq," in *Middle Eastern Affairs*, ed. Albert Hourani, pp. 106–136. This is one of the best studies of the effects of the land code in lower Iraq. It describes how the reforms of Midhat Paşa in Iraq from 1869 to 1871 were detrimental to tribal cultivators. Through inexperience, bribes, and ignorance, deeds (*tapus, seneds*) were given to heads of tribal confederations, tribal chiefs residing in towns, or rich merchants. In Iraq the consequences of Midhat Paşa's attempted reforms contributed to the breakup of tribal confederations. Although the situation in lower Iraq was different than in Kurdistan, there is a parallel between the effects of the land code in lower Iraq, which reduced the power of chiefs of tribal confederations, and the destruction of the great Kurdish emirs and *derebeys* (literally, lords of the valley, who controlled vast tracts of territory), which contributed to the rise of sheikhs such as Ubaydallah. The granting of deeds (*tapus*) to tribal leaders was continued by the British as part of their policy of making the tribal leaders a fulcrum of their colonial rule. See Albertine Jwaideh, "Midhat Pasha," p. 135.

9. Jwaideh, "The Kurdish Nationalist Movement," p. 212.

10. Van Bruinessen, *Agha, Shaikh and State*, pp. 228–229.

11. For a full text of the Treaty of Berlin, see J. C. Hurewitz, *Diplomacy in the Near and Middle East: A Documentary Record: 1535–1914*, I, pp. 189–191; see also Sir Edward Hertslet, *The Map of Europe by Treaty*, IV, *1875 to 1891*, pp. 2759–2799 (article 61 on p. 2796). Hertslet's volumes have the advantage of being accompanied by maps.

12. Jwaideh, "The Kurdish Nationalist Movement," p. 231. Article 16 of the Treaty of San Stefano seemed to imply protection for the Armenians by Russia. But the Treaty of Berlin, which superseded the Treaty of San Stefano, abrogated Russia's ability to provide such protection. Responsibility for compelling the Ottomans to carry out the reforms was placed upon the European concert of nations. Richard G. Hovannisian, *Armenia on the Road to Independence, 1918*, p. 26, states that the Treaty of Berlin also elevated the "so-called Armenian question to a level of international diplomacy." The fact that article 16 of the Treaty of Berlin stimulated Kurdish nationalism was certainly detrimental to the creation of an Armenian state.

For the full text of the Treaty of San Stefano, see Hertslet, *The Map of Europe*, IV, pp. 2672–2696 (article 16 on p. 2686).

13. Jwaideh, "The Kurdish Nationalist Movement," p. 233, quoting Vice-Consul Clayton to Trotter, 11 July 1880 (Turkey, no. 5, 1881), p. 7.

14. Joseph, *The Nestorians and Their Neighbors*, p. 104, who quotes W. M. Ramsay, *Impressions of Turkey during Twelve Years' Wanderings*, p. 147. The British consuls were provided for in article I of the Convention of Defensive Alliance signed 4 June 1878. It is sometimes referred to as the Cyprus Convention. The text can be found in Hurewitz, *Diplomacy in the Near and Middle East*, pp. 188–189; Hertslet, *The Map of Europe*, IV, pp. 2722–2723. For the wider significance of the Cyprus Convention, see Dwight Ervin Lee, *Great Britain and the Cyprus Convention of 1878*, pp. 125–165.

15. Jwaideh, "The Kurdish Nationalist Movement," p. 224; his account on pp. 239–252 is the best source for the Kurdish League; see also Safrastian, *Kurds and Kurdistan*, p. 63. My version follows Jwaideh. Writing some twenty years after Jwaideh, a Turkish historian confirms that Abdulhamid II was supporting Ubaydallah and sending him arms. See Bayram Kodaman, "Hamidiye Hafif Süvari Alayları: II Abdülhamid ve Doğu-Anadolu Aşiretleri," *Tarih Dergisi* 32 (1979): 436.

16. Jwaideh, "The Kurdish Nationalist Movement," pp. 266–267. One of the consequences of Ubaydallah's invasion of Iran was the establishment of diplomatic relations with the United States; some members of Congress were outraged by the sheikh's attacks on the Nestorians.

17. Ibid., p. 281; van Bruinessen, "Vom Osmanismus," pp. 119–120.

18. I rely on four major works for this discussion of the Hamidiye. The best account is Kodaman, "Hamidiye Hafif Süvari Alayları," pp. 427–480, the only article dealing with the Hamidiye that utilizes the original documents; M. Nuri Dersimi, *Kürdistan Tarihinde Dersim*, pp. 76–93, has some information about the areas of the Sheikh Said rebellion; M. Şerif Firat, *Doğu Illeri ve Varto Tarihi*, devotes chapter 7, pp. 113–127, to the Hamidiye; Stephen Duguid, "The Politics of Unity: Hamidian Policy in Eastern Anatolia," *Middle Eastern Studies* 9 (May 1973): 139–155, provides a good interpretation of Sultan Abdulhamid II's policies (quotation on p. 139).

19. As an example of this policy, Kodaman, "Hamidiye Hafif Süvari Alayları," p. 437, suggests that Grand Vizer Said Paşa wanted to make some reforms for the Armenians. Abdulhamid II himself, however, thought that Said Paşa only advocated the reforms because he had received bribes from the Armenians. Kodaman suggests that Said Paşa's enthusiasm for the reforms indicates that he was dissembling.

20. Ibid., pp. 438–439, discusses the reason for these six objectives, which should be clear from the earlier discussion.

21. Duguid, "The Politics of Unity," p. 152.

22. Kodaman, "Hamidiye Hafif Süvari Alayları," pp. 450, 465; van Bruinessen, "Vom Osmanismus," pp. 121–122. Firat, *Doğu Illeri*, p. 114, suggests

that there were 1,200 men in each regiment, but this would mean that each regiment had a complete roster, which rarely occurred. Ismail Beşikçi, *Doğu Anadolu'nun Düzeni: Sosyo-Economik ve Etnik Temeller*, p. 237, repeats Firat's figures.

23. Kodaman, "Hamidiye Hafif Süvari Alayları," pp. 463–471, discusses Abdulhamid's order in detail (pp. 467–469 include the names of the tribes and the regiments to which they belonged); van Bruinessen, "Vom Osmanismus," p. 122.

24. Kodaman, "Hamidiye Hafif Süvari Alayları," p. 476.

25. Ibid., p. 478; Firat, *Doğu Illeri*, pp. 114, 117.

26. Halid Beg was the son of Mahmud Beg, the commander of the second Cibran regiment, who had been killed in 1902. Halid Beg replaced him as commander of the regiment. See Firat, *Doğu Illeri*, pp. 124, 149–153; van Bruinessen, "Vom Osmanismus," p. 123.

27. Bayram Kodaman, *Abdülhamid Devri Eğitimi Sistemi*, pp. 181–224.

28. Duguid, "The Politics of Unity," pp. 152–153.

29. Good short accounts of these Kurdish organizations are found in Jwaideh, "The Kurdish Nationalist Movement," pp. 297–386, and van Bruinessen, *Agha, Shaikh and State*, pp. 371–378, which I generally follow. The translator of Muhammad Amin Zakı, *Khulasat Tarikh al-Kurd wa Kurdistan min Aqdam al-Usur Hatta al-An*, Ali Avni, suggests that there may have been an organization preceding the Kürdistan Taali ve Terraki Cemiyeti (p. 319), called Kürdistan Azm-i Kavi Cemiyeti (Society for a Strong Kurdistan), which was established in 1900. A recent publication, *Kürt Milliyetçiliği ve Abdullah Cevdet*, p. 29, confirms that Ali Avni was correct. Ahmet Ramiz from Lice was one of its founding fathers.

30. Van Bruinessen, *Agha, Shaikh and State*, pp. 338–340.

31. Ibid., pp. 370, 50 (quotation); Jwaideh, "The Kurdish Nationalist Movement," pp. 291–293, 299 (where he gives the date as 1910).

32. Jwaideh, "The Kurdish Nationalist Movement," pp. 291–293, 302–303 (quotation).

33. Ibid., pp. 304–306 (quotation); Jwaideh lists the rebellions (pp. 307–329).

34. *Kürt Milliyetçiliği*, pp. 52, 53.

35. Zaki, *Khulasat Tarikh al-Kurd*, pp. 274–276; Jwaideh, "The Kurdish Nationalist Movement," pp. 361–363. According to Firat, *Doğu Illeri*, pp. 136, 139, the Russians suffered 30,000 dead and thousands were taken prisoner. It should be noted that Turkish soldiers were probably part of the casualties.

36. Hovannisian, *Armenia on the Road to Independence, 1918*, p. 36.

37. Justin McCarthy, *Muslims and Minorities: The Population of Ottoman Anatolia and the End of the Empire*, pp. 112, 115 (quotation); Hovannisian, *Armenia on the Road to Independence, 1918*, p. 67.

38. Justin McCarthy, "Population in Eastern Turkey during World War I," *Newsspot* 22 (February 1985): 5; van Bruinessen, *Agha, Shaikh and State*, p. 445 n. 11, who quotes FO 371, 1919: 44A/105775/3050.

39. Roberts and Ravensdale's report is in Bilal N. Şimşir, *Belgeleriyle Türkiye'dei "Kürt Sorunu" (1924–1938)*, pp. 263–290; see also pp. 126–148.

40. Zaki, *Khulasat Tarikh al-Kurd*, pp. 274–275; Jwaideh, "The Kurdish Nationalist Movement," pp. 363–369, gives detailed descriptions of the ruins and depleted population of northern Iraq; Bletch Chirguh, *La question kurde: Ses origins et ses causes*, p. 23; Sureya Bedir Khan, *The Case of Kurdistan against Turkey*, pp. 32–33; Nikitine, *Les Kurdes*, pp. 296–298.

41. Van Bruinessen, *Agha, Shaikh and State*, has the list (p. 446 n. 32 and n. 34); and Zinnar Silopi, *Doza Kürdistan*, pp. 52–54. I was not able to get access to this book. Silopi was a pseudonym of Qadri Beg Cemil Paşa, a leading member of the Kürt Taali Cemiyeti of Diyarbakır.

42. Kutschera, *Le mouvement national kurde*, p. 29; Jwaideh, "The Kurdish Nationalist Movement," pp. 374–378.

43. Stanford J. Shaw and Ezel Kural Shaw, *History of the Ottoman Empire and Modern Turkey, II: Reform, Revolution, and Republic: The Rise of Modern Turkey, 1808–1975*, p. 340; Erik Jan Zürcher, *The Unionist Factor: The Role of the Committee of Union and Progress in the Turkish Nationalist Movement, 1905–1926*, pp. 68–105.

44. Kutschera, *Le mouvement national kurde*, pp. 32–33.

45. Hurewitz, *Diplomacy in the Near and Middle East*, II, pp. 81–87, has a copy of the Treaty of Sèvres. Articles 62, 63, and 64 of section III deal with Kurdistan. Article 64 states that the Kurdish peoples would be able to ask for independence one year later (fall 1921).

2. Kurdish Nationalism

1. Van Bruinessen, *Agha, Shaikh and State*, pp. 445–446 n. 24; Hovannisian, *Armenia on the Road to Independence, 1918*, pp. 121–123.

2. Firat, *Doğu Illeri*, pp. 142–143.

3. Van Bruinessen, *Agha, Shaikh and State*, p. 371; Firat, *Doğu Illeri*, pp. 144–145.

4. Van Bruinessen, *Agha, Shaikh and State*, states that the Azadi was founded in 1923, but it may have been established in 1921. Firat, *Doğu Illeri*, gives the date as 1921 and Dersimi, *Kürdistan Tarihinde Dersim*, says it was founded in 1922 and named the Kurdish Independence Society (Kürt Istiklal Cemiyeti).

5. Firat, *Doğu Illeri*, p. 147.

6. There is only one account of the Koçgiri rebellion to which I had access: M. Nuri Dersimi, *Kürdistan Tarihinde Dersim*, pp. 120–172. I was not able to obtain a copy of the book or pamphlet entitled *Koçgiri Halk Hareketleri*.

7. Dersimi, *Kürdistan Tarihinde Dersim*, pp. 120, 127, states that there were 72 Kurdish members of Parliament at this time out of a total of 437; van Bruinessen, *Agha, Shaikh and State*, p. 446 n. 37; Frederick W. Frey, *The Turkish Political Elite*, appendix B, pp. 438–442, has a list of the members of the first Grand National Assembly.

8. Dersimi, *Kürdistan Tarihinde Dersim*, p. 129.

9. Ibid., p. 131, gives the name of two: Kango Oğlu Ahmet Ramizi and Major (Binbaşı) Hasan Hayriye (Hayri).

10. Ibid., pp. 134, 136; he accepted the grant of land, but only hesitatingly, in order to facilitate the spread of Kurdish nationalism in that area (Koçhisar).

11. At least according to Dersimi, ibid., p. 141.

12. Ibid, pp. 143, 149–154, 159–162, gives a figure of 6,185 for the Kurds. The employment of the Turkish forces would seem to indicate an approximate figure. The telegraph was signed by two leaders of the Koçgiri tribes, Muhammad and Taki, and for the tribal leaders of Dersim by Mustafa, Seidhan, Muhammad, and Munzur.

13. Ibid., pp. 120–172.

14. Ibid., p. 171.

15. Van Bruinessen, *Agha, Shaikh and State*, p. 374.

16. Ibid., pp. 9, 455.

17. Ismail Beşikçi, *Doğu Anadolu'nun Düzeni: Sosyo-Ekonomik ve Etnik Temeller*, p. 270.

18. Kemal Atatürk, *Nutuk*, III, *vesika* (document), 47, 48, 49, 50, 51, 52, 53, pp. 937–945. Mustafa Kemal also wrote letters that are included in the volume III documents to Küfrevizade Şeyh (Sheikh) Abdulbaki Efendi (Bitlis); Abdurrahman Ağa (Şirnak-Şcrnak); Ömer Ağa (Derşevli); Resul Ağa (Musaşlı); and Sheikh Mahmud Efendi and Cemil Ceto Beg (Garzan).

19. FO 371/6369, November 1921 from commander, GOC Allied Forces Constantinople to War Office. There was no treaty between Iran and Turkey until 22 April 1926. My account of the committee or commission and the draft law concerning the administration of Kurdistan is based on FO 371/7781 E 3553/96/65, a dispatch from Horace Rumbold, British ambassador to Turkey, to Lord Curzon, the foreign secretary, dated 29 March 1922. The British apparently possessed a full copy of the proposed draft law.

20. Van Bruinessen is the first scholar to point out the activities of the Azadi, *Agha, Shaikh and State*, pp. 373, 446–447 n. 42; Air Ministry (Air) 23/411: the earliest account of the mutiny of Beyt Şebab, as it was usually called, is found in Air 23/411 in a dispatch from air intelligence Baghdad to Air Headquarters Baghdad dated 8 November 1924. A list of the leaders of the mutiny was recorded as early as 5 November. There were two reports before that dated 8 October and 21 October from air intelligence officers designated as SSO (Special Service Officers) at Baghdad and Mosul, respectively (no. D6 of 10/8/24 and no. J/62 of 10/21/24). The Baghdad report was based on sources other than the Kurdish informants. I could not find these reports, but the report of 8 November seems to incorporate all of the information in them with the exception of a few details. Van Bruinessen has written that there is a similar report in FO 371, 1924, E 11093/11093/65; see p. 442 n. 43 and n. 44. I did not use this document, but it must have originated from the air intelligence reports, which had the special intelligence responsibility in Iraq. There are also accounts of the Beyt Şebab mu-

tiny in Air 5/556, 23/471, 23/436, and 23/279. Accounts subsequent to these seem to be based on the 8 November report, including the FO 371 document used by van Bruinessen. Air Ministry records are fuller than the FO 371 or Colonial Office records since it was the originating ministry, in charge of intelligence for Iraq and, in many instances, eastern Turkey. I rely on the Air Ministry documents. The FO 371 document does not give the names of deserters, but the Air Ministry reports do.

21. Air 23/411, 5 November 1924.

22. Air 23/411 8 November 1924.

23. Air 5/556, received by the Colonial Office on 27 November 1924, is fifteen pages long, whereas the 8 November report is only nine pages. It usually took six to seven days for dispatches from Baghdad to reach London, which means that between 8 November and 20 November more information was added to the report. It seems likely that some information from the SSO in Mosul was added to the account. The officer writing the report noted in handwriting, "if names wanted see original," to which he referred as S15428.

24. In the 8 November 1924 report it is also mentioned that Kurdish tribesmen were made to carry grain for Turkish army units. Receipts were then given for less grain than had been received. Turkish commanders also took animals from the Kurds without compensation. There is also a list of the earlier grievances in van Bruinessen, *Agha, Shaikh and State*, p. 447 n. 43; the same list is included in his "Popular Islam, Kurdish Nationalism and Rural Revolt: The Rebellion of Shaikh Said in Turkey (1925)," in *Religion and Rural Revolt*, ed. János M. Bak and Gerhard Benecke (Papers Presented to the Fourth Interdisciplinary Workshop on Peasant Studies, University of British Columbia), p. 294. There is also a list in his "Vom Osmanismus," pp. 143–144. Van Bruinessen's list comes from the FO 371 document referred to above. The list I give is fuller. There is also a list of grievances in the Air 23/411 report of 8 November stated in a slightly different way. Actually, there was a summary of similar Kurdish grievances as early as November 1921: seven demands that the Turks thought the Kurds would make if they were able to send a mission to Europe, similar to the eleven that I have listed. See FO 371/6369, no. 464, November 1921, commanding officer of Allied Forces GOC Constantinople, to War Office.

25. Air 23/411 8 November 1924. This is another example of the miscalculation and poor organization of the Azadi, especially in Iraq. There was little understanding of Sayyid Taha's position. On 15 June 1925, SSO in Arbil, H. W. Foote, reported that he had failed to discover what Sayyid Taha's relations were with Ihsan Nuri, Tewfik (Tevfik) Cemil, or Ahmet Rassim. Sayyid Taha appeared to be loath to discuss the three deserters with Foote. He told Foote that he thought the three men were genuine patriots and that he had a high opinion of Ihsan Nuri's intelligence and capacity. Taha professed complete ignorance of their recent activities or their connections with "any Kurdish Committee." He said that the three deserted officers had "told him very little." Sayyid Taha did agree that they could remain in

Rawanduz, a place they wanted to be, he speculated, "in case further orders should come from the north." See Air 23/436, "Investigation of Bayt-Ash-Shabab," 15 June 1925.

26. Air 23/436, 7 February 1925. This report was written by an SSO (captain) at Air Headquarters, Baghdad. It is unclear whether Ihsan Nuri was the source of any of this information.

27. For example, British intelligence checked out Ihsan Nuri's career with four prominent Kurds then present in Iraq. Since they were under British protection and sought British help to obtain jobs in the Anglo-Iraqi government, their accounts were accepted as true. Zayn al-Abidin, former secretary of the Kürt Taali Cemiyeti in Istanbul; Salih Zaki Beg, a former staff officer in the Turkish army; Lieutenant Faikh (Faik), a deserter from the Turkish army; and Mustafa Paşa, former head of the judicial branch of the Turkish army in Istanbul during 1919–1920. All four men thought it improbable that Ihsan Nuri or the other deserters were spies. See Air 23/436, 7 February 1925. Copies of the Turkish letters can be found in the abovementioned report. By 6 August 1926, the British had deciphered all of the Turkish letters in the confiscated mail bag. Air 23/436, 6 August 1925, also contains the Turkish and Kurdish proclamations with English translations.

28. The only account of this congress is in van Bruinessen, *Agha, Shaikh and State,* pp. 377–378, based on oral accounts. I could find no documents in the Public Record Office that mentioned this congress. This could be an indication that the Azadi was quite good at concealing its movement. It seems likely that Turkish intelligence was aware of it. My account here follows van Bruinessen.

29. FO 424/261, Henderson (British ambassador to Turkey) to MacDonald (British foreign secretary); Air 5/556, p. 12, states that another Turkish-Kurdish congress was held in Jezira (Cezire).

30. Air 23/411, 8 November 1924.

31. Air 5/556, 27 November 1924.

32. Ibid.

3. The Second Time Around

1. I wish to thank the editors of *Die Welt des Islams* for permission to use material from my "The Second Time Around: British Policy towards the Kurds, 1921–1922" (27 [1987]: 91–102).

2. E. W. C. (Edward William Charles) Noel had a very long, fruitful, and adventurous career by all accounts. There is extensive coverage in the Colonial Office records of his exploits in the Caucasus during World War I and among the Jangalis of Kuchak Khan in Gilan in 1919, where he was imprisoned, and among the Bakhtiyar and the Kurds. He was also active among the Pathans and the tribes of the Northwest Frontier in India, to which government he was assigned. There is a good portrait of Noel in Sir Arnold T. Wilson, *Mesopotamia 1917–1920: A Clash of Loyalties,* pp. 31–37, 127–129. Noel wrote a 77-page treatise on his reconnaissance and espionage among the Kurds: *Diary of Major Noel on Special Duty in Kurdistan, from*

June 14th to September 21st, 1919. A copy of this report can also be found in FO 371/5068. Noel wrote one other published piece, *Note on the Kurdish Situation.* He was also present at the Cairo conference during March 1921. For his role there, see Aaron S. Klieman, *Foundations of British Policy in the Arab World: The Cairo Conference of 1921,* p. 110; also see FO 371/6343, where the original reports of the Cairo conference can be found, especially appendix 10, "Fourth Meeting of the Political Committee of the Middle East Department 15 March 1921."

3. Dersimi, *Kürdistan Tarihinde Dersim,* p. 122.

4. Jwaideh, "The Kurdish Nationalist Movement," p. 485; C. J. Edmonds, *Kurds, Turks, and Arabs: Politics, Travel and Research in North-Eastern Iraq, 1919–1925,* pp. 264–385.

5. FO 371/5068, 13 April 1920.

6. Ibid., see appendix A.

7. There are thousands of documents relating to the "Air Scheme" for Iraq. See especially CO 730/32; Air 20/526. For the political concerns see Peter Sluglett, *Britain in Iraq, 1914–1932,* pp. 254–270.

8. Ibid.

9. The best discussion of the significance of the Cairo conference is Klieman, *Foundations of British Policy;* FO 371/6343 has copies of the original documents, some 157 pages.

10. FO 371/6343, p. 21.

11. Klieman, *Foundations of British Policy,* p. 110; FO 371/6343, pp. 59–61.

12. CO 730/2, Mesopotamia Intelligence Report no. 13, 15 May 1921, with minutes by Reader Bullard.

13. CO 730/2, no. 153, 2 June 1921, Cox to Churchill.

14. CO 730/2, no. 148, 9 June 1921, Churchill to Cox; no. 169, 8 June 1921, Cox to Churchill; 15 June 1921, Churchill to Middle East Department.

15. CO 730/2, no. 201 and folio p. 612, received at the Colonial Office on 21 June 1921. This is a paraphrase of a dispatch from Cox to Churchill.

16. Ibid., folio p. 614.

17. FO 371/6346, no. 209, 21 June 1921, Cox to Churchill. No. 201 was received at the Colonial Office at 11 A.M.; no. 204 was received at 5:18 P.M.

18. CO 730/9, no. 476, 11 May 1921, Rumbold to Curzon.

19. FO 371/6369, 11 November 1921, intelligence report, Constantinople to Foreign Office.

20. CO 730/7, 26 November 1921, intelligence report, Constantinople to Colonial Office.

21. FO 371/6346, no. 521, 25 May 1921, Rumbold to Curzon; 1 June 1921, Rumbold to Amery (secretary of the Colonial Office before Winston Churchill).

22. FO 371/6346, no. 162, 13 May 1921, Curzon to Churchill.

23. FO 371/6346, 5 May 1921, Shuckburgh to political undersecretary at Foreign Office.

24. FO 371/6346, 24 May 1921, Shuckburgh to Foreign Office; 31 May 1921, Curzon to Churchill; 14 June 1921, Churchill to Cox.

25. CO 730/2, no. 196, 24 June 1921, Churchill to Cox.
26. CO 730/2, no. 109, 25 May 1921, Churchill to Cox.
27. CO 730/2, no. 211, 2 July 1921, Churchill to Cox; FO 371/6346, no. 162, 13 May 1921, Curzon to Churchill; CO 730/2, no. 216, 21 June 1921, Cox to Churchill (minute by J. H. Hall).
28. CO 730/4, no. 433, 21 August 1921, Cox to Churchill; no. 424, 26 August 1921, Cox to Churchill.
29. CO 730/4, no. 433, 21 August 1921, Cox to Churchill; 8 September 1921, Churchill to Cox.
30. CO 730/5, no. 503, 20 September 1921, Cox to Churchill.
31. Ibid.
32. CO 730/5, 27 September 1921, Reader Bullard's minute on Cox's 20 September telegram.
33. CO 730/5, no. 423, 3 October 1921, Churchill to Cox.
34. CO 730/5, no. 534, 29 September 1921, Cox to Churchill; 31 September 1921, Oliphant (Foreign Office) to Cox; FO 371/7781, 18 October 1921, Cox to Churchill.
35. CO 730/6, no. 616, 25 October 1921, Cox to Churchill.
36. Ibid.
37. CO 730/6, no. 519, 11 November 1921, Churchill to Cox. Churchill is obviously talking about the pourparlers to the London conference of March 1922.
38. CO 730/6, 28 October 1921, Cox to Churchill. Cox's proposals are found in a section marked "Very Special" (pp. 485–489). Cox's telegram is sometimes referred to as 55824. The quotes in the text come from this telegram.
39. FO 371/6346, no. 209, 21 June 1921, Cox to Churchill.
40. CO 730/6, Bullard's minute of 9 November 1921.
41. Ibid., Meinertzhagen's minute.
42. Ibid., Shuckburgh's minute.
43. CO 730/7, no. 700, 21 November 1921, Cox to Churchill.
44. CO 730/7, 1 December 1921, Churchill to Cox.
45. Ibid., Churchill's minute of 7 December 1921; CO 730/28. Rawlinson's report and the accompanying minutes of Colonial Office personnel are dated from 4 March to 17 March 1922 and consist of pages 200–209. Reference is to these pages unless otherwise indicated in the text.
46. Soon after his release from prison in Turkey, Rawlinson wrote *Adventures in the Near East*, about his activities in Turkey (see pp. 351–353). See also Salahi Ramsdan Sonyel, *Turkish Diplomacy, 1918–1923*, pp. 24, 35–85. According to Sonyel, Rawlinson's reports were of some interest and importance to British officials, especially regarding the differences among the nationalist leaders such as Rauf Orbay, Selaheddin Bey, and Vehbi Hoca and Kemal Atatürk (*Turkish Diplomacy*, p. 163). See Roderic H. Davison, "Turkish Diplomacy from Mudros to Lausanne," in Gordon A. Craig and Felix Gilbert, *The Diplomats, 1919–1939*, pp. 172–209; Briton Cooper Busch, *Mudros to Lausanne: Britain's Frontier in West Asia, 1918–1923*, pp. 163–

319; Ömer Kürkçüoğlu, *Türk-Ingiliz Ilişkileri (1919–1926)*, pp. 137–250; CO 730/28, p. 207.

47. Rawlinson, *Adventures in the Near East*, pp. 208 (quotation), 130–140. One of Rawlinson's duties during his mission in Turkey in 1920–1921 was to learn of and, if possible, to create dissension among the various nationalist officers (ibid., pp. 267–334; Sonyel, *Turkish Diplomacy*, p. 163; CO 730/28, p. 208). Rawlinson observed or undoubtedly heard firsthand of the insurrections and rebellions of the Dersim Kurds during 1919–1920.

48. These events can be traced in Sonyel, *Turkish Diplomacy*, pp. 91–182; Davison, "Turkish Diplomacy from Mudros to Lausanne," pp. 172–196; Kürkçüoğlu, *Türk-Ingiliz Ilişkileri*, pp. 137–250. Detailed accounts of published British documents are in *Documents on British Foreign Policy*, first series, XVLII, *Greece and Turkey*, 1 January 1921–2 September 1922.

49. Phebe Marr, *The Modern History of Iraq*, p. 41; Sluglett, *Britain in Iraq*, pp. 86–87. Interestingly, Sheikh Mahmud was forced from power in February 1923 and Sir Percy Cox retired the same month. Cox was replaced by Sir Henry Dobbs as high commissioner.

50. One of the latest and best accounts is Marian Kent, "British Policy, International Diplomacy and the Turkish Revolution," *International Journal of Turkish Studies* 3 (Winter 1985–1986): 33–51; also the same author's "Great Britain and the End of the Ottoman Empire," in *The Three Great Powers and the End of the Ottoman Empire, 1900–1923*, ed. Marian Kent, pp. 172–205.

51. Ibid., pp. 45, 46 n. 88. The Churchill-Cox correspondence also indicates that Curzon was willing to take a softer line than he took publicly or in his opening negotiations at Lausanne. Kent states that the reason for this was that Curzon and Lord Eyre Crowe, permanent under-secretary of state and foreign affairs, accepted E. G. Forbes-Adams's view that the British "desired as far as possible to maintain the legal theory that the government at Constantinople was the government of Turkey in the hope that eventually Constantinople and Angora would merge in a common government of more moderate views." The Churchill-Cox correspondence and the British policy toward the Kurds and developments in Iraq would also be at variance with this policy. It was, at any rate, the policy made in the field that triumphed.

52. Air 23/397, "Intelligence Reports on Turkish Internal Affairs 1924–25." The report of 7 October was entitled "The Projected Militarisation of the Executive" and the 2 January 1925 report "The 'Oriental' and 'Occidental' Policies." This would seem to suggest that the decision to drop the "pseudo-oriental" policy was influenced by the negotiations at Mudanya; the armistice was signed on 11 October 1922.

53. Ibid.

54. Ibid.

55. Ibid.

56. Ibid., 28 January 1925. For an account of these and other events during this period, see Walter F. Weiker, *Political Tutelage and Democracy in Turkey: The Free Party and Its Aftermath*, pp. 44–51, 73–75; Kemal H. Karpat,

Turkey's Politics: The Transition to a Multiparty System, pp. 42–48; Mete Tuncay, *T. C. 'nde Tek-Parti Yönetimi'nin Kurulması (1923–1931)*, pp. 138–139, says that Mustafa Kemal created the new naval (marine) post simply to have another supporter in Fethi's cabinet. Fuad Cebesoy saw it as strictly a political move on the part of the ardent supporters of Mustafa Kemal and Ismet Inönü.

57. British intelligence reported that Inönü received the telegram at 10 P.M. Thursday night, 19 February 1925—obviously, the British had access to telegraph communications; Air 23/397, 21 February 1925, p. 9.

58. Ibid., 2 March 1925, entitled "Turkey: Internal, Ismet Pasha and the Revolt in Kurdistan."

59. Ibid.

60. Ibid.

4. Mobilization for Rebellion

1. Van Bruinessen, *Agha, Shaikh and State*, p. 378.

2. Shaw and Shaw, *The Rise of Modern Turkey*, II, p. 384; Chirguh, *La question kurde*, p. 31; van Bruinessen, *Agha, Shaikh and State*, pp. 379 (quotation), 447.

3. Dersimi, *Kürdistan Tarihinde Dersim*, p. 174, states that Yusuf Ziya Beg had spoken to the Progressive Republican party and other opposition to Mustafa Kemal in spring 1921. But since the Progressive Republican party was not formed until October 1924, that would have been impossible. It is possible, however, that he spoke to members of the opposition since he knew many of them. After the rebellion, as we shall see later, the Kemalists tried to discredit the Progressive Republican party by implicating its members as having connections with the perpetrators of the rebellion. The accusation was hotly denied by all Progressive party members and other opposition to Mustafa Kemal.

4. Van Bruinessen, *Agha, Shaikh and State*, p. 379.

5. Firat, *Doğu Illeri*, pp. 151 (lists Babakurdi tribes), 155; Dersimi, *Kürdistan Tarihinde Dersim*, p. 174 (I follow Firat for these events; Dersimi's account seems to rely on it as well); van Bruinessen, *Agha, Shaikh and State*, p. 447 n. 54.

6. Firat, *Doğu Illeri*, p. 157; van Bruinessen, *Agha, Shaikh and State*, p. 383.

7. Firat, *Doğu Illeri*, pp. 157, 158–159 (n. 1 has a Turkish transliteration of the *fetva* that Sheikh Said gave to the independence tribunal in Diyarbakır during his trial and a copy of the letter that he sent to the tribal leaders of the Hormek tribe).

8. Here I follow van Bruinessen, *Agha, Shaikh and State*, pp. 384, 385, which is based on the account of his informant, Mela Hesen. He was not present at these meetings, but van Bruinessen thinks that his account is probably more accurate than that of Firat, *Doğu Illeri*, pp. 159–160. Van Bruinessen gives no date for the meeting at which the fronts were established, but the information given indicates that it was at the 8 January meet-

ing in Melekan; ibid., p. 447 n. 59. If the meeting that established the fronts was on 8 January, it would mean that the meeting at which the March date for the rebellion was agreed upon occurred before the beginning of Sheikh Said's January tour. It could have taken place during the 4 January meeting in Kırıkan.

9. Behçet Cemal, *Şeyh Sait Isyanı*, p. 24; Metin Toker, *Şeyh Sait ve Isyanı*, p. 38 (in the portion of his book dealing with the events of the Sheikh Said rebellion, Toker follows closely, sometimes verbatim, the account of Cemal, which is usually more detailed on aspects of the rebellion itself); Dersimi, *Kürdistan Tarihinde Dersim*, p. 177; Firat, *Doğu Illeri*, p. 161, gives the date 8 February for the outbreak of the rebellion, as does van Bruinessen, *Agha, Shaikh and State*, p. 385; it is unclear if van Bruinessen accepts the date as given by Firat or that of his informant, Mela Hesen. Cemal and Toker both give the date of the rebellion as 13 February, a Friday, which would mean that the events leading to the rebellion occurred on Sunday, 8 February 1925.

10. Van Bruinessen, *Agha, Shaikh and State*, p. 397, 131–132; Dersimi, *Kürdistan Tarihinde Dersim*, pp. 42–57, has a list of tribes speaking Zaza and those speaking Kurmanci. The Gurani-speaking Kurds also seem to have originated in north-central Iran.

11. Van Bruinessen, *Agha, Shaikh and State*, pp. 397 (quotation), 30; Firat, *Doğu Illeri*, pp. 6–19, 151, 152, gives a description of the origins and differences among Zaza, Kurmanci, and Babakurdi. Firat mentions that the Zaza did not even consider themselves Kurds. See also Beşikçi, *Doğu Anadolu'nun Düzeni*, p. 353. Beşikçi does not separate the Zaza from the Kurmanci.

12. Van Bruinessen, *Agha, Shaikh and State*, pp. 397, 398.

13. Air 23/333, 5 April 1925. This is a nine-page summary concerning the rebellion to that date. The informant got most of his information from a Dr. Ziya Beg, who was at the time a medical officer in the Second Division stationed in Siirt.

14. It also meant that in the rebellions staged subsequently (e.g., in 1937–1938 by the Alevi Dersim Kurds) the Zaza and Sunni tribes would not come to the aid of the Alevis.

15. Van Bruinessen, "Vom Osmanismus," p. 146.

16. Van Bruinessen has a whole chapter on the establishment and evolution of the Nakşbandi and Qadiri orders in Kurdistan, *Agha, Shaikh and State*, pp. 299–352; see also pp. 379, 402–403, where he gives a list of some of the most important sheikhs in the rebellion area.

17. Toker, *Şeyh Sait ve Isyanı*, p. 31; Cemal, *Şeyh Sait Isyanı*, p. 18, says that he was "past sixty." Toker and Cemal's dates are based on testimony that Sheikh Said gave during his trial in Diyarbakır.

18. Air 23/236, 3 March 1925, quoting from the newspaper *Al-Istiklal* in Baghdad; Toker, *Şeyh Sait ve Isyanı*, p. 31. Judging from his narrative it is apparent that Toker visited Palu.

19. Ibid., pp. 32–33; Cemal, *Şeyh Sait Isyanı*, pp. 18–19.

20. Van Bruinessen, *Agha, Shaikh and State*, pp. 259, 260–261, 404.

21. Air 23, enclosure 12, 16 March 1925, estimated the rebels at "15,000

fighting men." The report also estimated the total population of the area in rebellion to be 150,000; see also Air 23/399B, which quotes reports of the rebels as being anywhere from 7,000 to 15,000 men. One intelligence source estimated that Haco, chief of the Hoverli and paramount chief of the Midyat tribes, could raise 12,000 fighters just from the tribes under his control (Air 23/236, 28 May 1925). Haco apparently never did so.

22. Air 23/399B. The report was marked "SECRET."

23. Ibid. This is a draft of the quoted report.

24. Şimşir, İngiliz Belgeleriyle, pp. 68–69. Harenc miscalculated his total estimates for rifles. His total was 49,000, but the figures he gives total 54,000. Şimşir quotes from FO 242–263, pp. 2–3, no. 2/2. Harenc's figures seem to be based on estimates made during the last part of May or early June by air intelligence in Baghdad. All of this information is in Air Ministry files that Şimşir and van Bruinessen did not consult. In this regard, compare FO 371/10867, in which Harenc gives the same estimates. In a report, Air 23/397, 11 March 1925, air intelligence reported that "it was known that Fethi Bey had approached the French in order to obtain the necessary permission, as had been stipulated in Turkish-French agreements, for the transport by rail through Syria of Turkish troops to Kurdistan." The French granted permission for the troops to pass, but Fethi Bey was also counting, thought the British, on securing the connivance of France by the offer of attractive concessions to the French capitalists to let about 100,000 men into the Mosul frontier area. The troops were to be used ostensibly against the Kurds but in reality to make a demonstration against Britain and the Iraq government. For this purpose, Fethi Bey had decreed a mobilization of all men between the ages of twenty and forty in Konya and Adana and in all of the "oriental vilayets," including those of Kurdistan. The report then stated that "this may have touched off the rebellion." Another intelligence officer noted that the 100,000 figure sounded like an exaggeration; on the other hand, it was known that the Turkish military authorities had been canvassing the local market for the immediate supply of 30,000 portable tents, 3,000 "lull tents," 50,000 uniforms (used or unused), socks (quantity unspecified), and 200,000 meters of jute sacking. If the Turks could not purchase this material locally, it was to be purchased abroad.

After Ismet Inönü assumed power on 2 March, the number of recruits to be mobilized was reduced. A minute on the report notes that it was possible that Inönü had suspended Fethi Bey's order simply because of the impossibility of procuring sufficient equipment for all those recruits who were to be called up. The conclusion of the report speculates that the rebellion may have been touched off by Fethi Bey's recruitment order. This, of course, is not true. Since the new recruits were to be sent "against the insurgents," this would mean that Fethi's order would have to have been issued before 8 February 1925, which was not the case. As discussed in the text, plans for the rebellion to be begun in March had been decided in one of the Azadi's meetings during the last days of December 1924 or early days of January 1925. It is possible that Fethi Bey could have given the mobilization order for demonstrative reasons against Britain before the outbreak of the Sheikh

Said rebellion. Many incidents occurred before 8 February 1925 that could have been labeled "insurgency" by the Turkish government.

5. The Rebellion and Its Aftermath

1. See chapter 3, n. 15. For accounts of the rebellion as it unfolded, I rely on van Bruinessen, *Agha, Shaikh and State,* pp. 385–393; Cemal, *Şeyh Sait Isyanı,* pp. 25–37; Firat, *Doğu İlleri,* pp. 160–183; Toker, *Şeyh Sait ve Isyanı,* pp. 38–43 and 85–88. Toker seems to follow closely the account of Cemal, who in turn follows the account of Firat. When these accounts differ, I follow van Bruinessen and his sources, who seem to provide the best reconstruction of events. I also used the Air Ministry files and on occasion the Foreign Office records. The Air Ministry files add immensely to our knowledge. They are the only contemporary records of the rebellion, kept systematically and chronologically by air intelligence, which took great interest in the rebellion because of its potential influence in Iraq.

For example, there are four fat dossiers in the Air Ministry files that are entitled "Kurdish Rising in Anatolia." Part I, Air 23/236, has 66 enclosures dealing with the period 26 February 1925 to 6 June 1925. Part II, Air 23/237, contains 54 enclosures and deals with the period 18 June 1925 to 9 September 1925. Part III, Air 23/238, has 101 enclosures and deals with the period 15 September 1925 to 15 April 1926. Part IV, Air 23/239, has 83 enclosures and covers the period 15 April 1926 to 3 January 1927. All of the documents in these files are virtual goldmines in terms of the Turkish military operations against Sheikh Said. Air 23/333, 23/334, 23/279, 23/333, 23/399, 23/399B, and 23/525 also contain substantial information on the rebellion. The Air Ministry files also have a nearly complete record of the Sheikh Said rebellion as it appeared in the Turkish press, especially the newspaper *Tanin;* see Air 23/236, 5 April 1925.

One gets a flavor of the Turkish accounts by the rendering of Toker, who asserts that one of the factors contributing to the "Piran Event" and hence the rebellion was that Sheikh Said, who had three wives and many children, had heard that, according to the soon-to-be-announced civil law, he would have to give equal inheritance to his heirs; also, the new civil law was to forbid polygamy (*Şeyh Sait ve Isyanı,* p. 39).

2. Firat, *Doğu İlleri,* p. 162 n. 1 and n. 18. Given the total figure of around 15,000 fighters mobilized by the Kurds, this figure seems too high.

3. Air 23/279, a long report that incorporates diverse intelligence concerning the rebellion. Two other officers escaped and were not imprisoned: Colonel Arif and Lieutenant Colonel Azan (Adhan).

4. Ibid. The British were now estimating the insurgents were 8,000 strong. On about 1 March, Najib (Naceb) Ağa, chief of the Balu tribes, joined the rebels with another estimated 1,000 men. Firat gives the figure of "20,000 in the command" of Sheikh Said, *Doğu İlleri,* p. 163. This number seems much too high according to my previous calculations. If we were to accept Firat's figures, it would mean that at least 25,000 men joined in the rebellion. Fighting was going on at other fronts simultaneously with the battles

in Diyarbakır, in which at least several thousand men were engaged. According to Sheikh Said's own testimony during his trial, he had 3,000 men. The Turkish government estimated his forces at 5,000. A resident of Diyarbakır speculated that 10,000 men laid siege to the city after the rebels were unable to conquer it (FO 371/100869). This is an eyewitness account written in French entitled, "Sur l'insurrection du Kurdistan de février à avril 1925." Van Bruinessen quotes a similar or perhaps the same source, Agha, Shaikh and State, p. 447 n. 62 and FO 371 E 3340/1091/44.

5. "Sallallahu alayhim! Ya Allah! Teslim! Teslim!" (Cemal, Şeyh Sait Isyanı, p. 32); Firat, Doğu İlleri, pp. 163–164, 167–169 (lists the congratulatory telegrams from Turkish authorities, including Mustafa Kemal to the people of Kiğı and the Hormek tribes); Cemal, Şeyh Sait Isyanı, p. 35, states that the big battle during which the wall was breached occurred on 7 March.

6. Firat, Doğu İlleri, p. 164; Dersimi, Kürdistan Tarihinde Dersim, pp. 180–181.

7. Dersimi, Kürdistan Tarihinde Dersim, p. 165, gives the figure of 5,000 rebels, which seems high; p. 181 states that Sheikh Yado remained in the Çapakçür mountains and staged guerrilla warfare against Turkish forces until 1927, when he fled to Syria.

8. FO 371/10837. The full title of the report is "Diary of Events at Mezreh [Mamouret-el-Aziz], 23 March to 15 April" (from a letter written by a European inhabitant of the town; see appendix VIII); compare van Bruinessen, FO 371 E2359/362/65, which may be the same document. Van Bruinessen gives a partial description of the report, Agha, Shaikh and State, p. 389. See n. 4, above. I refer to the sources used in this book. Obviously, there are accounts of Sheikh Said's rebellion in the archives, especially the archives in Germany, the Soviet Union, Greece, and Turkey. The French archives should be rich in this regard. I have indicated elsewhere, however, that many of the French intelligence reports are included in the British archives that I used.

9. Firat, Doğu İlleri, pp. 167–169; Dersimi, Kürdistan Tarihinde Dersim, p. 178.

10. Firat, Doğu İlleri, pp. 169, 170, also gives the four major areas of rebellion; Dersimi, Kürdistan Tarihinde Dersim, p. 178.

11. Firat, Doğu İlleri, p. 171; van Bruinessen, Agha, Shaikh and State, p. 388. Firat, Doğu İlleri, pp. 173–176, duly records the telegrams of thanks from the Turkish commanding officer at Hınıs on 13 and 14 March 1925.

12. Firat, Doğu İlleri, pp. 176, 177; Dersimi, Kürdistan Tarihinde Dersim, p. 178.

13. Firat, Doğu İlleri, p. 177; Dersimi, Kürdistan Tarihinde Dersim, p. 179, says that it was Sheikh Said's son Abbaseddin. Ali Riza in the following months and year remained in close contact with the British in Iraq, seeking their aid for rebellion, and with the Armenian-Kurdish organization Tashnak-Hoybun (Khoybun). There are many accounts of his activities in the Air Ministry files. Hasananlı Halid returned to Malazgird in spring 1926.

14. Firat, Doğu İlleri, p. 180. He stated this in a telegram or letter to Şerif Efendi (Firat), commander of the Hormek tribal militia.

15. Van Bruinessen, *Agha, Shaikh and State,* p. 312, states that Sheikh Said was captured on 14 April. He gives no footnotes and apparently relies on his informants and on Cemal (*Şeyh Sait Isyanı,* p. 72). Cemal's date of 15 April relies on an official Turkish government announcement of that date. Metin Toker (*Şeyh Sait ve Isyanı,* p. 98), following Cemal, says that Sheikh Said was captured on the night of 14–15 April and that it was officially announced on 15 April. Shaw and Shaw (*The Rise of Modern Turkey,* p. 381), following Cemal, give the date as 15 April. Firat and Dersimi, the two Kurdish accounts, state that Sheikh Said was captured on 27 April at Abdurrahman Paşa bridge. British intelligence gives the date as 15 April. While it is possible that the Turkish government's announcement of the capture of Sheikh Said was premature, the weight of evidence seems to indicate that Said was captured on or about 15 April.

16. Firat, *Doğu Illeri,* p. 181, n. 1. There are discrepancies of dates. For example, Firat states that Sheikh Said and the other rebel leaders left Çapakçür on 10 May, whereas Cemal, *Şeyh Sait Isyanı,* p. 93, states that they arrived in Diyarbakır on 5 May. Van Bruinessen, *Agha, Shaikh and State,* pp. 390–394, 396, has many cartoons from the *Cumhuriyet* newspaper that depict the Turkish version of the suppression of the rebellion.

17. There is a voluminous literature dealing with the negotiations regarding the Turkish-Iraqi boundary negotiations. One of the best surveys accompanied by excellent maps is *Question de la frontière entre la Turquie et l'Irak 16 à 30 septembre 1924.* There are literally thousands of pages concerning this problem in the Air Ministry files (e.g., Air 367, 5/403, 5/389, CO 730/9, 730/66, 730/67, 730/83, 730/98, 730/100). The last two volumes contain the negotiations leading to the treaty and the treaty itself.

18. The Brussels Line decision was given by the League of Nations at 6 P.M. during the Thirty-first Session of the council; CO 730/83. Some reports state the award was made on 17 December.

19. Air 23/278.

20. See especially Cemal, *Şeyh Sait Isyanı,* pp. 27–29, who discusses this at some length. See n. 1 above for a discussion of these sources; Air 23/236, 13 March 1925.

21. French intelligence in Syria shared its information with the British. French estimates of Turkish troops that were passing to the area of rebellion were usually higher than those of the British. Both the British and French estimated that the Turks intended to have a force of 100,000 in the area of rebellion and, of course, north of the Iraqi frontier. In addition to the French intelligence reports, Air 23 files have extensive coverage of the Turkish newspapers, especially *Tanin;* Air 23/236.

22. The source was a business associate of Friedrich Wilhelm Hayer of the German firm Hayer, Schroeder, and Froehlich of Wittenburg-Dessau (Air 23/399A, 4 March 1925).

23. Air 23/236. These included the chiefs of the villages of Dariş, Karzi, Boçal, Karnak, Kundak, Çamalla, Teppe, and Sor. The names of the chiefs are also included in the report, 10 June 1925.

24. For an account of early Ottoman aviation, see Pierre Oberling, "The

State as Promoter of Technology Transfer: The Early Years of Ottoman Aviation," in *Turks, Hungarians and Kipchaks: A Festschrift in Honor of Tibor Halasi-Kun (Journal of Turkish Studies* 8 [1984], ed. Şinasi Tekin and Gönül Alpay Tekin), pp. 209–214. By the beginning of the first Balkan war in October 1912, the Ottoman air force had eight pilots and ten planes. Air 23/425 has substantial information on the Turkish air force for the years 1925–1927. These reports were written by the British military attaché, Major Harenc, with the collaboration of Commander Neyroni, the Italian naval attaché, who took a keen interest in the development of the air force. The Italians were major suppliers of aircraft to Turkey.

25. Apparently in March or so. See Air 23/236, 23/279, 23/280.

26. Air 23/225 (gives the salaries of the various officers), 23/279.

27. Air 23/280, 23/237, 23/280.

28. Firat, *Doğu İlleri*, pp. 181, 182. Nuh Beg remained with Sheikh Mahmud in Iraq for two years. In May 1928, he was executed by Sheikh Mahmud in revenge for the treachery of his nephew, Hacı Oğlu's son Medeni, for killing Hayderanlı Huseyin Paşa, one of the men Sheikh Mahmud had sent to start a Kurdish rebellion in the Ararat (Ağrı) mountain region.

29. See n. 1 above. Air 23/237 includes 54 enclosures between these dates.

30. Toker, *Şeyh Sait ve Isyanı*, p. 119; Air 23/237, 3 September 1925.

31. Air 23/238, 16 September 1925.

32. Toker, *Şeyh Sait ve Isyanı*, pp. 22, 23, characterizes İnönü and his group as the "Radical Team" (*radikal takımı*); Cemal, *Şeyh Sait Isyanı*, p. 12.

33. Toker, *Şeyh Sait ve Isyanı*, p. 26; van Bruinessen, *Agha, Shaikh and State*, p. 390, gives the date as 23 February, but he gives no source. Cemal, *Şeyh Sait Isyanı*, pp. 41, 53, gives the date as 21 February and includes a copy of the martial law proclamation. For a detailed interpretation of the domestic effects of the rebellion, see Tuncay, *Tek-Parti*, pp. 127–148.

34. Shaw and Shaw, *The Rise of Modern Turkey*, II, p. 381. Some refer to the law in English as the Maintenance of Order Law: see Karpat, *Turkey's Politics*, p. 47; Weiker, *Political Tutelage*, p. 45; Toker, *Şeyh Sait ve Isyanı*, pp. 67–68. Toker (pp. 48–49) relates a colorful story as to why Mustafa Kemal preferred Ismet İnönü rather than Fethi Okyar as prime minister as a result of Sheikh Said's rebellion. The independence tribunals were first established on 29 April 1920. They were used to suppress separatist movements and guerrilla armies and Communist or allegedly Communist groups. Toker, *Şeyh Sait ve Isyanı*, pp. 75, 76–77 (on p. 82 Toker gives a list of the newspapers and their editors).

35. Tuncay, *Tek-Parti*, p. 142, gives the names of the members of the Ankara tribunal; Toker, *Şeyh Sait ve Isyanı*, pp. 118–119; Cemal, *Şeyh Sait Isyanı*, pp. 112–114; Shaw and Shaw, *The Rise of Modern Turkey*, II, p. 381, like Toker, follow Cemal, giving the date as 29 June. Van Bruinessen, *Agha, Shaikh and State*, p. 392, states that Sheikh Said was hanged on 4 September along with 47 others; Toker, p. 131, gives a partial list of those hanged. See also Air 23/238, 16 September 1925; Şimşir, *İngiliz Belgeleriyle*, p. 89; 23 March 1926, Hoare to Chamberlain.

36. Tuncay, *Tek-Parti*, p. 168; Zürcher, *The Unionist Factor*, pp. 108–109, 144; 12 January 1927, Clerk to Chamberlain, 9 August 1927, Clerk to Chamberlain, 14 December 1927, Hoare to Chamberlain; Şimşir, *Ingiliz Belgeleriyle*, pp. 107, 108, 114. Major Harenc stated that he had seen groups of Kurds, one numbering 150 around Niğde and another group of 300 between Karaman and Konya, and a camp of Kurds numbering 600 at Çumrah near Konya.

37. Şimşir, *Ingiliz Belgeleriyle*, pp. 114, 119–120; 11 January 1928, Clerk to Chamberlain, 26 June 1928, Clerk to Chamberlain, enclosure in no. 46, "Aux Vilayets Orientaux: Une nouvelle proclamation d'Ibrahim Taly Bey"; 14 August 1928, Clerk to Chamberlain. The British documents in Şimşir, *Ingiliz Belgeleriyle*, provide continuing coverage of Kurdish affairs, rebellions, and revolts up to 1938.

38. Tuncay, *Tek-Parti*, pp. 136–137 n. 16. Tuncay, a Turkish scholar, quotes and apparently accepts the figure of Sureya Bedir Khan in *The Case of Kurdistan against Turkey*. Tuncay also quotes Abdul Rahman Ghassemlou, *Kurdistan and the Kurds*, who states that the Turks suffered 15,000 to 20,000 killed; *Tek-Parti*, p. 136 n. 16, quoting Ghassemlou, gives this figure and that of Bedir Khan, who states that the Turkish government spent 60,000,000 Turkish lira in suppressing the rebellion.

39. Tuncay, *Tek-Parti*, pp. 127–128 n., gives a list of eighteen rebellions as recorded in *Türkiye Cumhuriyeti'nde Ayaklanmaları (1924–1938)*, which is an official version of Turkish military history as written by the General Staff of the Turkish Armed Forces in 1972. Tuncay considers the Nestorian (Nasturi) rebellion of September 1924 not directly connected to the Kurdish rebellions. The following list is from Tuncay. (1) Nestorian (Nasturi) rebellion (12–28 September 1924); (2) Sheikh Said rebellion (13 February–31 May 1925); (3) Raçkotan and Raman pacifying operations (9–12 August 1925); (4) Sason (Sasun) rebellion (1925–1937); (5) First Ağrı (Ararat) rebellion (16 May–17 June 1926); (6) Koçuşağı rebellion (7 October–30 November 1927); (7) Mutki rebellion (26 May–25 August 1927); (8) Second Ağrı (Ararat) rebellion (13–20 September 1927); (9) Bicar suppression (7 October–17 November 1927); (10) Asi Resul rebellion (22 May–3 August 1929); (11) Tendürük rebellion (14–27 September 1929); (12) Savur suppression (26 May–9 June 1930); (13) Zeylan rebellion (20 June–beginning of September 1930); (14) Aramar rebellion (16 July–10 October 1930); (15) Third Ağrı (Ararat) rebellion (7–14 November 1930); (16) Pülümür rebellion (8 October–14 November 1930); (17) Menemen rebellion (December 1930); (18) Tunceli (Dersim) suppression (1937–1938).

6. The International Aspects of the Sheikh Said Rebellion

1. CO 730/28, 4–7 March 1922.

2. Şimşir, *Ingiliz Belgeleriyle*; Kürkçüoğlu, *Türk-Ingiliz Ilişkileri*, p. 30, quotes the newspaper *Cumhuriyet* of 17 February as an example of such charges; Tuncay, *Tek-Parti*, pp. 130–131, in his discussion of Great Britain's involvement in the rebellion, states that he agrees with Kürkçüoğlu that it

was not in the interest of Great Britain to support the Kurds against the Turks, especially by 1925.

3. FO 371, E 1229/1091/44, a minute by D. A. Osborne of the Foreign Office made on 3 March 1925. This same phrase is quoted in van Bruinessen, Agha, Shaikh and State, p. 394, but he uses "indissolubly" whereas my notes indicate that the word is "indivisibly" and that the minute was written by D. A. Osborne and was not anonymous as stated by van Bruinessen in note 72 (p. 448); also, van Bruinessen did not use the abbreviations employed by Osborne.

4. FO 371/10867, E 2195/1091/44, 14 April 1925, no. 322, 22 April 1925, Lindsay to Chamberlain. This same sentence is quoted in Kürkçüoğlu, Turk-Ingiliz Ilişkileri, p. 311 n. 3.

5. Kürkçüoğlu, Turk-Ingiliz Ilişkileri, pp. 311–313, FO 371/10867, E 1360/1091/44, 4 March 1925, for James Morgan's memorandum on the Kurdish revolt. Morgan perhaps related the Sheikh Said rebellion to the attempts of the Turks after 1918 to encourage Kurdish nationalism. According to Wadie Jwaideh, "In fact, at the time of Turkey's defeat and weakness, the Turks themselves, fearful of losing the eastern provinces to the Armenians, had done much to foster Kurdish nationalist aspirations and to encourage the Kurds to demand the creation of an independent Kurdish state in eastern Asia Minor. Their vociferous Kurdish demands had borne some tangible results, for in the Treaty of Sèvres, provisions had been made for such a state. But then came the miraculous Turkish revival under Mustafa Kemal Ataturk" ("The Kurdish Nationalist Movement," pp. 383–397, 595).

6. Ibid.

7. Kürkçüoğlu, Türk-Ingiliz Ilişkileri, p. 313; also FO 371/10837. Harenc's report is included in the 15 April report of Lindsay to Chamberlain.

8. FO 371/1087, 24 March, Paris, no. 435, 2 June 1925, Lindsay to Chamberlain, no. 408, 9 June 1925, Lindsay to Chamberlain.

9. FO 57, no. 193, dispatch no. 38, 18 April 1926, Lindsay to Chamberlain; also reported in CO 730/99, 17 April 1926, Lindsay to Chamberlain.

10. Kürkçüoğlu, Türk-Ingiliz Ilişkileri, p. 314.

11. Ibid.

12. Ibid.

13. Sluglett, Britain in Iraq, pp. 125, 138 n. 68; Kürkçüoğlu, Türk-Ingiliz Ilişkileri, pp. 301–302. There are many reports to this effect in the records of the Colonial Office, Foreign Office, and Air Ministry. See also Peter J. Beck, "A Tedious and Perilous Controversy: Britain and the Settlement of the Mosul Dispute, 1918–1926," Middle Eastern Studies 17 (April 1981): 256–276; Jon Jacobson, Locarno Diplomacy: Germany and the West, 1925–1929, pp. 3–91.

14. Beck, "A Tedious and Perilous Controversy," pp. 269, 270 n. 59, 276 (see p. 275 n. 54 for references); FO 371/10826, 2 November 1925.

15. Kürkçüoğlu, Türk-Ingiliz Ilişkileri, p. 302; Beck, "A Tedious and Perilous Controversy," p. 270; Peter Edwards, "The Austen Chamberlain–Mussolini Meetings," Historical Journal 14 (March 1971): 154–160.

16. Edwards, "The Austen Chamberlain–Mussolini Meetings," pp. 158, 159; FO 424/264; Kürkçüoğlu, *Türk-Ingiliz Ilişkeri*, p. 300.

17. FO 371/10867, E 6883/362/65, 28 October 1925.

18. FO 371/10867, 9 November 1925, Crewe, British ambassador to France, to Foreign Office.

19. See Beck, "A Tedious and Perilous Controversy"; CO 730/86.

20. FO 371/10867, E 6412/362/64. For more details of the Druze rebellion, see Safiuddin Joarder, *Syria under the French Mandate: The Early Phase, 1920–27*, pp. 140–206; Tabitha Petran, *Syria*, pp. 65–68; Stephen Hemsley Longrigg, *Syria and Lebanon under French Mandate*, pp. 148–177; A. L. Tibawi, *A Modern History of Syria, Including Lebanon and Palestine*, pp. 345–349; also see Philip S. Khoury, "Factionalism among Syrian Nationalists during the French Mandate," *International Journal of Middle East Studies* 13 (November 1981): 441–469.

21. FO 371/10869, no. 751 (confidential), October 1925, Lindsay to Chamberlain. It should be noted that, in spite of German and British opinion that there was little substance to the Turkish-Soviet treaty, it did last with some changes and emendations until 19 March 1945, when it was denounced by the Soviet Union. For the text of the treaty, see Hurewitz, *Diplomacy in the Near and Middle East*, II, pp. 123–124.

22. Kürkçüoğlu, *Türk-Ingiliz Ilişkileri*, pp. 303, 304; FO 371/10808, 12 October 1925, Lindsay to Chamberlain.

23. Rouhallah K. Ramazani, *The Foreign Policy of Iran: A Developing Nation in World Affairs, 1500–1941*, pp. 269–271, has a summary of the treaty. The full text of the treaty is in *League of Nations Treaty Series*, VI, pp. 261–265. There is also a copy in French with an English summary in FO 427/264, no. 83, pp. 73–74, FO 427/264, dispatch of Sir Percy Loraine, British ambassador to Iran, to Chamberlain on 25 May 1926; the quotations are from this dispatch. Iran did not recognize Iraq until 25 April 1929, when diplomatic representatives were exchanged and a provisional agreement between the two countries was signed. A final boundary agreement was not signed until 4 July 1932. See Ramazani, *The Foreign Policy of Iran*, pp. 259–266, and FO 424/264, no. 71, where Loraine states, "Persian circles believe it will pave the way for a Persian-Irak treaty."

24. Ramazani, *The Foreign Policy of Iran*, p. 270; FO 427/264, no. 83, pp. 73–74.

25. Air 125, 15 March 1925.

26. There is extensive coverage of the Turcoman-Kurdish rebellion in FO 416/112, Persia: Annual Reports, 1924 (beginning on p. 57) and also in Air 23/122 from November 1924 to 31 November 1926; FO 416/112.

27. CO 730/86, Oliphant to under-secretary of the colonies, 4 December 1925; FO 406/56, E 7602/32/65, has Dobbs's detailed arguments against Lindsay's proposals.

28. Tarik Z. Tunaya, *Türkiye'nin Siyasi Hayatında Batılılaşma Hareketleri*, p. 103.

29. Kürkçüoğlu, *Türk-Ingiliz Ilişkileri*, p. 306.

30. FO 371/10868, E 1927/1786/44, 30 March 1926, Lindsay to Chamberlain, D. A. Osborne's minute of 3 March 1925; CO 730/86, 22 November 1925, Lindsay to Chamberlain; Kürkçüoğlu, *Türk-İngiliz İlişkileri*, pp. 308–309.

31. The literature on Zionism is voluminous. But with regard to the subject as I treat it here the best and most recent books are Mim Kemal Öke, *Siyonism ve Filistin Sorunu 1880–1914*, and the same author's *II. Abdülhamid, Siyonistler ve Filistin Meselesi*. Öke summarizes his conclusions in English in "The Ottoman Empire, Zionism, and the Question of Palestine (1880–1908)," *International Journal of Middle East Studies* 14 (August 1982): 329–341; Isaiah Friedman, *Germany, Turkey and Zionism, 1897–1918*.

32. FO 424 (Confidential Print), no. 50, July to December 1925; Lindsay to Chamberlain 16 October, no. 50, no. 52, 20 October 1925, Lindsay to Chamberlain.

33. FO 406/56, no. 62, 23 October 1925; the following discussion is based on this document.

34. Ibid.

35. CO 730/86, draft from Chamberlain to Lindsay, 5 November 1925. The same correspondence can be found in FO 424 (Confidential Print), no. 63, 30 November, Chamberlain to Lindsay; CO 730/98 and CO 730/102 have a full discussion of the council discussion with regard to paragraphs 3 and 4, which stipulated "regard must be paid to the desires expressed by the Kurds." The extent of Kurdish autonomy in northern Iraq as of March 1925 is detailed in a "Memorandum on Administration of Kurdish Districts in Irak," in CO 730/99, 24 February 1926; CO 730/98, Shuckburgh to Sir Samuel Wilson in January 1926.

36. CO 730/99, "Memorandum on Administration of Kurdish Districts in Irak," paragraph 12. An official copy of the treaty can be found in Great Britain, *Parliamentary Papers Treaty Series*, no. 18 (1927), cmd. 2912. There is a draft of the treaty in cmd. 2679. There is also a copy in Hurewitz, *Diplomacy in the Near and Middle East*, II, pp. 143–146, but the citation for the treaty (1930, Treaty Series no. 7, cmd. 3488) is incorrect. CO 731/98 has several copies and drafts as well as commentary on the treaty.

37. CO 730/98. In a memorandum by the Middle East Department on the treaty, an official noted that in regard to article 14, "It seems desirable to dwell as little as possible on this matter in any public statement, as it can not be denied that the arrangement is somewhat in the nature of a bribe." CO 730/98 and CO 730/100 have detailed accounts of the negotiations, drafts, and counterdrafts of the treaty negotiations.

38. See *Documents on British Foreign Policy*, series 1a, vol. 1, pp. 828–829, for Lindsay's instructions. William Stivers, *Supremacy and Oil: Iraq, Turkey, and the Anglo-American World Order, 1918–1930*, p. 171 n. 95, approaching the subject from the question of oil, also comes to the same conclusion; also see the same author's "A Note on the Red Line Agreement," *Diplomatic History* 7 (1983): 23–34.

39. Helmut Mejcher, *Imperial Quest for Oil: Iraq 1910–1928*, and the

same author's *Die Politik und das Öl im Nahen Osten* and "Iraq's External Relations 1921–26," *Middle Eastern Studies* 13 (October 1977): 340; Sluglett, *Britain in Iraq,* esp. pp. 79–80, 103–104, 110–115; Marian Kent, *Oil and Empire: British Policy and Mesopotamian Oil, 1900–1921,* pp. 126–128, 155–157; Karl Hoffman, *Ölpolitik und Angelsächsicher Imperialismus;* Elizabeth Monroe, *Britain's Moment in the Middle East,* p. 103; Stivers, *Supremacy and Oil,* pp. 108–193, and his "International Politics and Iraqi Oil, 1918–1928," *Business History Review* 55 (Winter 1981): 517–540.

40. For the internal impact of the rebellion on Turkish politics, see Robert W. Olson and William F. Tucker, "The Sheikh Said Rebellion in Turkey (1925): A Study in the Consolidation of a Developed Uninstitutionalized Nationalism and the Rise of Incipient (Kurdish) Nationalism," *Die Welt des Islams* 18/3–4 (1978): 210–211. Alex K. Helms, a British consular officer in Izmir in July 1927, asked Edib Servet Bey, one of the Turkish parliamentary deputies from Istanbul, if the Mosul settlement had been good for Turkey. "No," he said, "but it was not in our hands, the Ghazi and Ismet Pasha decided at any price to reach a settlement with England and so it had to be. Nevertheless, we want to advance along the road with England" (FO 267/424 [Confidential Print], part 14, July–December 1927, note 3).

41. Kürkçüoğlu, *Türk-İngiliz İlişkileri,* pp. 322–323, quoting a dispatch from Lindsay to Chamberlain in which he summarizes a conversation he and Sir Henry Dobbs had with Mustafa Kemal and Tevfik Rüstü in FO 371/11557, E 6677/6677, 24 November 1926. Mustafa Kemal himself apparently believed that the backwardness of the Kurds' Islamic beliefs and the deficiencies of the East, to which they belonged, would prevent the Kurds from ever being able to rule themselves.

42. The 30 May 1926 treaty had been initialed by France on 18 February 1926, but the French apparently wanted to see the results of the negotiations between Great Britain and Turkey before signing the treaty, one article of which dealt with the unobstructive passage of Turkish goods along the Pozanti-Nusaybin railway, which France had impeded while there was a possibility of war between Turkey and Great Britain during fall 1925 and early 1926 (see Kürkçüoğlu, *Türk-İngiliz İlişkileri,* pp. 315–321).

43. I found no evidence of the Soviet Union's incitement or support of the rebellion as asserted by Shaw and Shaw, *The Rise of Modern Turkey,* II, p. 381. The argument I present demonstrates that the Soviet Union had diplomatic goals that compelled it to forego supporting Kurdish nationalism at this time; the Soviet Union especially wanted to reduce its isolation resulting from the Locarno treaties and wanted to join the League of Nations; Tuncay, *Tek-Parti,* p. 131; Kürkçüoğlu, *Türk-İngiliz İlişkileri,* pp. 312–314.

Conclusion

1. Van Bruinessen, *Agha, Shaikh and State,* p. 379, emphasizes this as well.

2. Tuncay, *Tek-Parti*, p. 129; van Bruinessen, *Agha, Shaikh and State*, p. 405.

3. Amal Vinogradov, "The 1920 Revolt in Iraq Reconsidered: The Role of Tribes in National Politics," *International Journal of Middle East Studies* 3 (April 1972): 124–125. This article contains a good bibliography of works concerning the rebellion. For the Jangali movement, see Ervand Abrahamian, *Iran: Between Two Revolutions*, pp. 110–113; Sepehr Zabih, *The Communist Movement in Iran*, pp. 14–44. Both books have good bibliographies.

4. Vinogradov, "The 1920 Revolt in Iraq Reconsidered," p. 125.

5. For the policy of the Kemalist regime in this regard, see Ergun Özbudun, *Türkiye'de Sosyal Değişme ve Siyasal Katılma*, pp. 37–47; Tuncay, *Tek-Parti*, pp. 132–134; M. Ciwan, "Şeyh Sait Ayaklanması," in *1925 Kürt Ayaklanması (Şeyh Sait Hareketi)*, pp. 62–66; Ergun Özbudun, "Established Revolution versus Unfinished Revolution: Contrasting Patterns of Democratization in Mexico and Turkey," pp. 380–405, esp. pp. 389–390, where he states that the Kemalists, in spite of being largely from the lower middle classes and salaried middle class, favored an alliance with the landed notables for two reasons: the contribution of the local nobility to the war of independence; and the belief that the local nobility would be more supportive of their modernization program than the conservative religious masses. Thus, says Özbudun, "an implicit trade off materialized between the two groups. The local nobility supported the modernization program of the national military-bureaucratic elite, in return for which it was allowed to retain its land, status, and local influence, as evidenced in the conspicuous absence of any real land reform under the Republican governments." See the same author's *Social Change and Political Participation in Turkey*, p. 44; and Şerif Mardin, "Center-Periphery Relations: A Key to Turkish Politics?" *Daedalus* (Winter 1973): 164–190. As indicated in the text, the Kurdish landowners were among the first and major supporters of the "Defense of Rights Association": seventy-two Kurds were members of the first Grand National Assembly.

6. Certainly the Turks thought so. See Toker, *Şeyh Sait ve Isyanı*, pp. 50–59, for the elaborate Tampling scheme of the Turks to implicate Sayyid Abdul Qadir in the Sheikh Said rebellion.

7. Zürcher, *The Unionist Factor*, pp. 140–167. I use this book as an example because it is the latest book concerning this period utilizing the latest available sources and bibliography. It is also the best account, in my opinion, of this period of Turkish history.

8. Tuncay, *Tek-Parti*, pp. 142–143. Throughout their books, both Cemal and Toker state criticism of the press; see also Zürcher, *The Unionist Factor*, pp. 139–140, 148, 154 n. 38.

9. The best account is in Zürcher, *The Unionist Factor*, pp. 142–167, and Tuncay, *Tek-Parti*, pp. 161–183.

10. For a list of the reforms and laws passed during this period, see Shaw and Shaw, *The Rise of Modern Turkey*, II, pp. 375–395; Toker, *Şeyh Sait ve Isyanı*, introduction.

11. The charges that the Progressive Republican party "had had a hand in

the Kurdish revolt of 1925" continued to be made right up to the time of the Izmir trial. At the trial the charge was made by the chief prosecutor, Necip Ali Küçüka. See Zürcher, *The Unionist Factor*, p. 153; Weiker, *Political Tutelage*, p. 50; Karpat, *Turkey's Politics*, p. 47; Lord Kinross, *Ataturk*, pp. 452–455; Irfan Orga and Margarete Orga, *Ataturk*, p. 250.

12. For an earlier view of the consequences of the rebellion, see Olson and Tucker, "The Sheikh Said Rebellion in Turkey (1925)," pp. 195–211.

13. Jafna L. Cox, "A Splendid Training Ground: The Importance to the Royal Air Force of Its Role in Iraq, 1919–32," *Journal of Imperial and Commonwealth History* 13 (1985): 158, 174, states that 1919–1923 was the "most consequential portion for the genesis of the RAF's role in maintaining security in Iraq, and the importance of that role to the air service."

14. Ibid., p. 175 n. 112, quoting from a speech given by L. S. Amery at the annual dinner of the Central Asian Society, 30 June 1925.

15. A. J. P. Taylor, *English History, 1914–1945*, pp. 230, 232.

16. Uri Bialer, *The Shadow of the Bomber: The Fear of Air Attack and British Politics, 1932–1939*, p. 157. Cox, "A Splendid Training Ground," pp. 175, 176, also notes that the British persisted in their bombing policy throughout the 1930s even though "the 1929 riots in Palestine seemed to indicate that air power was of little use in heavy centres of population, unless high civilian casualties were accepted." While it is outside the scope of my study, I also agree with Cox's observation (p. 174) that the efficacy of air power contributed to "inhibiting the development of a true democracy in Iraq as the Sunni government came to rely too much upon military repression." The British air power policy may also have contributed to the concatenation of military coup d'états, beginning with Bakr Sidqi's in 1936 and persisting to the present.

Bibliography

Archival: Public Record Office, Kew Gardens, Great Britain
Colonial Office (CO)

CO 730: 1, 2, 3, 4, 5, 6, 7, 8, 9, 10, 28, 29, 32, 45, 46, 47, 48, 49, 52, 64, 65, 67, 82, 83, 84, 85, 98, 99, 100.

Foreign Office (FO)

FO 371: 5067, 5068, 5069, 5070, 6340, 6346, 6347, 6369, 6485, 7780, 7781, 7782, 7824, 10089, 10121, 10158, 10229, 10821, 10822, 10823, 10824, 10825, 10826, 10835, 10836, 10837, 10867, 10868, 10869, 10893.
FO 406: 53, 54, 55, 56, 57, 58, 59.
FO 416: 110, 111, 112, 113, 114.
FO 424: 258, 259, 260, 262, 263, 264, 265, 266, 267, 268, 269.

Air Ministry (Air)

Air 5: 256, 292, 338, 389, 403, 433, 449, 477, 543, 558, 566, 762.
Air 23: 122, 125, 126, 142, 151, 236, 237, 238, 239, 262, 263, 278, 279, 333, 334, 374, 379, 399A, 399B, 407, 411, 412, 424, 436, 449, 543, 544, 559. These folios also include a substantial number of French intelligence reports. British air intelligence and French intelligence exchanged information with regard to the Sheikh Said rebellion and on other matters as well.

Documents

Treaty between the United Kingdom and Iraq and Turkey regarding the Settlement of the Frontier between Turkey and Iraq Together with Notes Exchanged. Angora, 5 June 1926 (with a map), cmd. 2679. There is a facsimile of this treaty in cmd. 2912 after ratifications were exchanged. The cmd. number 3488 in J. C. Hurewitz, *Diplomacy in the Near and Middle East: A Documentary Record: 1914–1956*, II, p. 143, is incorrect.

Books

Abrahamian, Ervand. *Iran: Between Two Revolutions*. Princeton: Princeton University Press, 1982.
Allen, Henry E. *The Turkish Transformation*. Chicago: University of Chicago Press, 1935.
Arfa, Hassan. *The Kurds: An Historical and Political Study*. London: Oxford University Press, 1966.

Armstrong, Harold. *Grey Wolf.* New York: Minton and Balch, 1933.

Atatürk, Kemal Mustafa. *Nutuk.* 3 vols. Istanbul: Milli Eğitim Basımevi, 1934.

Bak, János M., and Gerhard Benecke, eds. *Religion and Rural Revolt.* Manchester: Manchester University Press, 1984.

Bedir Khan, Sureya. *The Case of Kurdistan against Turkey.* Philadelphia: Kurdish Independent League, 1928.

Beşikçi, Ismail. *Doğu Anadolu'nun Düzeni: Sosyo-Ekonomik ve Etnik Temellor.* Ankara: E. Yayınları, 1969.

Bialer, Uri. *The Shadow of the Bomber: The Fear of Air Attack and British Politics, 1932–1939.* London: Royal Historical Society, 1980.

Boyle, Andrew. *Trenchard.* London: Collin, 1982.

Busch, Briton Cooper. *Mudros to Lausanne: Britain's Frontier in West Asia, 1918–1923.* New York: State University of New York Press, 1976.

Cemal, Behçet. *Şeyh Sait Isyanı.* Istanbul: Sel Yayınları, 1955.

Chirguh, Bletch. *La question kurde: Ses origins et ses causes.* Cairo: Paul Barbey, 1930.

Craig, Gordon A., and Felix Gilbert. *The Diplomats, 1919–1939.* Princeton: Princeton University Press, 1953.

Dersimi, M. Nuri. *Kürdistan Tarihinde Dersim.* Aleppo: Ani Matbaası, 1952.

Edib, Halide. *Conflict of East and West in Turkey.* Lahore: Sheikh Muhammad Ashraf, 1935.

Edmonds, C. J. *Kurds, Turks and Arabs: Politics, Travel and Research in North-Eastern Iraq, 1919–1925.* London: Oxford University Press, 1957.

Firat, M. Şerif. *Doğu Illeri ve Varto Tarihi.* Istanbul: Saka Matbaası, 1948.

Foster, Henry A. *The Making of Modern Iraq: A Product of World Forces.* New York: Russell and Russell, 1935.

Frey, Frederick W. *The Turkish Political Elite.* Cambridge, Mass.: MIT Press, 1965.

Friedman, Isaiah. *Germany, Turkey and Zionism, 1897–1918.* London: Oxford University Press, 1977.

Froembgen, Hans. *Kemal Atatürk.* New York: Hillman Curl, 1937.

Ghassemlou, Abdul Rahman. *Kurdistan and the Kurds.* Prague: Publishing House of the Czechoslovak Academy of Sciences, 1965.

Gologlu, Mahmut. *Devrimler ve Tepkiler, 1924–1930.* Ankara: Turhan Kitabevi, 1972.

———. *Erzurum Kongresi.* 2 vols. Ankara: Nüve Matbaası, 1968.

Hasretyan, M. A., K. M. Ahmad, and M. Ciwar. *1925 Kürt Ayaklanması (Şeyh Said Hareketi).* Uppsala: Jina Nû Yayınları, 1985.

Hay, W. R. *Two Years in Kurdistan: Experiences of a Political Officer, 1918–20.* London: Sedgewick and Jackson, 1921.

Hertslet, Sir Edward. *The Map of Europe by Treaty.* Vol. IV: *1875 to 1891.* London: Her Majesty's Stationery Office, 1891.

Hoffman, Karl. *Ölpolitik und Angelsächsicher Imperialismus.* Berlin: Ringverlag, 1927.

Hourani, Albert, S. M. Stern, and Vivian Brown, eds. *Islamic Philosophy and the Classical Tradition.* London: Oxford University Press, 1972.

Hovannisian, Richard G. *Armenia on the Road to Independence, 1918.* Berkeley: University of California Press, 1967.

―――. *The Republic of Armenia.* 2 vols. Los Angeles: University of California Press, 1971 and 1982.

Huntington, S. P., and C. H. Moore, eds. *Authoritarian Politics in Modern Society.* New York: Basic Books, 1970.

Hurewitz, J. C. *Diplomacy in the Near and Middle East: A Documentary Record: 1535–1914.* 2 vols. Princeton: D. van Nostrand, 1956.

Ibrahim, Ferhad. *Die Kurdische Nationalbewegung in Irak: Eine Fallstudie zur Problematik ethnischer Konflikte in der Dritten Welt.* Islam Kundliche Untersuchungen, vol. 88. Berlin: Klaus-Schwartz, 1983.

Jacobson, Jon. *Locarno Diplomacy: Germany and the West, 1925–1929.* Princeton: Princeton University Press, 1972.

Jelavich, Barbara. *History of the Balkans: Eighteenth and Nineteenth Centuries.* 2 vols. New York: Cambridge University Press, 1983.

Joarder, Safiuddin. *Syria under the French Mandate: The Early Phase, 1920–27.* Dacca: Asiatic Society of Bangladesh, publication no. 31, 1977.

Joseph, John. *The Nestorians and Their Neighbors: A Study of Western Influence on Their Relations.* Princeton: Princeton University Press, 1961.

Jwaideh, Wadie. "The Kurdish Nationalist Movement: Its Origins and Development." Ph.D. Dissertation, Syracuse University, 1960.

Karpat, Kemal H. *Turkey's Politics: The Transition to a Multiparty System.* Princeton: Princeton University Press, 1959.

Kent, Marian, ed. *The Great Powers and the End of the Ottoman Empire, 1900–1923.* London: George Allen and Unwin, 1984.

―――. *Oil and Empire: British Policy and Mesopotamian Oil, 1900–1921.* New York: Barnes and Noble, 1976.

Khoury, Philip S. *Syria and the French Mandate: The Politics of Arab Nationalism: 1920–1945.* Princeton: Princeton University Press, 1987.

Kinross, Patrick Balfour (Lord). *Ataturk.* New York: William Morrow, 1965.

Klieman, Aaron S. *Foundations of British Policy in the Arab World: The Cairo Conference of 1921.* Baltimore: Johns Hopkins University Press, 1970.

Kodaman, Bayram. *Abdülhamid Devri Eğitimi Sistemi.* Istanbul: Ötüken Neşriyat, 1980.

Kruger, Karl. *Kemalist Turkey and the Middle East.* London: George Allen and Unwin, 1932.

Kürkçüoğlu, Ömer. *Türk-Ingiliz Ilişkileri (1919–1926).* Ankara: Ankara Üniversitesi Basımevi, 1978.

Kürt Milliyetçiliği ve Abdullah Cevdet. Uppsala: Jina Nû Yayınları, 1986.

Kutschera, Chris. *Le mouvement national kurde.* Paris: Flammarion, 1979.

League of Nations Treaty Series. Geneva: Printed for Secretariat of the League, 1920–1946.

Lee, Dwight Ervin. *Great Britain and the Cyprus Convention of 1878.* Cambridge, Mass.: Harvard University Press, 1934.

Lewis, Bernard. *The Emergence of Modern Turkey.* London: Oxford University Press, 1961.

Longrigg, Stephen Hemsley. *Four Centuries of Modern Iraq.* Oxford: At the Clarendon Press, 1925.

———. *Iraq, 1900 to 1950: A Political, Social, and Economic History.* Oxford: Oxford University Press, 1953.

———. *Syria and Lebanon under French Mandate.* Oxford: Oxford University Press, 1958.

McCarthy, Justin. *Muslims and Minorities: The Population of Ottoman Anatolia and the End of the Empire.* New York: New York University Press, 1983.

Marr, Phebe. *The Modern History of Iraq.* Boulder, Colo.: Westview Press, 1985.

Medlicott, W. N., Douglas Dakin, M. E. Lambert, eds. *Documents on British Foreign Policy, 1919–1939.* Series 1A, 1925–1929. 7 vols. London: Her Majesty's Stationery Office, 1966–1975.

Mejcher, Helmut. *Die Politik und das Öl im Nahen Osten.* Stuttgart: Klett-Colya, 1980.

———. *Imperial Quest for Oil: Iraq, 1910–1928.* London: Ithaca Press, 1976.

Melek, Kemal. *Ingiliz Belgeleriyle Musul Sorunu (1890–1926).* Ankara: Üçdal Neşriyat, 1983.

Monroe, Elizabeth. *Britain's Moment in the Middle East.* Baltimore: Johns Hopkins University Press, 1963.

Mumcu, Ahmet. *Tarih Açısından Türk Devriminin Temelleri ve Gelişimi.* Istanbul: Inkilap ve Aka Basımevi, 1979.

Nikitine, Basil. *Les Kurdes: Etude sociologique et historique.* Paris: Imprimerie Nationale, 1956.

Noel, Edward William Charles. *Diary of Major Noel on Special Duty in Kurdistan, from June 14th to September 21st, 1919.* Basrah: Government Press, 1920. Also in Foreign Office 371/5068.

———. *Note on the Kurdish Situation.* Baghdad: Government Press, 1920.

Öke, Mim Kemal. *II. Abdülhamid, Siyonistler ve Filistin Meselesi.* Istanbul: Kervan Kitapçılık, 1981.

———. *Siyonism ve Filistin Sorunu, 1880–1914.* Istanbul: Üçdal Neşriyat, 1982.

Orga, Irfan, and Margarete Orga. *Ataturk.* London: Michael Joseph, 1967.

Özalp, Kazım. *Milli Mucadele, 1919–1922.* Ankara: Türk Tarih Kurumu, 1971.

Özbudun, Ergun. *Social Change and Political Participation in Turkey.* Princeton: Princeton University Press, 1976.

———. *Türkiye'de Sosyal Değisme ve Siyasal Katılma.* Ankara: Üniversitesi Hukuk Fakültesi Yayınları, no. 363, 1975.

Petran, Tabitha. *Syria.* New York: Praeger, 1972.

Popoviç, Alexander, and Marc Gaborieau, eds. *Les confréries soufies dans le monde arabo-islamique: Les Naqshbandis.* Forthcoming.

Question de la frontière entre la Turquie et l'Irak 16 à 30 septembre 1924. With map. Geneva, 1925.

Ramazani, Rouhallah K. *The Foreign Policy of Iran: A Developing Nation in World Affairs, 1500–1941.* Charlottesville: University of Virginia Press, 1966.

Rambout, Lucien. *Les Kurdes et le droit.* Paris: Editions du Cerf, 1947.

Ramsay, William Mitchell. *Impressions of Turkey during Twelve Years' Wanderings.* London: Hodder and Staughton, 1891.

Rawlinson, A. *Adventures in the Near East, 1918–1922.* New York: Dodd, Mead, 1924.

Safrastian, Arshak. *Kurds and Kurdistan.* London: Arwell Press, 1948.

Selek, Sabahattin. *Anadolu Ihtilali.* Istanbul: Istanbul Yayınları, 1968.

Shaw, Stanford J., and Ezel Kural Shaw. *History of the Ottoman Empire and Modern Turkey.* 2 vols. Vol. II: *Reform, Revolution, and Republic: The Rise of Modern Turkey, 1808–1975.* New York: Cambridge University Press, 1977.

Silopi, Zinnar. *Doza Kürdistan.* Beirut, 1969.

Simon, Reeva S. *Iraq between the Two World Wars: The Creation and Implementation of a Nationalist Ideology.* New York: Columbia University Press, 1986.

Şimşir, Bilal N. *Ingiliz Belgeleriyle Türkiye'de "Kürt Sorunu" (1924–1938).* Ankara: Dişişleri Bakanlığı Basımevi, 1975.

Sluglett, Peter. *Britain in Iraq, 1914–1932.* London: Oxford by Ithaca Press, 1976.

Sonyel, Salahi Ramsdan. *Turkish Diplomacy, 1918–1923.* Beverly Hills, Cal.: Sage Publications, 1975.

Stivers, William. *Supremacy and Oil: Iraq, Turkey, and the Anglo-American World Order, 1918–1930.* Ithaca and London: Cornell University Press, 1982.

Tapper, Richard, ed. *The Conflict of Tribe and State in Iran and Afghanistan.* London: Croom-Helm, 1983.

Taylor, A. J. P. *English History, 1914–1945.* Oxford: At the Clarendon Press, 1965.

Tibawi, A. L. *A Modern History of Syria, Including Lebanon and Palestine.* New York: Macmillan and St. Martin's Press, 1967.

Toker, Metin. *Şeyh Sait ve Isyanı.* Ankara: Ruzgarlı Matbaası, 1968.

Toynbee, Arnold J., ed. *Survey of International Affairs, 1925.* London: Oxford University Press, 1927.

Tunaya, Tarik Z. *Türkiye'nin Siyasi Hayatında Batılılaşma Hareketleri.* Siyaset Ilmi Serisi, vol. 2, no. 8. Istanbul: Hukuk Fakültesi Yayınları, 1960.

Tuncay, Mete. *T.C.'nde Tek-Parti Yönetimi'nin Kurulması (1923–1931).* Ankara: Yürt Yayıncılık, 1981.

Turan, Ilter. *Cumhuriyet Tarihimiz: Temeller, Kuruluş, Milli Devrimler.* Istanbul: Cağlayan Kitabevi, 1969.

Türkiye Cumhuriyeti'nde Ayaklanmaları (1924–1938). Ankara: Genel Kurmay Harb Tarihi Başkanlığı, 1972.

van Bruinessen, Maarten [Martin] M. *Agha, Shaikh and State: On the Social and Political Organization of Kurdistan.* Published Ph.D. dissertation. Utrecht: Ryksuniversiteit, 1978.

van Bruinessen, Martin, and Jochen Blaschke, eds. *Jahrbuch zur Geschichte und Gesellschaft des Vorderen und Mittleren Orients 1984.* Berlin: Express Edition, 1985.

Weiker, Walter F. *The Modernization of Turkey: From Ataturk to the Present Day.* New York: Holmes and Meier Publishers, 1981.

———. *Political Tutelage and Democracy in Turkey: The Free Party and Its Aftermath.* Leiden: E. J. Brill, 1973.

Wilson, Sir Arnold T. *Mesopotamia 1917–1920: A Clash of Loyalties.* Oxford: Oxford University Press, 1931.

Wolf, Eric. *Europe and the People without History.* Berkeley: University of California Press, 1982.

Wortham, H. E. *Mustafa Kemal of Turkey.* Boston: Little, Brown, 1931.

Zabih, Sepehr. *The Communist Movement in Iran.* Berkeley: University of California Press, 1966.

Zaki, Muhammad Amin. *Khulasat Tarikh al-Kurd wa Kurdistan min Aqdam al-Usur Hatta al-An.* Cairo: as-Saʿada Press, 1939.

Ziemke, Kurt. *Die neue Turkei.* Stuttgart: Deutsche Verlagsanstalt, 1930.

Zürcher, Erik Jan. *The Unionist Factor: The Role of the Committee of Union and Progress in the Turkish National Movement, 1905–1926.* Leiden: E. J. Brill, 1984.

Articles

Abu Manneh, Butros. "The Naqshbandiyya in the Ottoman Lands in the Early 19th Century." *Die Welt des Islams* 22/1–4 (1984): 1–35.

Algar, Hamid. "The Naqshbandi Order: A Preliminary Survey of Its History and Significance." *Studia Islamica* 44 (1977): 124–152.

Beck, Peter J. "A Tedious and Perilous Controversy: Britain and the Settlement of the Mosul Dispute, 1918–1926." *Middle East Studies* 17 (April 1981): 256–276.

Ciwan, M. "Şeyh Sait Ayaklanması." In *1925 Kürt Ayaklanması (Şeyh Sait Hareketi).* Uppsala: Jina Nû Yayınları, 1985, 46–75.

Cox, Jafna L. "A Splendid Training Ground: The Importance to the Royal Air Force of Its Role in Iraq, 1919–32." *Journal of Imperial and Commonwealth History* 13 (1985): 157–184.

Davison, Roderic H. "Turkish Diplomacy from Mudros to Lausanne." In *The Diplomats, 1919–1938,* ed. Gordon A. Craig and Felix Gilbert, 172–209.

Duguid, Stephen. "The Politics of Unity: Hamidian Policy in Eastern Anatolia." *Middle Eastern Studies* 9 (May 1973): 139–155.

Edwards, Peter. "The Austen Chamberlain–Mussolini Meetings." *Historical Journal* 14 (March 1971): 153–160.

Finefrock, Michael. "Laissez-Faire, the 1923 Izmir Economic Congress and Early Turkish Development Policy in Political Perspective." *Middle Eastern Studies* 17 (July 1981): 375–392.

Hourani, Albert. "Shaikh Khalid and the Naqshbandi Order." In *Islamic Philosophy and the Classical Tradition*, ed. Albert Hourani, S. M. Stern, and Vivian Brown, 89–104.

Jwaideh, Albertine. "Midhat Pasha and the Land System of Lower Iraq." *Middle Eastern Affairs*, ed. Albert Hourani, St. Antony's Papers, no. 16. London: Chatto and Windus, 1963, 106–136.

Kent, Marian. "British Policy, International Diplomacy and the Turkish Revolution." *International Journal of Turkish Studies* 3 (Winter 1985–1986): 33–51.

———. "Great Britain and the End of the Ottoman Empire, 1900–1923." In *The Great Powers and the End of the Ottoman Empire, 1900–1923*, ed. Marian Kent, 172–205.

Khoury, Philip S. "Factionalism among Syrian Nationalists during the French Mandate." *International Journal of Middle East Studies* 13 (November 1981): 441–469.

Kodaman, Bayram. "Hamidiye Hafif Süvari Alayları: II Abdülhamid ve Doğu-Anadolu Aşiretleri." *Tarih Dergisi* 32 (1979): 427–480.

Mardin, Şerif. "Center-Periphery Relations: A Key to Turkish Politics?" *Daedalus* (Winter 1973): 164–190.

McCarthy, Justin. "Foundations of the Turkish Republic: Social and Economic Change." *Middle Eastern Studies* 19 (April 1983): 139–151.

———. "Population in Eastern Turkey during World War I." *Newsspot* 22 (February 1985): 5.

Mejcher, Helmut. "Iraq's External Relations, 1921–26." *Middle Eastern Studies* 13 (October 1977): 340–357.

Noel, Edward. "The Character of the Kurds as Illustrated by Their Proverbs and Popular Sayings." *Bulletin of the School of Oriental Studies* 1/4 (1921): 79–90.

Oberling, Pierre. "The State as Promoter of Technology Transfer: The Early Years of Ottoman Aviation." In *Turks, Hungarians and Kipchaks: A Festschrift in Honor of Tibor Halasi-Kun*, ed. Şinasi Tekin and Gönül Alpay Tekin (vol. 8 of the *Journal of Turkish Studies* [1984]: 209–214).

Öke, Mim Kemal. "The Ottoman Empire, Zionism, and the Question of Palestine (1880–1908)." *International Journal of Middle East Studies* 14 (August 1982): 329–341.

Olson, Robert W. "The Second Time Around: British Policy toward the Kurds (1921–1922)." *Die Welt des Islams* 27 (1987): 91–102.

Olson, Robert W., and William F. Tucker. "The Sheikh Said Rebellion in Turkey (1925): A Study in the Consolidation of a Developed Uninstitutionalized Nationalism and the Rise of Incipient (Kurdish) Nationalism." *Die Welt des Islams* 18/3–4 (1978): 195–211.

Özbudun, Ergun. "Established Revolution versus Unfinished Revolution: Contrasting Patterns of Democratization in Mexico and Turkey." In *Authoritarian Politics in Modern Society*, ed. S. P. Huntington and C. H. Moore, 380–405.

Stivers, William. "International Politics and Iraqi Oil, 1918–1928." *Business History Review* 55 (Winter 1981): 517–540.

————. "A Note on the Red Line Agreement." *Diplomatic History* 7 (1983): 23–34.

van Bruinessen, Martin. "Kurdish Tribes and the State of Iran: The Case of Simko's Revolt." In *The Conflict of Tribe and State in Iran and Afghanistan*, ed. Richard Tapper, 364–400.

————. "Popular Islam, Kurdish Nationalism and Rural Revolt: The Rebellion of Shaikh Said in Turkey (1925)." In *Religion and Rural Revolt*, ed. János M. Bak and Gerhard Benecke, 281–295.

————. "Vom Osmanismus zum Separatismus: Religiöse und ethnische Hintergründe der Rebellion des Scheich Said." In *Jahrbuch zur Geschichte und Gesellschaft des Vorderen und Mittleren Orients 1984*, ed. Jochen Blaschke and Martin van Bruinessen, 109–165.

Vinogradov, Amal. "The 1920 Revolt in Iraq Reconsidered: The Role of Tribes in National Politics." *International Journal of Middle East Studies* 3 (April 1972): 123–139.

Index

ments of, 47; in Piran, 95, 107;
Turkish suppression of
rebellion, 105–107, 119–122,
125–152
Saip (Ursavaş), Ali, 124
Sakarya, 66, 70, 82
Salih Efendi, 39, 40
Salih, Hınlı (Beg), 108
Salmond, Sır John, 83, 121, 161
Sami, Bekir, 65
Sami (Bey), Kemaleddin, 118
Sami Bey (Colonel), 111
Sanussi order (*tarikat*), 101
Sarıkamış, 114, 118
Sasunah, 109
Sayım Bey (Colonel), 116
Sebilürresat (newspaper), 123
Septi, 99
Serbesti (newspaper), 18
Settlement Law (Iskan Kanunu),
32
Shari'a (corpus of Islamic law), 17,
48
Shaw, Ezel, 23
Shaw, Stanford, 23
sheikhs, 90, 93, 97, 98, 99, 100,
145; as leaders of Kurdish na-
tionalism, 2–3, 4; reduction of
role of, 14. See also Jwaideh,
Wadie
Shi'is, 35, 113, 156. See also
Alevis; Kızılbaş
Shuckburgh, Sir John, 54, 55, 62,
65, 74, 75, 79, 147
Siirt, 42, 117
Silvan (Farkın), 94, 104
Simko, Ismail (Ağa), 67, 75, 115,
139, 141
Sivas, 19–21, 29, 33, 36, 38, 96
Siverek, 110, 116
Sluglett, Peter, 149
Soane, E. B. (Major), 62, 66
Society for Kurdish Freedom
(Ciwata Azadi Kurd), 41
Society for Kurdish Independence
(Ciwata Kweseriya Kurd), 28,
41. See also Azadi

Society for the Propagation of
Kurdish Education (Kürt Neşri
Maarif Cemiyeti), 15
Society for the Rise and Progress
of Kurdistan (Kürdistan Taali ve
Terraki Cemiyeti), 15, 21, 27,
28, 29, 63, 64, 72, 93, 117
Solhan, 28, 112, 115
South Kurdish Confederation, 53
Soviet Union, 87, 88, 134, 138,
138, 140, 145, 146, 151, 155;
policy of, toward Kurds, 138,
151; policy of, toward question
of Mosul, 139; policy of, toward
Turcoman rebellion, 141; policy
of, toward Turkey, 86, 87, 138,
142, 151
Special Organization (Teşkilat-i
Mahsusa), 23
Stivers, William, 149
Stresemann, Gustav, 135
Sudan, 162
Sukuti, Işak, 16
Sulaymaniya, 53, 59, 60–61, 62,
95
Sunnis, 35, 94, 99, 113, 156; and
Koçgiri rebellion, 35; and
Sheikh Said rebellion, 97–98
Syria, 136, 137

Şafii (school of Islamic law), 17
Şemdinan, 122, 123
Şerafettin mountains, 113, 114
Şerif, Sheikh, 94, 95, 110, 111
Şerif Paşa, 22, 24
Şerif Paşa, Muhammad, 15
Şeriyet (corpus of Islamic law), 17,
48, 91, 110
Şernak, 73, 96
Şimşir, Bilal, 126–128
Şukri Mehmet, 22

Taha, Sayyid, 50
Tali, Ibrahim Bey, 125
Talu, Ibrahim, 9, 11, 26
Talu, Zeynel, 11, 12, 94
Tamplin [?], 131